MORT WALKER'S

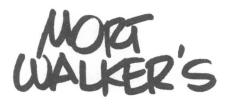

PRIVATE SCRAPBOOK

Mort Walker's

PRIVATE SCRAPBOOK

Celebrating a Life
of Love and Laughter

**Andrews McMeel
Publishing**

Kansas City

Mort Walker's Private Scrapbook copyright © 2000 by Mort Walker. All rights reserved. Printed in China. No part of this book may be used or reproduced in any manner whatsoever without written permission except in the case of reprints in the context of reviews. For information, write Andrews McMeel Publishing, an Andrews McMeel Universal company, 4520 Main Street, Kansas City, Missouri 64111.

00 01 02 03 04 RDS 10 9 8 7 6 5 4 3 2 1

Library of Congress Cataloging-in-Publication Data

Walker, Mort.
    Mort Walker's private scrapbook : celebrating a life of love and laughter.
      p. cm.
    ISBN 0-7407-1126-1 (pbk.)
    1. Walker, Mort. 2. Cartoonists—United States—Biography. I. Title: Private scrapbook.
NC1429.W23 A2 2000
741.5'092—dc21
[B]   00-042015

Design and composition by Kelly & Company, Lee's Summit, Missouri

---

To my wife, Cathy,
and our children,
Greg
Brian
Polly
Morgan
Margie
Neal
Roger
Whitney
Cathy Jr.
Priscilla

May none of us ever
fully grow up.

My Philosophy

Be friendly and you'll make friends.

Be honest and people will be honest with you.

Be good and you'll sell two or three
copies of your autobiography
(to your mother).

Contents

Introduction

If there is such a thing as being born into a profession, it happened to me. From my very first breath, all I ever wanted to be was a cartoonist. Everything I did or learned or aspired to was for that one goal, to draw cartoons. It was my identity in school and later throughout the world, and it was my door to prosperity. I had many opportunities in other professions, including acting, art, architecture, writing, music, and editing, but I never had any doubts that I was born to be a cartoonist.

Strangely enough, all my other pursuits worked to make my cartoons better. Drawing a comic strip is like producing a little play each day, requiring you to be casting director, author, and set designer, as well as a humorist who observes life and comments on the human condition. Producing a daily comic strip is an all-encompassing art.

Although other careers might have made me far richer, I never regretted my choice to pursue cartooning. My life has been full and fun and exciting every day that I sit down to "work"—without the stress that other jobs have. I "commute" to a room in my home, sit down, and draw funny pictures, and they send me money and give me awards. I'm also glad that my work has made other people happy and won me friends around the world. I can't think of a better way to live.

I'm thankful for the good life cartooning has given me, and I try to give back to the profession and the public. I've spent much time and effort on the National Cartoonists Society and the Newspaper Features Council, I was the founder of the International Museum of Cartoon Art and Hall of Fame, and every week I do free cartoons for schools, charities, and other good causes that write to me for help. Many people gave me a hand along the way, and this book is how I want to show my appreciation.

CHAPTER ONE

The Early Years

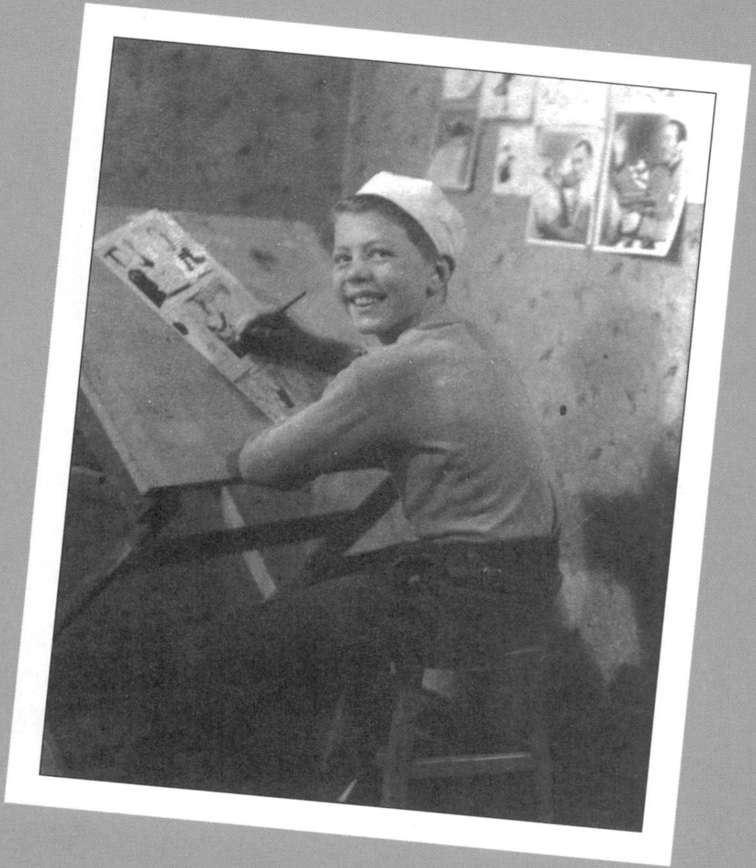

Knasen *is what* Beetle Bailey *is called in Sweden. This photo was taken at a Swedish book fair and shows me before and after.*

My ancestors came to America from Scotland, Ireland, and England (my great-great-great-great-great-great-great-great-great-great-grandfather was a doctor on the *Mayflower*). They spread out across the northern part of the country, eking out a living any way they could. They tried restaurants, hotels, music shops, farming, and anything else requiring hard work with no assurance of success. One ancestor sold organs. He would put one in the back of his cart and ride off, visiting church after church, until he sold it. One time he came home to find his entire town burned down and his family gone. Another ancestor founded the town of Waverly, Iowa. Still another wrote a series of books called *From Log Cabin to White House;* I'm sure you've heard of *them.* My father rode a bicycle from a farm in Lincoln, Nebraska, to Kansas City, Missouri, to study architecture at the YMCA night school. Nobody ever got rich, but they were ethical, friendly, hard-working . . . and very successful as human beings. ❖

I was very young when I was a little boy, so I shouldn't be held responsible for any of the bad things I did. Only the good things.

My grandmother wrote to her son Julian in 1923: "Rob and Carolyn [my parents] certainly have a baby that leads them a life. He has a temper that can't be beat and we can't imagine where he got it. He won't let anyone scold him or he makes them wish they hadn't." El Dorado, Kansas, is a beautiful town now, but when I was born there in the early twenties it was dusty and dirty, and the smell of oil filled the air. You might show a little temper, too.

In a couple of years we moved to Amarillo, Texas, where a blight had killed all the trees. In retaliation I promptly sat on a cactus. Mother had to stay up all night pulling out the needles with a pair of tweezers. Several days later I mistook a bottle of pills for candy red hots and ate the whole bottle. I lay comatose for twenty-four hours (not a bad state to be in when you're in Amarillo). Eventually I recovered and ran away from home as fast as my little legs would take me. When they caught me and asked where I was going, I said, "Way, way far."

Maybe they took the hint, because we soon moved to another booming oil town, Bartlesville, Oklahoma. My father figured that oil attracts people, people have children, and children need schools. So he'd follow the oil and build schools for them . . . or churches . . . or hospitals—whatever they needed. My father was a good man, but he wasn't as good to himself as he was to others. He never charged enough, and so we never had enough. In Bartlesville we lived in a tiny house that had no lights, no heat, and no plumbing. We bathed in a galvanized tub in the backyard and read our Sears catalog in a much smaller house farther out back.

About that time I developed my philosophy of life: "Poverty sucks."

Our family moved to Kansas City, Missouri, in late 1927.

My father was an architect by trade, but he was also an accomplished musician, the poet laureate of Kansas, and a great impressionist painter. He also loved cartoons.

My mother was a newspaper illustrator who did drawings like this.
She also painted landscapes and decorated trays.

Christmas

Hang up the garlands
    Open the blind
Home and in far-lands
    Joy to mankind
Open the portals
    Turn on the light
Smile, oh ye mortals,
    'Tis Christmas tonight.

Business cares banished
    Strife put away,
Worries all vanished
    Joy reigns today.
Glow your hearts mellow
    Gleam your souls bright,
Smile on your fellow.
    'Tis Christmas tonight.

Hushed is your sadness
    Gone are your woes,
Spread around gladness
    Bright your smile glows.
Look on faults blindly
    Clasp their hands tight,
Greet the world kindly
    'Tis Christmas tonight.
        Robin A. Walker.

A few of my father's illustrated poems

The TRAIL O' MEMORY

SOME trails lead out Westward,
   And some go toward the East;
      Others over mountains to the sea.
But one I often travel
Leads not to West or East,
      But down a winding pathway into memory.

Some trails lead to splendor,
And some to deserts bare,
      Others lead to laughter gay and free;
But the trail where joy is brimming
And the sky is ever fair
      Is where I sit and travel down the trail o' memory.

Back to the sunny, happy days,
When life was glad and young,
      And friends of joyous childhood romped with me;
We step out from the present
And list to gay songs sung,
      Down the winding path that leads through memory.

And time nor tide can never dim,
Nor wash away this trail,
      For love has touched with charm each face I see;
And peace is at each turning,
And joy shall never fail,
      With friends who, near me, travel down the trail o' memory.
                                    ROBIN A. WALKER.

The Resurrection

THE tomb was open, Christ was gone!
As Mary stood at break of dawn,
    All breathless and with fear.
Two angels fair appeared and said
"Thy lord hath risen from the dead,
    He is no longer here."

So Mary hastened back again,
To beg the weeping ones refrain
    As wonderous news she told.
Then just as children leap and run,
They hurried, while the morning sun
    Sent forth its shafts of gold.

"Whom seek ye here?" A stranger spoke,
And they, entreating, did invoke
    The place where He was lain.
But smiling he held forth his hands,
Nail-pierced and torn by Pilate's bands
    And marked with red blood stain.

" 'Tis Christ!" They whispered low in fear,
And dared not even venture near,
    But stood in awe and gazed.
" 'Tis I!" He said, and so they knew
His promise to them He held true;
    The temple He had raised.

And so, wherever men may dwell,
This resurrection story tell,
    And children sing the lay,
Since He did from the dead arise,
And prove Himself before their eyes,
    We worship on this day.
                    ROBIN A. WALKER.

The UNQUENCHABLE FLAME
By ROBIN A. WALKER

UP ON the height or down in the deep
  A mother's love still is the same.
 Constantly o'er us its brightness will keep,
  For it burns with unquenchable flame.

Though we may travel over the sea
  Or stray from the path that is right:
Forgetting, neglecting, scorning, still she
  Is praying the same prayer tonight.

Her hands that are thin and faded from age
  Still hold the same touch as of old
And fain would she turn, in life's book, every page
  To the day when her child she could hold.

For we still are the same in our mother's eyes,
  No matter how badly we fare;
Her love is as constant and true as the skies,
  Her heart holds no place for despair.

Time cannot dim nor disaster affect ,
  For mother-love's ever the same;
It fades not in poverty, trouble, neglect,
  For it burns with unquenchable flame.

*Two of my father's poems
illustrated by my mother
for the Kansas City Star*

The HIDDEN CHORD
BY ROBIN A. WALKER

THERE'S a chord in the soul of every man,
  A chord that is hidden away,
Though he lives his life in selfish strife
  And blackens every day.

You can touch this chord and change the tune
  To a sweeter and tenderer song;
You can lift his soul toward a higher goal
  If your touch is trained and strong.

A hating heart may melt to tears,
  Soft words from lips most vile,
If you know the way this chord to play,
  If your music is worth while.

There's a chord in the soul of every man
  Hidden deep and away,
But the pity is this, so many men miss
  The learning this chord to play.

One of my mother's drawings of my sister Peggy

THE SCARRITT SCOUT

February, 1933.

Price 1¢

In the fourth grade I did editorial cartoons for the *Scarritt Scout,* our mimeographed school newspaper. Here I fearlessly illustrate a 1933 attack on tea and coffee, candy, and bad eating habits. We championed soap and water, tooth brushing, and vegetables, fruit juices, and milk. We were for good health against bad health. We even took on the battle between clean thoughts and unwholesome thoughts to determine who ruled the mind. Finally, sickness surrendered and health won. "Health shall rule the human body!" we declared. Oh, but we were a brave bunch of kids!

Me with my brother Bob and sister Peggy

Me with my brother Bob and puppy

Me, age two. I was a happy guy from the start.

At age sixteen I performed as a comedian for a high school show. I also painted the backdrop.

My mother, Carolyn Richards Walker

My father, Robin Adair Walker

My father was an inventor of sorts . . . the sort who never made any money from his inventions. He invented an illuminated street sign, an indoor golf course, and a machine for cutting pumice stone, among other things. He spent years trying to find a way to cure baldness. He'd get in the bathroom at night, press a plumber's plunger onto his bald pate, and pull it off, hoping it would suck out some hairs. *Shoosh-pluck! Shoosh-pluck!* We'd hear him for half an hour. Another idea involved hedge apples, which are strange, round, prickly green things that grow on bushes in the Midwest. They aren't edible, so my father figured God put them on earth for some other good reason. Maybe they were here to cure baldness. He'd bring home a basketful and cook them into a paste, which he spread on his head. After this failed to produce results, he got a calf's bladder from the stockyards and put it on his head. His theory was that the bladder would dry and shrink, pulling the scalp up and allowing hair to grow through. It was ugly and smelly, and Mother made him wear a tam to hide it. Continuing that train of thought, he turned to rubber cement as a substitute for the bladder. Finding that a jar of the stuff was hardening, he put it on the stove to warm. It blew up, and he staggered from the kitchen bleeding from the glass shards. That was it, my mother announced, and they both lived out their lives with his shiny dome. ❖

Peggy, Bob, me, and Marilou, 1940

Muscles

Drawing at age six

My father's frontier mentality required every male to be equipped to defend his family. Our house was outfitted with chinning bars, weights (a box filled with bricks was all we could afford), a punching bag, and boxing gloves. We worked out almost every day, went for long hikes and runs, and kept ourselves in top condition. I couldn't wait for someone to come along and threaten our family.

At one point I honestly believed I was the toughest kid in the county. The gym teacher in my grade school had me parade in front of the class and flex my muscles. I got in fistfights constantly and even went out looking for fights if they didn't come often enough naturally. I heard the Morrell Street gang was tough, so I recruited some Jackson Street boys to go mix it up one night. I was striding purposefully toward Morrell Street when suddenly one of their gang jumped out of a bush behind me and decked me with one blow. *He* was the toughest kid in the county. *I* was a kid who didn't like to get hurt.

The last time I fought was in the army. The sergeant found out I knew how to box and booked me into a bout with my best buddy. It was a three-round exhibition in the theater. We came out of our corners, and my buddy (soon to be my ex-buddy) struck the first blow—*wham!*—a roundhouse shot to my shin. My legs turned to spaghetti. My eyes took off in different directions, and my pugilism was reduced to flailing at unidentified objects. But I was rendered a much wiser person. At the safe age of nineteen I retired from fighting and devoted the rest of my life to making friends. ❖

The Early Years ❖ 13

Two drawings done when I was seven

The Run

The energy displayed by young people is amazing, and their ability to amuse themselves is profoundly underrated.

My father had an office on the eleventh floor of a building in Kansas City. He would often take me to work with him and let me "help" him with his plans, which I would deliver to the blueprint company. I had to go down a wonderful square iron stairway with an open well. I would stand at the top and drop pieces of paper, watching them swirl down the funnel. Running out of paper, I'd see how far spit would go before hitting a railing. The biggest thrill was to run all the way to the bottom and back up to the eleventh floor. Then down again two steps at a time, swinging off the posts at each floor, and back up again, two steps at a time. Then, holding the railing, I'd slide down with my feet barely touching the stairs. Then it was up to the top again.

Eventually my father would finish work, come out, take me by the hand, and ask if I'd like to take a walk. "Sure," I'd say, eager for a little exercise. ❖

My Era

I probably grew up in the most astounding period in history, the 1920s. I saw the first automobiles, the first airplanes, the first of almost everything we take for granted today. A man landing on the moon was pure fiction. Only one person on our block had a telephone. If we got a call, they'd run down to get us. When you made a call you got "central," who would plug you into your number. Another family had a radio and would invite us to hear the fights. My grandfather had a radio eventually, but he'd sit in the corner with earphones on, laughing at something we'd never hear. My brother built his own radio out of a cigar box, a coil of wire, and a screw that was used for tuning. We'd sit in bed sharing an earphone each and listen to music coming from *Chicago!*

Movies cost ten cents, a hamburger five (or six for a quarter), and a brand-new Chevy was $500. My father bought our first home in Kansas City for $1,000, and my uncle built a mansion on the lake for $10,000. I used to work for ten cents an hour and caddy eighteen holes for twenty-five cents. (In yesterday's paper they quoted a real estate agent telling a client, "Well, for a million dollars you will get a very modest home.")

Most roads were dirt in those days, and you always brought along a board or something to help you get out of a mud hole. Cars weren't very speedy, and the phrase, "He was going like sixty!" was an overstatement. A full day's trip then could be done today in a few hours on our superhighways.

The first TV I saw was in a rich man's house. It had a seven-inch screen. Later, a neighbor got a set, and a bunch of us would get together to watch Milton Berle. It was a miracle. It was going to kill the movies.

I got one of the first home movie cameras and began taking pictures of our children. Later came the video cameras, and now I've got a digital camera and six computers. (Keeping up with the times has taken a lot of energy and a lot of foaming and fuming over the instruction books.)

We used to sleep on the porch or in the park during the

hot summer months. Eventually we could afford a fan. Many years later we got window air conditioners. Now central air-conditioning is a must. I remember going through the South and seeing people lounging in the shade or walking slowly. There was no relief. Air-conditioning has made half of our country livable.

Our ice was always delivered by a horse-drawn cart; we'd put a card in the window when we needed it. My job was to empty the drip pan under the icebox. Today's refrigerator and freezer have eliminated my job.

We had many scourges in the old days. People died of pneumonia, tuberculosis, flu, polio, and all kinds of other illnesses. We didn't have antibiotics. A popular book of the

Early published drawings in Cargo *magazine, for which I received $1 each*

time was *Life Begins at Forty*, to give people hope. Life expectancy is now almost double that. If this trend goes on, geezers will eventually outnumber boomers and we'll

Drawing by Mort Walker

get *Graywatch* on TV instead of *Baywatch*.

In 1947 I made history by having one of my cartoons sent over facsimile (now called fax). It was an experimental machine at the University of Missouri, and they'd never tried sending cartoons before. Today I couldn't live without fax machines, or e-mail, computers, and cell phones either.

I've been through all the fads from yo-yos to zoot suits, spats, straw hats, the Hula-Hoop, Hetacol, sloppy joe sweaters, ascots, blackstrap molasses, black chinos, baggy pants, skin-tight pants, long

hair, beards, tattoos, rings in noses, lips, ears, navels, you name it. Every generation tries to shock or challenge convention but usually comes back to what is generally accepted.

The Depression has been described as a plague that spread over our country. It was sad to see so many people out of work and desperate. We often didn't have anything to eat and were sent out to bring back dandelion leaves or anything else edible for Mother to throw in the pot. But it was also a great period of helping and sharing. We all cooperated. Grocers gave us food. The milkman gave us credit. Neighbors gave us clothes. We found a spare corner in our homes for old people. I remember there was a warm, friendly feeling in the community, compared to today, when people don't want to get involved. ❖

"I'm all dressed up to see my gal. I hope she doesn't have another pal."

(*Eleven years old*)

── My Friends at the *Kansas City Star* ──

The *Kansas City Star* had a lot of artists on the staff back in the thirties. They would hand-letter many of their headlines and draw portraits of famous people rather than use photos. The *Star* had its own comic strip, its own editorial cartoonist, and a guy who did a wrap-up in cartoons of the week's events.

My father would take me with him when he went to turn in his weekly poems, and the staff artists would allow me to hang around and watch them draw and go through their files of old artwork. If I wanted one, they usually let me have it, and my room at home was wallpapered with their drawings.

They would also look at my work and give me advice. "When you're drawing a woman, don't have any sharp angles. Keep women smooth and curvy." They were very kind and helpful. ❖

Darrell Porter was a kind of "cartoonist at large," taking on any assignment. He gave chalk talks to various groups and would take me with him and have me draw on the stage. It was great experience and a lot of fun.

S. J. Ray had a lot of talent and was very intelligent. He had his own strong style. When my strip started, he was helpful in getting the Star to run it.

Dale Beronius was a great cartoonist with good ideas. I always wondered why he didn't go to New York and get syndicated.

A Pro at Eleven

My father could never afford to give his four children an allowance, so we had to work if we wanted to buy or do anything. I sold magazines from door to door. I delivered newspapers, mowed lawns, caddied, and delivered for the drugstore on my bike for ten cents an hour. I painted signs, decorated jackets at two bits apiece, and dug dandelions for the same price a basket. Nothing was too menial if I wanted to spend a dime on a movie or buy a nickel hamburger.

So you can imagine the thrill I got when I was eleven and sold my first cartoon to *Child Life* magazine for a whole dollar. "Wow!" I said. "That's where the *real* money is!"

Within a short time I sold a few others and then more and more. By the time I was fifteen I'd sold more than three hundred cartoons and could actually afford to go into a hockshop and buy a sport jacket for $5. I was getting between $2 and $7 for each cartoon. I was *rich!* ❖

When I was twelve, I started collecting original cartoons from famous cartoonists. They were very generous in those days, and I ended up with a great collection, the origins of the International Museum of Cartoon Art that I founded in 1974. Above is the envelope for a letter I wrote to Walt Disney in 1935. It turned up in a flea market fifty years later, and the purchaser sent me a copy of it.

Gag cartoons from the Kansas City Journal, *1937*

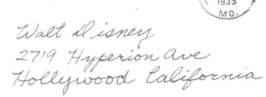

"Hm! . . . shall I stay out here and get wet, or go inside and get soaked?"

By Morton Walker.

"We had to take down the other windmill—there was only wind enough for ONE!"

"Guess I'll take a little nap!"

I learned to read before I went to school. God, I loved to read! By the time I was seven, I was devouring three or four books a week. When I discovered the library, I forced my best friend to check out books with me, read them, compare notes, and go back for more.

They weren't necessarily great books, mostly adventure and humorous tales involving pirates or West Point cadets, although I once embarked on the task of reading the entire set of *World Book* encyclopedias. I liked history and certain textbooks, and I took notes and wrote my own summations.

During the war I carried around an entire barracks bag full of books. I kept a vocabulary list and tried to learn new words as I read along. I kept a diary and read the Bible several times. But I think the book that had the greatest effect on me was Dale Carnegie's *How to Win Friends and Influence People*. It taught me not to bore people by talking too . . .

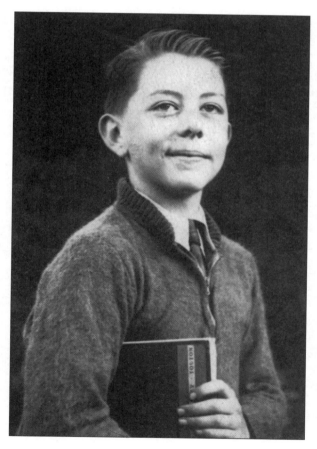

My favorite teacher was Miss Browdy. She taught fifth grade. Miss Browdy made the classroom interesting and colorful with artwork, posters, slogans, decorations, and her own personal energy and intelligence, which inspired her students to participate. I hadn't been too interested in school up to that point, preferring to fight and cause mischief and explore other fascinating pursuits, usually involving girls. I had also considered myself a little dumb, an attitude encouraged by my older brother.

Miss Browdy changed all that, at least as much as humanly possible, considering the raw material she had to work with. First of all she seemed to like me, a rarity among teachers heretofore. She also saw something in me that no one had ever noticed, having lacked her extraordinary insight. *She thought I had talent and promise.* Under her greenhouse effect, I flowered. I worked to please this woman who had faith in the wretched child I was, and to my astonishment (and surely my parents') I began to make A's. I stopped fighting. I became popular. Mary Jane Powell kissed me. I was happy with myself and with the world.

Love, faith, and encouragement are magical ingredients in the teaching profession—also, in the case of Miss Browdy, laser-keen eyesight—and should be employed instead of the stick. Anyway, it worked for me. ❖

I was visiting my Aunt Florence on January 3, 1936 (I was thirteen), and she took me downtown for lunch. Something didn't agree with me and I upchucked. She hailed a cab to take me home. The cab driver didn't want me to mess up his car and made me stick my head out the window. The next day I woke up with the flu. I had never been sick before and it frightened me.

My diary records my feelings at the time.

I HAVE NOT BEEN TO SCHOOL LATELY. IT'S SO MONOTONOUS, I GET TIRED AND FEEL SICK. MOTHER MAKES ME STAY IN BED WITHOUT ANY COMIC BOOKS. I DREW A COMIC STRIP CALLED THE LIMEJUICERS ABOUT SOME SAILORS AND SENT IT TO THE POST TO SEE IF THEY WOULD PRINT IT. IT WOULD BE A GOOD START FOR ME. I DREAD TO THINK OF TOMORROW. SCHOOL!

January 20

WHEN I GOT UP THIS MORNING I DIDN'T FEEL WELL. MOTHER DOESN'T BELIEVE ME. [SHE] GIVES ME A NASTY-TASTING MEDICINE [QUININE?] EVERY TWO HOURS. IT MAKES ME SHIVER EVERY TIME I TAKE IT.

January 24

TODAY THE PAPER COMES OUT THAT MAYBE WILL HAVE MY COMIC STRIP IN IT. SOME OF THE BOYS FROM SCHOOL CAME OVER TO SEE ME. EVERYBODY TELLS ME I SHOULD COME BACK TO SCHOOL OR I WON'T GRADUATE. I HAVE BEEN WAITING IMPATIENTLY FOR THE PAPER. I CAME DOWNSTAIRS TO SEE IF IT HAD COME YET. DADDY WAS GRINNING FROM EAR TO EAR. MY COMIC STRIP WAS IN IT, MY FIRST PRINTED STRIP. BOY, AM I EXCITED AND PROUD! WE SENT MARILOU OUT ASKING THE NEIGHBORS FOR COPIES.

January 27

I STARTED BACK TO SCHOOL TODAY . . . THE FIRST DAY IN THIRTY-SIX DAYS. MOTHER WILL GIVE ME $1 IF I GO STEADY FOR THIRTY DAYS.

June 3

I MISSED TWELVE DAYS OF SCHOOL BECAUSE BOB ELLIS HAD THE SCARLET FEVER AND THEY MADE ME STAY OUT. UP TO TODAY I HAVE HAD OVER SEVENTY-FIVE DRAWINGS PUBLISHED.

I didn't graduate and was held back a semester, but my career was launched.

I was thirteen when my first comic strip, The Limejuicers, *ran for a year in 1936 in the* Kansas City Journal.

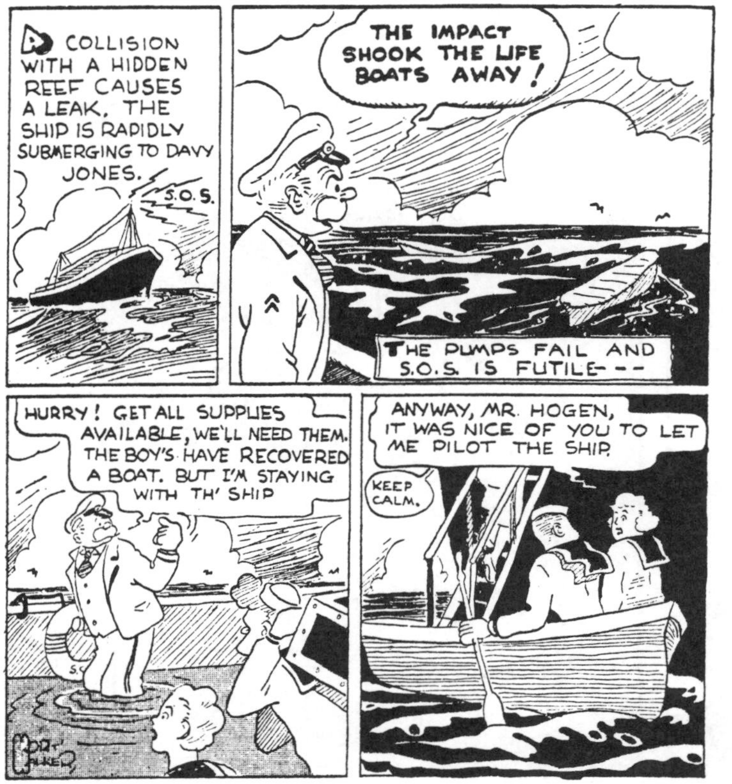
A COLLISION WITH A HIDDEN REEF CAUSES A LEAK. THE SHIP IS RAPIDLY SUBMERGING TO DAVY JONES.
S.O.S.
THE IMPACT SHOOK THE LIFE BOATS AWAY!
THE PUMPS FAIL AND S.O.S. IS FUTILE---
HURRY! GET ALL SUPPLIES AVAILABLE, WE'LL NEED THEM. THE BOY'S HAVE RECOVERED A BOAT. BUT I'M STAYING WITH TH' SHIP
ANYWAY, MR. HOGEN, IT WAS NICE OF YOU TO LET ME PILOT THE SHIP.
KEEP CALM.
MORT WALKER

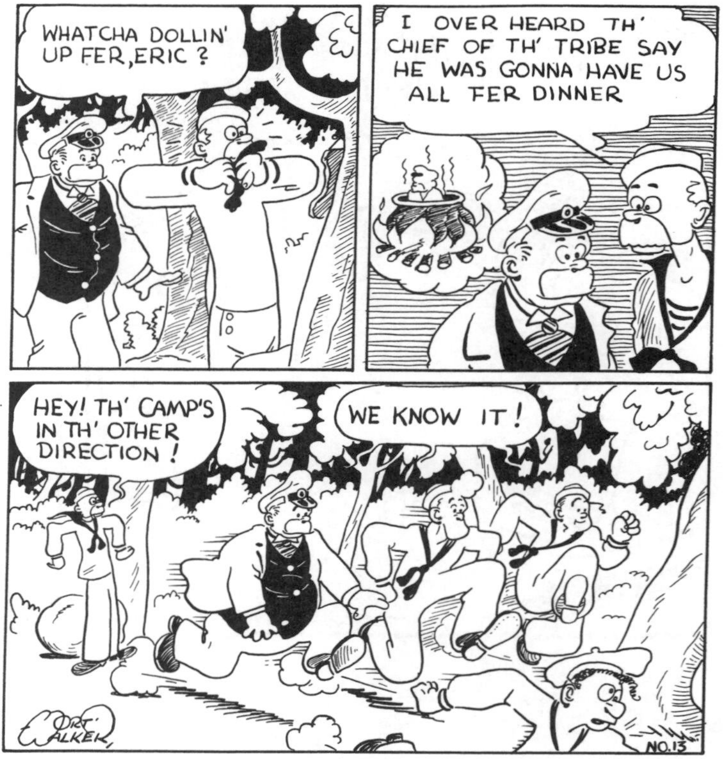
WHATCHA DOLLIN' UP FER, ERIC?
I OVER HEARD TH' CHIEF OF TH' TRIBE SAY HE WAS GONNA HAVE US ALL FER DINNER
HEY! TH' CAMP'S IN TH' OTHER DIRECTION!
WE KNOW IT!
MORT WALKER
NO. 13

Tip Top Comics, *1936, age thirteen*

Kansas City Journal, *1936*

Tip Top Comics, *1937, age fourteen*

Cartoonist Draws Pay As Well as Pictures

It looks like Morton Walker's all set. For two years the 14-year-old has been earning a living with his cartooning.

And a newspaper has a job waiting for him just as soon as he's old enough!

Mort's been drawing ever since he could hold a pencil. But he was 11 before his first cartoon was published.

Since, he's sold more than 70 drawings.

"My first drawings were printed without pay," Mort writes from 3910 Windsor, Kansas City, Mo., "but for the last two years they have brought as much as $5 each.

"Also I have a large collection of rejection slips."

Draws More Than He Plays.

Mort uses his room for a studio, confesses he spends more time drawing than playing. His hobby is collecting cartoon originals by famous artists.

Mort Walker—He Also Gets Rejection Slips.

1938 syndicated news story

"Heck! A swell serial story, and I'm getting hung tomorrow!"

Inside Detective, for which I was paid $7.50 (Fifteen years old)

"*Fessenden, you'll have to bail out. I simply CAN'T work with anyone looking over my shoulder.*"

Flying Aces, for which I was paid $2.50 (Fifteen years old)

The FOLLOW THROUGH IS THE THING—!! ———:

BILL, HERE'S A GOOD TIP ON A NEW ACCOUNT

2 WEEKS LATER!

I'LL DO IT TOMORROW!

STRIKE ONE!

O'BOY

APRIL

Drawing by Mort Walker

In the Wake of the Wanderer, *age fifteen, the first strip I submitted to a syndicate*

Sunshine and Shadow

Sunshine and Shadow

Sunshine and Shadow *was a regular strip I did for the* American Dairy Review *when I was sixteen.*

And I filled the letters with sketches.

When I was fifteen, I always decorated the envelopes when I wrote letters.

When I drew cartoons for my high school newspaper, I had to carve them into a chalk plate, then pour in molten metal to make a printing plate.

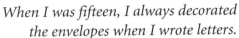

HERE'S A SKETCH OF MY STUDIO !!

This drawing commented on the amount of rain that spring.

I was a real whirlwind in high school. Coming back with the confidence of my success on the national cartoon scene, nothing fazed me, plus I was blessed with good health and a lot of energy. I was into everything and president of most. I found I could get by without studying, and I was out with a girl almost every night.

I had been a whiz in sandlot football and went to the coach to see if I could be on the team. I was five feet tall and the coach was six-five. He looked down and asked how tall my father was. I looked up and said six feet. He gave me a uniform and a shake of the head. In my first scrimmage, the runners came thundering at me. I had vowed I'd show the coach I had guts and stood my ground. They ran right over

My early form

me and I had to be carried off the field, bleeding.

All the athletes got big letter Ns for Northeast High School to wear on their sweaters and got all the girls. So I decided to start a golf team to get my N. A neighbor had an old rusty set of clubs on his back porch and I offered to buy them. "How much?" he asked. "Fifty cents," I offered. He said okay, and I got some guys to join the team. None of us knew anything about golf, but we went to our first tournament at the city's swankiest high school across from the public golf course with our rusty clubs and scrubby clothes. My first drive hit a tree and bounced back at my feet.

That was one of my better shots, so I became a cheerleader. I also edited the school

MORTON WALKER: Absolutely TOP-NOTCH in everything. Class Day Comm. 4; N.S.D. 2, 3, 4; V. Pres 3; Pres. 4; Lit. Contest 3; Art Club 2, 3, 4; V. Pres. 2; Pres. 3; Art Honor Society 2, 3; Annual Art Staff 2, 3, 4; Cartoonist for Annual 4; V. Pres. Jr. Class 3; Sergeant-at-Arms Sr. Class 4; Hi-Y 3, 4; Cabinet 3, 4; Pres. 4; Safety Pins 4; Safety Fair 4; Student Council 4; V. Pres. 4; Courier Staff 4; Vik. Var. 3, 4; Golf Team 4; Cheerleader 4; Jr.-Sr. Prom Comm. 3, 4; Class Day 3; Field Day; H.R. Officer 2, 3, 4; All-City Student Council 4; M.I.P.A. Meet 4.

newspaper and was art editor of the yearbook, performed onstage, acted in a radio show, ran a neighborhood teen center, and belonged to a dozen organizations.

The principal called me into his office and told me I had to get out of half my activities. I asked why, and he said they'd had a boy like me who overdid it and had a nervous breakdown. So I resigned from a bunch of stuff. But it didn't keep me out of trouble. I thought it would be fun to create a Hobo Day where everyone came dressed like tramps. It got me kicked out of school for two weeks. The principal called me in again and suggested I join the navy, where I might make something of myself, but I never followed this suggestion either.

From my high school yearbook

*One of the drawings that
got me a job at Hallmark*

"This brings them so close, they
look like they're in back of me!"

From my high school yearbook

In 1939, Open Road for Boys *magazine had a monthly contest with prize money. Many now-famous cartoonists entered this contest and became pen pals.*

The old joke goes, "When did you decide to become a cartoonist?"

"When I was a baby and was dropped on my head."

There may be more truth than fiction to this joke, because I do have a lumpy head and I can't ever remember not being a cartoonist. I was drawing almost before I could talk. It was so natural to me that I was a teenager before I realized that some people *weren't* cartoonists. I thought it came with the package, like ears and feet.

Somewhere about that time it occurred to me that drawing was only half the job. A good cartoonist needed to be a good writer as well. I began taking writing courses and studying literature. I became editor of our school newspaper and, later on, editor of my college magazine.

The Captains

MORT WALKER, KANSAS CITY CARTOONIST, WINS FIRST PLACE IN 1940 CAPTAINS CLUB CONTEST

Two hundred and fifty-eight contributions were printed on the Captains Club pages during 1940 and out of this number Mort Walker of 3910 Windsor, Kansas City, Mo., can claim 16 as his own original drawings. When this top-ranking Captain was asked to tell us something about himself and his hobby for publication with his picture shown at right, he said:

"Cartooning isn't my hobby; it is my career. I have many hobbies, including football, golfing, dates, hot dogs, books, eating, sleeping, studying, clothes, church, jokes, and the movies.

Mort Walker, 1940 Captains Club Winner

"I am cheer leader at our high school football games. Last year I was vice-president of my class. I am now a senior in high school and plan to go to college next year. After that I would like a course in art. My studies in art so far have been the school instruction, a course at the Kansas City Art Institute, and a correspondence course.

"I have been drawing since I was old enough to pick up a pencil and scribble on the wall paper and on the fly-leaves of my mother's best books.

"My first cartoon was sold and published when I was eleven years old. At present I am drawing a regular comic strip for a magazine published monthly in Kansas City." His latest contribution appeared in the November 10 issue of CARGO.

Although Mort has recently celebrated his 17th birthday he was sixteen at the time he submitted most of his drawings. The small cartoon accompanying this article is a sample of his work.

One of many drawings from my high school yearbook

OUR

SOCIAL

LIFE

*I kept drawing all kinds of things for my school
publications and anyone else who'd print my work.*

When I was fifteen, a couple of girls took me home after school to teach me to dance. How do girls always know how to dance? I guess it blossoms forth about the same time their breasts do. Anyway, they took this clod and laboriously plodded through the box step, showing me how the feet go, where the hands go, and where the hands *don't* go. Eventually it took, and within a month I was running a bimonthly dance at the Masonic Temple and was chairman of the prom. I'd jitterbug with Fanny, waltz with Jane, and clear the hall when my buddy Herb and I did a violent form of polka. Becoming more sophisticated, we created our own technique we called Slow Dance. We cut the beat in half, holding our partners' bodies close, feeling the inner rhythms of our partners. Someone dubbed it Why Dance? ❖

A few of my friends in high school felt that kids didn't have anywhere to go for fun. We decided to open our own recreation center. We rented an old mansion, cleaned it up, put in minimal furniture, and charged the kids an entrance fee to cover expenses. This is one of the oil paintings I did to help decorate the place.

I had just finished enduring a colonoscopy. I was sitting in the recovery room having my first bite of food in twenty hours, waiting for the doctor to come and give me the results of my test, which gave me time to think of something stupid.
The doctor comes in and I say, "You must have seen more assholes than the Speaker of the House of Representatives."
The doctor pats my knee and says, "You'll be all right."

Museum Nut

I must have seemed weird. When I was a little boy, thirteen or fourteen years old, I would walk ten miles to go to the Kansas City Museum, the Nelson Museum, and the Kansas City Art Institute. I'd go every week to visit my favorite paintings while my friends played. When I was in the army in Italy, I was in museums while my buddies were out chasing girls. Weird, now that I think back on it. When I married Cathy, I found she had similar interests, and we've been to museums all over the world. It's no wonder that she and I built the cartoon museum in Florida. I even took her back to Kansas City to visit my old favorites. After sixty years we were still able to find most of them. ❖

Some of the many caricatures of high school leaders I did for our yearbooks

Art Sail

When I was a senior in high school, I did a large pastel mural for the city home show and won a national oil painting contest sponsored by *American* magazine. My art teacher felt I had become a serious artist and gave me a large closet as my private studio. But when she came in to check on me one day and found me sailing paper airplanes out the window, I was immediately put back in the classroom.

Years later she was interviewed in the nursing home where she was living and they asked her about me. "Ah, Morton Walker," she said. "I couldn't tell him anything. He knew it all." ❖

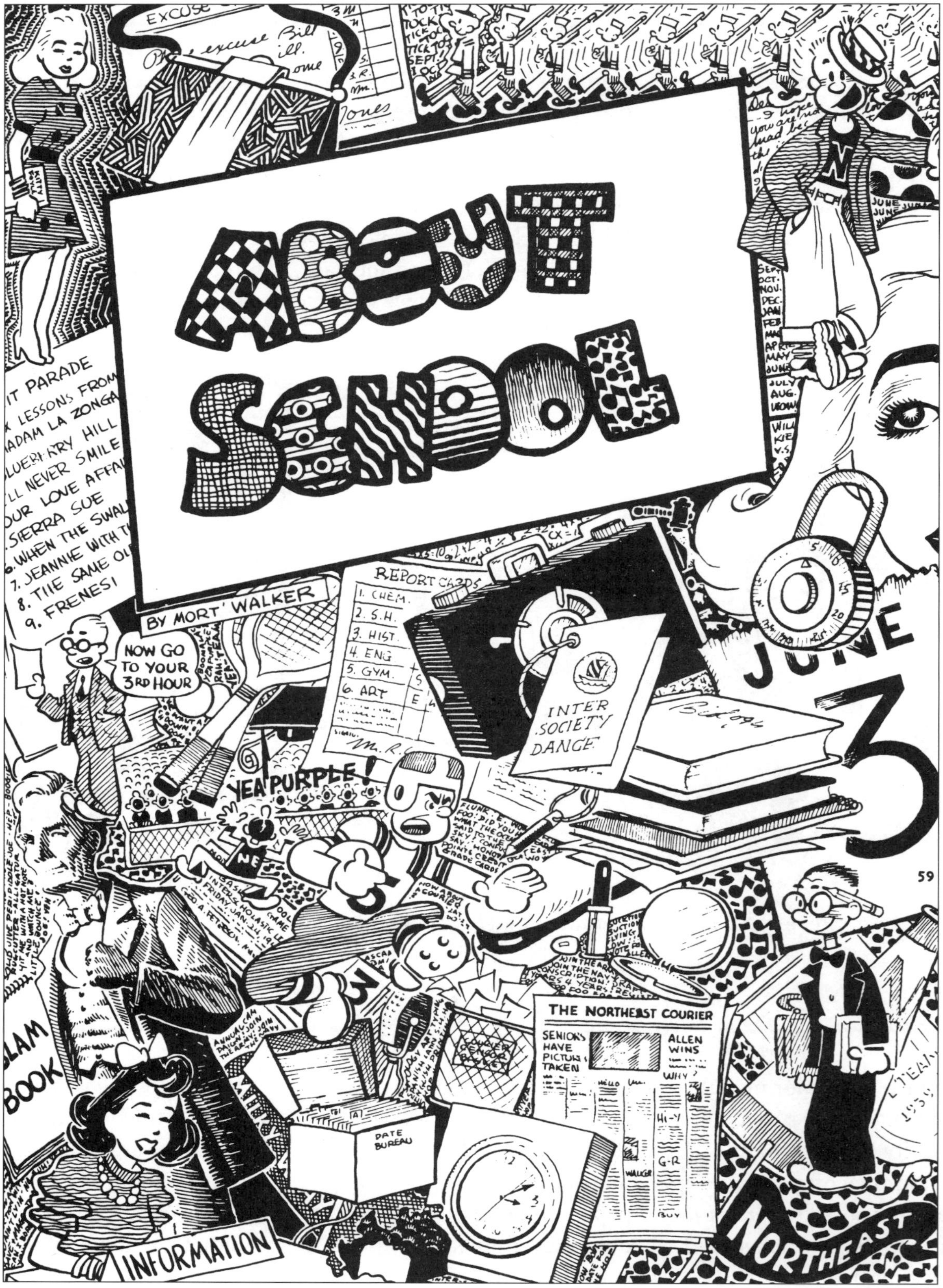
EXCUSE
ABOUT SCHOOL
BY MORT WALKER
IT PARADE
LESSONS FROM
ADAM LA ZONGA
LUEBERRY HILL
LL NEVER SMILE
OUR LOVE AFFA
SIERRA SUE
6. WHEN THE SWAL
7. JEANNIE WITH T
8. THE SAME OL
9. FRENESI
NOW GO TO YOUR 3RD HOUR
REPORT CARDS
1. CHEM.
2. S.H.
3. HIST.
4. ENG
5. GYM.
6. ART
INTER SOCIETY DANCE
JUNE 3
YEA PURPLE!
THE NORTHEAST COURIER
SENIORS HAVE PICTURES TAKEN
ALLEN WINS
WHY?
HI-Y
G-R
DATE BUREAU
SLAM BOOK
INFORMATION
NORTHEAST
59

My Hallmark Days

I had borrowed $25 to pay my first year's tuition to Kansas City Junior College and had to get a job to support myself while going to school. I found work on the night shift in the shipping department at Hallmark Cards (then called Hall Brothers). I left home each morning with two bags of food, one for lunch at school, the other for dinner in the park before going to work.

One day I saw an ad in the paper for an artist. I applied, and it turned out to be upstairs in the Hallmark editorial department. Their writers weren't happy with the way the art department interpreted their ideas. They wanted someone to sit with the writers and do drawings that made them happy. I brought some of my drawings to show them.

"How do you like our cards?" the vice president of the company asked.

"I don't like them at all," I said. A gasp went up from the group interviewing me.

"Why not?" he said, his curiosity aroused by this challenge from a brash seventeen-year-old kid.

"They're too mushy and sentimental. I wouldn't even send one to my grandmother."

Up to then, most greeting cards had been bought by women. Now the war had started, and they hoped to get soldiers as customers. Sensing a whole new huge market for cards, they wanted a male point of view. I got the job.

A writers' meeting was held every morning where yesterday's verses, or "sentiments," were projected on a screen and discussed. I became part of that meeting. I took all the approved verses back to my desk in the writers' section and drew them up for the art department to finish. My cartoon style was an innovation in the greeting card business. Most cards featured flowers, cute little bears they called "critters," and pretty scenes. Today the majority of cards are humorous. I hope I contributed to that change.

I also drew all the Disney cards; Bambi was the big star at that time. In fact, for several years I did rough designs for all the Hallmark cards, except for the flowers, the pretty scenes, and the critters, which the art department continued. Even when I left to go to the University of Missouri, they continued to send me verses, paying me $1 for each card. I was making $75 a week, more than my father pulled in. Occasionally he would borrow from me.

Merry Christmas

Examples of some of my Hallmark cards

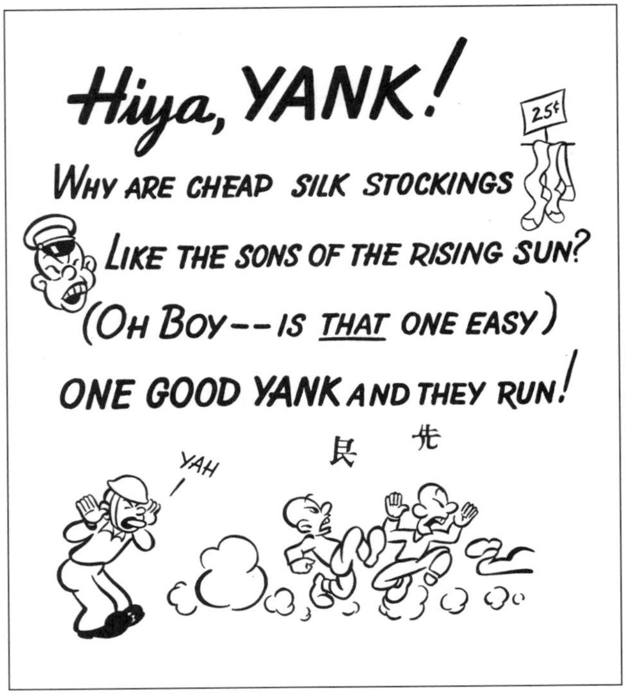
Hiya, YANK!
25¢
WHY ARE CHEAP SILK STOCKINGS
LIKE THE SONS OF THE RISING SUN?
(OH BOY--IS THAT ONE EASY)
ONE GOOD YANK AND THEY RUN!
YAH

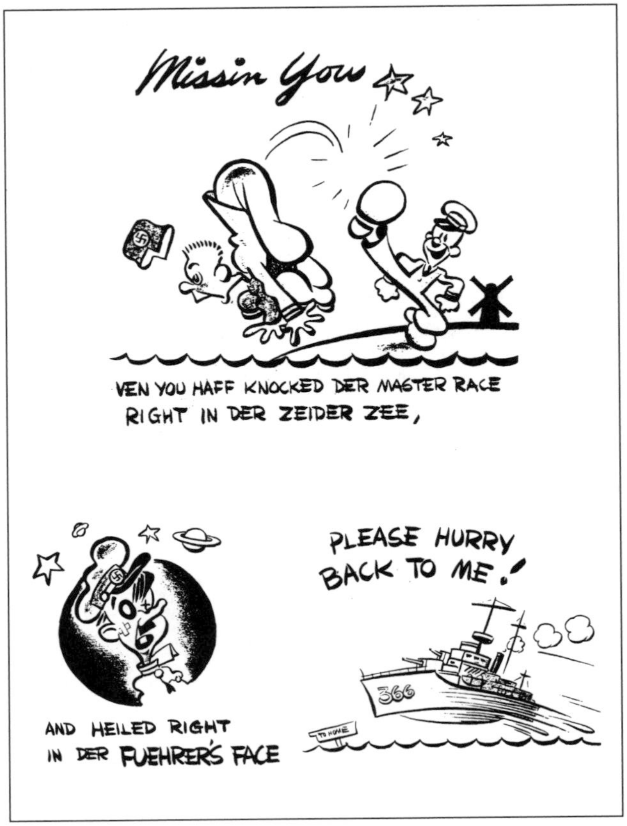
Missin You
VEN YOU HAFF KNOCKED DER MASTER RACE
RIGHT IN DER ZEIDER ZEE,
AND HEILED RIGHT
IN DER FUEHRER'S FACE
PLEASE HURRY
BACK TO ME!
366
TO HOME

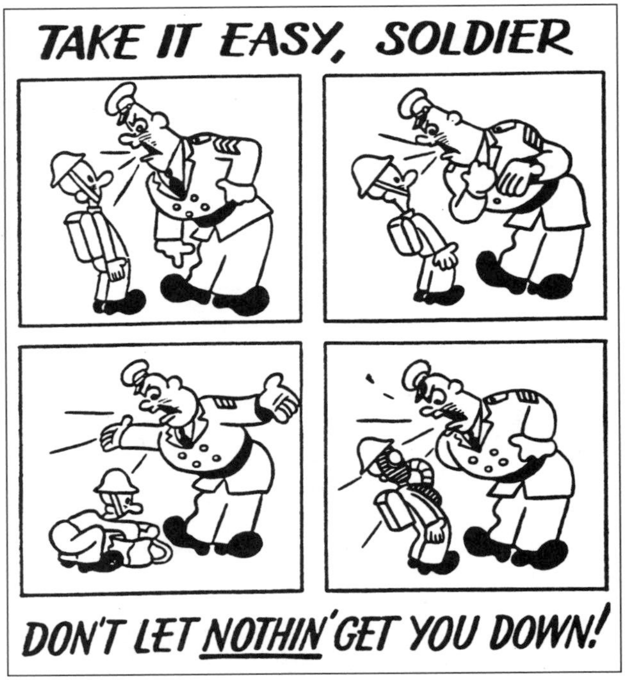
TAKE IT EASY, SOLDIER
DON'T LET NOTHIN' GET YOU DOWN!

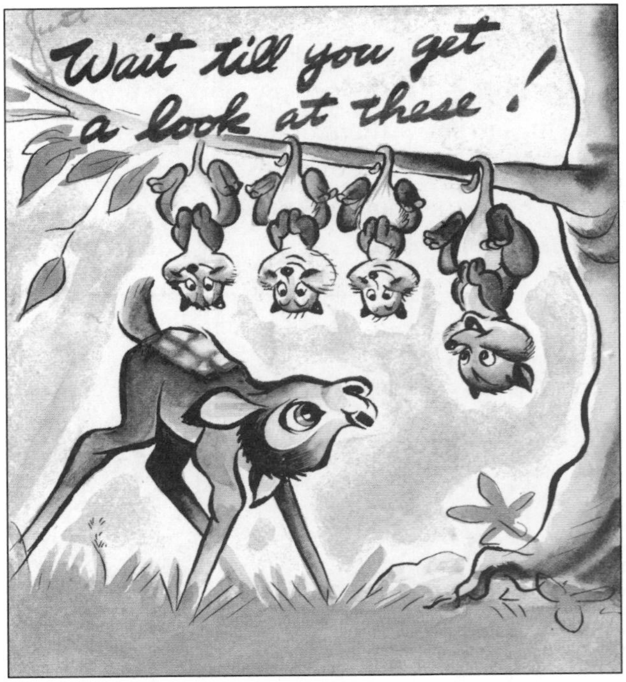
Wait till you get
a look at these!

When I started at Kansas City Junior College, I was amazed at how smart my classmates were and embarrassed by how little I knew. I realized I'd spent my high school days having fun, dating, and being a politician. Suddenly I had a tremendous desire to learn, so I threw myself into my studies. When I was drafted out of college, I took my textbooks with me. I made notes, worked on my vocabulary, kept a diary, and wrote reports on every book I read. In the army I got a diploma in engineering and found I had a talent for math. I don't think I've ever stopped trying to educate myself since. ❖

Me, lower right, as a high school cheerleader

Home
(Written when I was thirteen)

Everyone knows his own home, but a stranger would be lost in it. Certain instructions are required to make anything run in our house. When a visitor is trying to entertain himself while I am finishing eating, the conversation runs something like this: "Sit down and make yourself at home. You have to turn the lightbulb to make it go on because there's a double socket in the lamp and it's connected to the electric clock. You will find the latest *Life* on the table there. You might have some trouble getting some of the pages apart. We spilled some fudge on it last night. And be careful when you sit on the chair. Mother uses it as a pin cushion. Maybe you'd like to turn on the radio. It's about time for Jack Benny on WDAF. No, on our radio WDAF is 65. And if the sound fades out, you'll have to crawl under the piano and jiggle the ground wire a little. Just make yourself at home." About this time, the visitor is really enjoying himself.

When we have a guest over the weekend, we have to inform him that the hot water faucet produces cold water and the cold produces hot water—when we can get the heater to work. And don't pull too hard on the front doorknob, or it will come off. And we can't lock the door when we are outside, only when we are inside, and that doesn't do any good.

Now, don't think I live in a hole, because other homes I've visited have other things just as bad. ❖

CHAPTER TWO

Army and College Days

In the Army

Duh! A display of army intelligence.

Little did I know when I was drafted in 1942 that I was going to get almost four years of free research. I had no thoughts or ambitions at that time to do an army comic strip, but I was constantly sketching and trying to capture the humor that was so prevalent in military life. The army thoughtfully sent me to a number of places so that my experience would be broadened. I was in the Air Corps, the Signal Corps, the Engineers, Ordnance, the Infantry, and Intelligence and Investigating, and I had amphibious training with the navy. I ended up in charge of a German prisoner-of-war camp. I was a private, a corporal, a sergeant, and a lieutenant, and I was a goof-up in every rank.

When I was in Camp Crowder, Missouri, I got a three-day pass to go home to Kansas City. Before they would let us go they lined us up to see if we were dressed properly. As I was being inspected, a friend across the aisle made a funny face at me. I broke out laughing, and the officer took away my pass. My friend felt so bad about it, he lent me his. So for the next three days I was George Laskolin.

Lined up for a medical exam in the army

Induction center, Fort Leavenworth, Kansas, 1943

I was a private in the Infantry at Fort Leonard Wood, and we were preparing for a twenty-mile hike. Our company commander came out and said he needed a new company clerk. Could anyone type? My hand shot up. I'd seen a typewriter; my father had one, and I'd played around with it a little. I became the new company clerk and taught myself under fire. I was soon replaced by a real typist, but I missed the twenty-mile hike and I can still type fairly well.

HE GOT A LETTER FROM HIS GIRL

In Officer Candidate School I illustrated our graduation book with sketches of our four-month training period. Naturally, the page satirizing our officer instructors was a favorite with the students. Some of them look prophetically like Beetle Bailey. ❖

Naples, Italy, 1946

ADDISON M.

Home

My assignment overseas was with an Ordnance depot in Naples, Italy. I was made security officer of the installation in charge of the gates. When the war was over in Europe, we began to destroy everything in the depot rather than ship it home or dump it on the Italian market. Binoculars, watches, and other small items in our inventory were crushed by driving tanks over them. My job was to see no one stole anything before it was destroyed. I began to realize that army humor writes itself.

Along with my security duties I was the Intelligence and Investigating officer. I oversaw rape and murder cases as well as cases involving armed raids on the depot by Italian gangsters. The workers in the depot were German prisoners of war, and I was in charge of about ten thousand of them. Of course, I wasn't trained for any of these positions, which is typical of army assignments. But at least, at twenty-one years of age, I didn't know what I didn't know, so I muddled through.

Along the way I was picking up ideas for characters. ❖

The German major camp commander

My army sketches are signed "Addison M." My name is Addison Morton Walker.
Army rules are that everyone should be called by their first name, so I signed my
drawings that way while I was a soldier and occasionally afterward for various reasons.

The first day I took over the security office, two of our guards found an Italian civilian worker trying to leave with some items. They took him into a back room and began slapping him around. After a few minutes they stepped aside and said it was my turn. I raised my hand and then stopped. I couldn't hit him. I gave orders to stop that kind of treatment from happening again.

My office was a haven for informers. Everyone with information lined up to tell me about it, hoping, I guess, for special treatment. One day a German prisoner told me that a group of prisoners were going to escape that night. I got a few fellow officers to arm themselves, and we lay low outside the fence and waited. There was some shuffling, and then some shadows got up and started to run. We fired into the air and ordered them to halt. There were four of them. It turned out they had been leaving every night, spending several hours with girls, and returning every morning for roll call. They didn't really want to escape. They were waiting to be repatriated.

They had to be punished, of course, but how? They were already imprisoned. I remembered an old fraternity hazing trick and ordered them to dig

a six-foot ditch with spoons. I left them in the hot Vesuvius sun, digging in the rocky soil. After an hour I went to check on how they were doing and found they were finished; their friends must have come out with

shovels and helped. I grinned and told them to fill it in.

While I was in charge of the POW camp, the German officers really ran everything. I just sort of oversaw and approved. I used to sit around with the officers and ask about Germany and Hitler. They told me how anyone who griped about what was going on would just suddenly disappear with no questions asked. They also were curious about America. They couldn't comprehend the freedom we had in this country. They asked, "When you want to move to another city, what do you do?" You just move, I said. "Don't you have to get permission, some papers or anything?" Nope, I said, you just move. They were bewildered. "But how do you keep track of everybody?"

One of the Italian employees in my office invited me for Sunday dinner in his home. It was a nice house, reflecting more affluent days before the war. We enjoyed a little vino in his living room before his wife called us to the dining room. There were two place settings and two large plates of pasta. The two of us were the only ones at the table, although I could hear female voices in the kitchen and saw women peeking through the door to see if we were finished. Thinking it was the main course, I made an effort to finish my pasta so as not to disappoint them, but then they brought out a platter of fish for each of us. I thought I would burst. Then came the meat. I felt I was headed for the famous

Addison M. Naples, Italy 1946.

Roman vomitorium and excused myself. I felt bad about leaving, but at least I didn't leave feet first, killed by Italian hospitality.

P/W Camp No. 9 (Naples P/W No. 1)

The attendance of

Lt. Walker

is respectfully solicited to inspect

The handicraft exhibition

taking place at this camp on

Sunday, May 26, 1946 at 1500 hours.

GERMAN CAMP COMMANDER

CAPTAIN

My German POWs lived in rickety shacks with no amenities, but they worked hard to keep some form of intellectual life going. Above is a hand-drawn invitation they sent me to attend a craft show. I was astonished at the quality of their work, but I was also worried about where they got all their materials, carving knives, and tools.

One night I was invited to see a play they had produced. They had costumes, dresses, and many props. At one point in the show a pistol came into play. Suddenly I realized I was the only American in a room full of the former enemy . . .

and they had a *gun*. I didn't care if it *was* carved out of wood. I started to sweat, excused myself, and got the hell out of there.

When the war was over, I put them all on freight cars, went with them to Switzerland, and turned them over to the Red Cross. It was quite an education.

While the other guys were out boozing and getting laid I thought I'd take advantage of a free trip to Europe and visit museums and historic sites. I had my own jeep and an interpreter, so it was a breeze to go all over Italy and Switzerland.

Everywhere I went I made sketches and took photographs. I had a hard time getting prints made from my Speed Graphic camera, so I set up a darkroom in a closet in one of the warehouses on the depot grounds. I didn't have an enlarger so I improvised, using a projector I found in the lecture room. With a German soldier who knew something about photography, I was in business. We developed film and made prints for everyone.

I went home after a year with a treasure trove of photos and sketches and a great deal of knowledge about Italy. I had learned to speak Italian and made many friends. I loved the country so much I took Cathy back on our honeymoon to some of the same spots I had enjoyed.

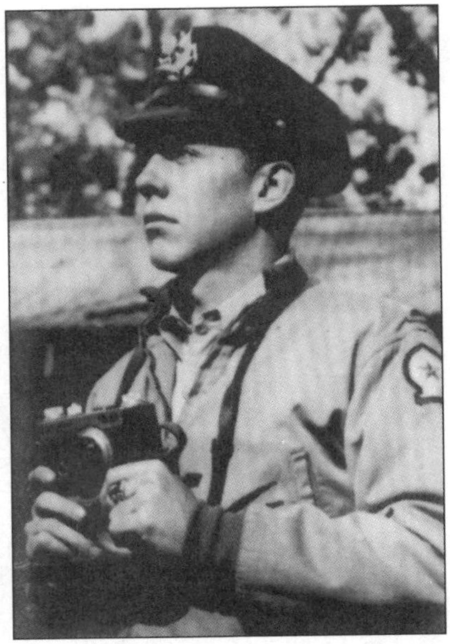

Me and my ever-present camera

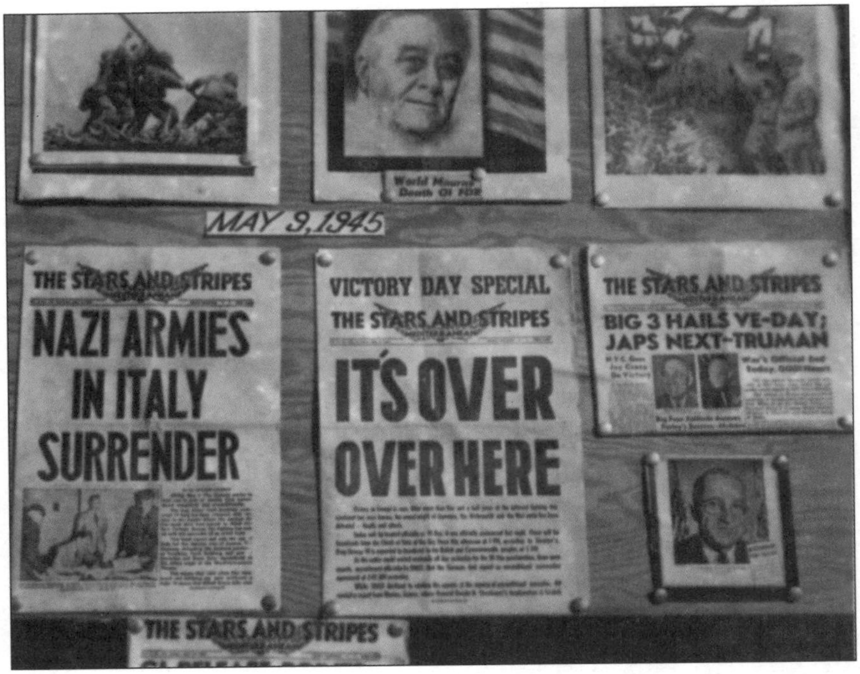
MAY 9, 1945
THE STARS AND STRIPES
NAZI ARMIES IN ITALY SURRENDER
VICTORY DAY SPECIAL
THE STARS AND STRIPES
IT'S OVER OVER HERE
THE STARS AND STRIPES
BIG 3 HAILS VE-DAY; JAPS NEXT—TRUMAN
THE STARS AND STRIPES

Our bulletin board announced the news we'd all been waiting for.

For those who lived through it, World War II was a real breakthrough. Men like me were lifted from their rural homes and shown the world. We met people and saw things we never would have encountered, isolated as we had been by no money or transportation. The war opened up vistas and opportunities. While we all wanted to get home and see our friends and families, we were all imbued with the urge to make up for lost time and do something with our lives. The survivors enriched our country. ❖

Mt. Vesuvius stretches 4,000 ft into the sky and is constantly overhung by soft pink clouds.

Naples, Italy, 1945

Italian is spoken by some forty-two million people in Italy, Lybia, West Africa and --- -- Brooklyn. Most of our English words have their roots in Latin but have gone to seed so far that the best international conversations are carried on by a series of grunts, gestures, and grimaces.

Naples, Italy 1945

Cigarette, Joe!
Buy something, Sell, something!
Shack up!
Butts!
Arf!

Going Home - Naples, Italy 1945

Addison M.

"As the name implies, the uniform must be worn in a uniform manner according to published regulations. Do not decorate the uniform, avoid unauthorized clothing ----"
Soldiers Handbook 21-13 Chapt IV

World War II brought our youth of the Depression age from their basement homes and the backwoods to a world-wide experience. Our whole society matured and benefited. We learned so many things and opened up so many new opportunities. Our country and the world would never be the same. ❖

I used to do cartoon portaits of my friends; this one is of John Sloan.

Morton Walker

The army had sent me to Washington University in St. Louis, where I got an engineering diploma. When I returned to the University of Missouri, I didn't want to spend another two years taking the prerequisites for journalism school, so I just enrolled in journalism anyway. I was a straight-A student and became editor of the school magazine, the *Showme,* and a member of the honorary journalism fraternity, Sigma Delta Chi. One day the dean called me into his office and said, "What are you doing here? You didn't take my course on the history and principles of journalism." I replied that I was too busy saving the world for democracy. He kicked me out. I gathered all my credits into a category called Humanities, got my degree, and left.

My office in the journalism building

Kinsey had just published his famous study on sex in the United States, and I thought it would be highly interesting to do a similar study of campus activities. I drew this cover adapted from a Picasso painting and wrote ten questions that I intended to distribute among the students. Within minutes I was standing before the dean again—shot down. I invoked the First Amendment, but he thought his ideas were better than Thomas Jefferson's.

This little spot drawing won me an award.

Do you tune it in the way I think you do?

"It's awful nice, Jack, but won't
we be accused of exhibitionism?"

"Frankly, Reverend, I'm a little
worried about myself."

"I guess we'll have to move again.
Here comes another emergency classroom."

COMMUNISM AT MISSOURI

Appearing in January

I had read that one of the state legislators claimed our campus was riddled with Communists, which I thought was a ridiculous statement. Neither I nor any of my friends had seen any Communists, so I drew this cartoon for the magazine. The caption read, "The Missouri campus as the State Legislature sees it." The dean of the journalism school called me into his office and said I was irresponsible and the cartoon might hurt the school's funding. He ordered me to tear the page out of all 5,000 magazines before distribution. Several staff members resigned in protest. ❖

The Joke

I did this for the Showme *in 1947, a year before Norman Rockwell
did his famous Gossip cover for the Saturday Evening Post.
I used to send our magazine to the* Post, *and I often
wondered if it had inspired him. If so, I was flattered.*

Missouri U. Magazine Jibe at Red Teaching Charge Ordered Deleted

COLUMBIA, Mo., Jan. 28 (UP).—The University of Missouri's monthly humor magazine, Show-me, scheduled to appear on the campus today, will be delayed for several days because of an "objectionable" cartoon satirizing recent charges of Communistic teaching, directed at the school.

Decision to delete the cartoon and delay publication was made last night by Sigma Delta Chi, journalism fraternity, following a meeting with university officials.

Sy Weintraub, the magazine's business manager, announced his resignation in protest against the action. He said publication would be delayed at least a week.

The cartoon was displayed around the campus yesterday to promote sales. It depicted a university professor, resembling Joseph Stalin, speaking to students who also resembled the Russian premier.

Entitled "one man's interpretation of a government at the university," the cartoon was in answer to charges in Washington by a Missouri Congressman that Communism was being taught at the school.

After the Communist flap we arrived at our *Showme* office in the journalism building to find our stuff in the hall and the office door locked. Undaunted, we put everything in a friend's cellar and held our staff meetings in the "Shack," closer to the source of beer. I'm second from left, writing.

I did this large figure for the front of my fraternity for our homecoming football game with the University of Kansas.

Needless to say, my college days were not a complete bust.

Four samples of the teenage strip Dave Hornaday and I tried to sell in 1947. There were no takers.

Cut out and hang above your study desk or on your door

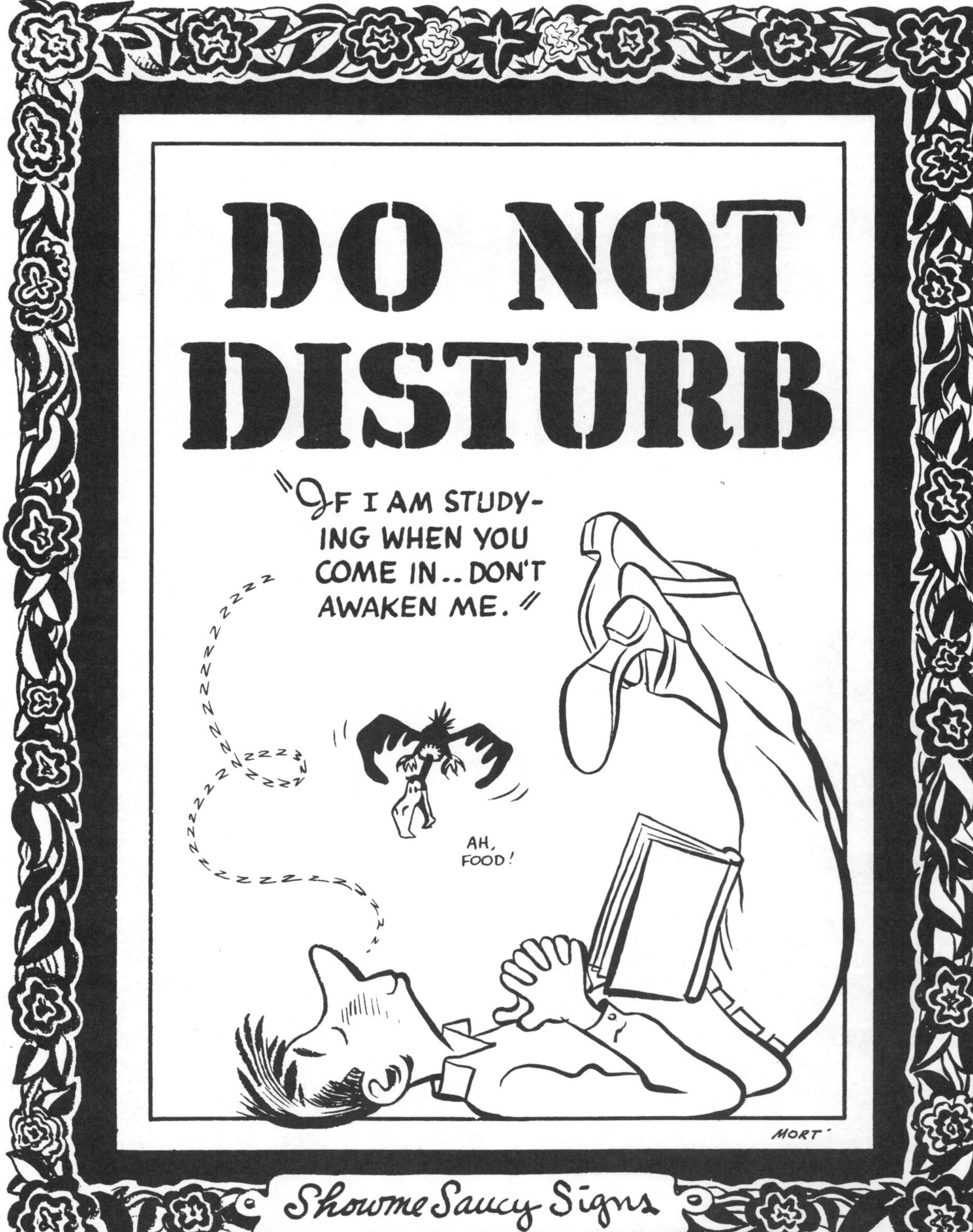
DO NOT DISTURB
"IF I AM STUDYING WHEN YOU COME IN.. DON'T AWAKEN ME."
AH, FOOD!
MORT
Showme Saucy Signs

How are you getting along on your G.I. Subsistence?

"Well, son, I hope that little talk
we had did you some good."

"Oh, we broke up as soon as
she made her New Year's resolutions."

CHAPTER THREE

New York, Here I Come!

SALUTE TO AUTRY!

Western Stars

WINTER 25c

DELL

For the FIRST time — — Gene's full life story
with episodes and photos never before published!
Extra! THE AUTRY RODEO!

"I sorta dread coming home on paydays."

paper, did my drawings in ink, and added a little blue wash color to make them more interesting. Then I decided to do more than the usual ten submissions. I did thirty ideas a week. The other cartoonists got mad at me. "There aren't thirty good ideas a week. I can only come up with seven," grumbled Tom Henderson, the top seller at the time. "Thanks to you, now we have to do finished drawings," another one griped. But I began selling—and selling a lot.

After we made the rounds, some of us would go have a drink together or take in a movie. One day we walked into a bar and found two old veteran cartoonists. I said hi. "Go back to where you came from," they growled, angry at the competition I was giving them. ❖

I went to New York in 1948 after graduating from college. I decided to try selling my cartoons to magazines. There were about twenty magazines that held open house for submissions on Wednesdays. I met a cartoonist who offered to show me around. As we sat waiting to see the editors, we showed our work to each other. The work was usually rough pencil sketches. I figured that to compete with these established veterans I had to outshine them, so I got heavier

"How can we start a club with only four members?"

When I was through with my studies at Missouri, I didn't wait for graduation ceremonies. I was too anxious to get going!

While struggling to stay alive in the Big Bad Apple, I showed my cartoons to an editor who said, "Weren't you editor of the magazine at Missouri University?" I said yes, and he offered me a job at Dell Publishing

Company, where he ran an editorial division. I really just wanted to be a cartoonist, but I also needed to eat, so I accepted. Dell at that time was one of the largest producers of popular-culture magazines, and I was brought in to be editor in chief of *1,000 Jokes* magazine, *Family Album,* and *Film Fun* and assistant editor on *Western Stars* and the new *Sport* magazine. I had a secretary and an assistant.

They hired me at $45 a week. The next day they changed their minds and said they were paying me $40 a week so I had "something to work up to." When they found out I could type, they fired my secretary. After a few weeks of watching me work they fired my assistant. I was doing the work of three people and never got a raise.

The work was interesting, though. I got to look at all the other cartoonists' work and dealt with humor writers. Rather than a joke book, *1,000 Jokes* was really a humor magazine. I wrote a lot of the articles. One was picked up and made into a Milton Berle show.

The head of my department was Charles Saxon, and we

became lifelong friends. He was promoted to editor of *Modern Screen* magazine and eventually left to become one of the best cartoonists *The New Yorker* ever had.

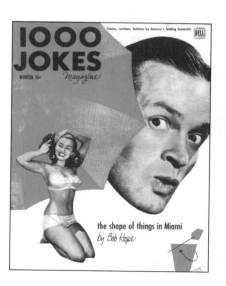

I only did magazine cartoons for three years. The last, 1950, was my best. A cartoonist publication took a count and said I was 1950's top-selling cartoonist. I only made about $8,000 that year, so I decided I'd better get into a better business. I had sold to almost every magazine in publication except *The New Yorker*. They wouldn't buy from me because they said I "drew too funny for them." However, they bought ideas from me and gave them to other cartoonists to draw.

While I was desperate to make some money, I was determined to protect my "ideals"—that is, not to go "money mad." It was a remote chance anyway, so I figured I might as well be noble about it. I wrote myself a note. *I will be happy to make $10,000 a year. That's enough.*

I've changed my mind a little since then. ❖

"I wonder what I said."

"Of course, I'm only wearing it till he can afford an engagement ring!"

"Just remember, I control two votes in the P.T.A."

"Nearest exit?"

THE SATURDAY EVENING POST

"Is this the day you wanted to get away a few minutes early?"

"Guess who's going to be a mother."

"I've rearranged my work schedule . . .
no dinner on washdays."

"I haven't really made up my mind yet, but I thought
I'd better take it while he was all worked up."

"Oh, oh, looks like I'm lost again."

"Did I ever tell you what
a scare you gave me?"

"See? Your hiccups are all gone."

— First Appearances of Beetle, Then Called Spider —

"Nothing, thanks, but you can bring
us a napkin to keep score on."

"I don't know the title, but it has a red cover and
my allowance is between pages 30 and 31."

"All right, recite Cicero's speech to the citizens
again, but this time turn the other way."

"Okay, Spider, heads we join the army,
tails we go on studying for final exams."

THE SATURDAY EVENING POST

"Separate checks?"

"Suppose there's any hope of the world being destroyed before final exams?"

CHAPTER FOUR

Beetle Begins

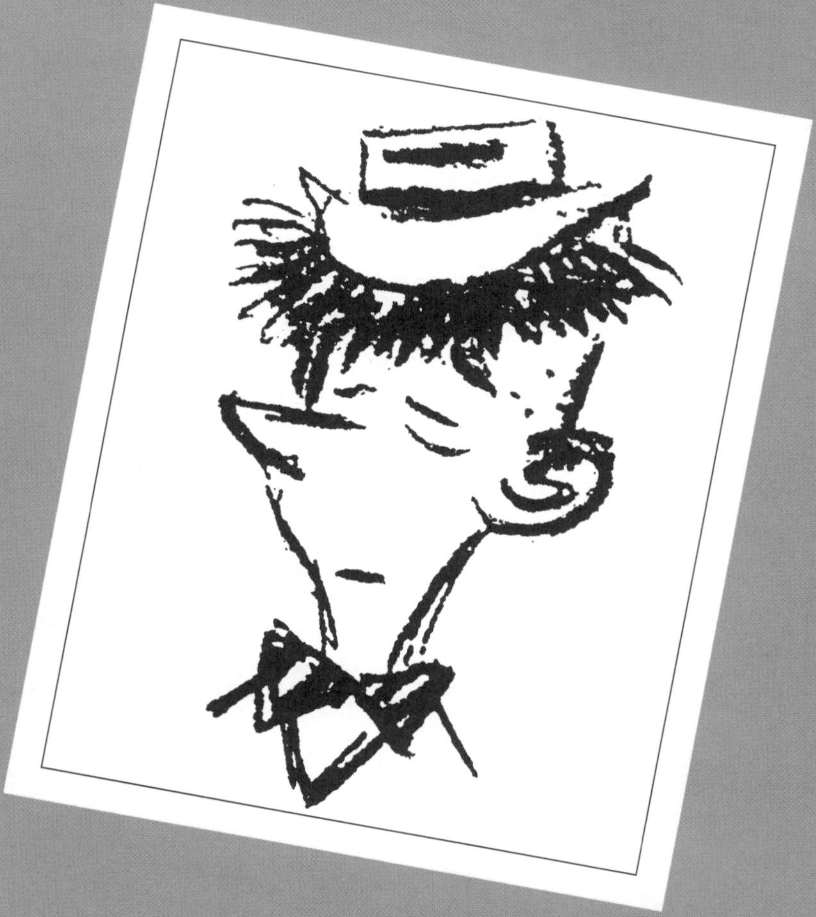

Living in a condemned building in New York in 1947 with only a few bucks in the bank was not the happiest of circumstances, especially when my first two hundred drawings had been rejected. Many of my college friends who had hoped to come to "the mountain" to make their fortune had already crawled back home. I wrote a card that said I WILL NOT BE DENIED and tacked it to the top of my drawing board. I laugh about it now. I was too naïve to know I *could* fail. ❖

It was time to do a comic strip. I took a character I'd created in my gag cartoons, Spider, changed him to Beetle, and took it to King Features, who bought it immediately.

The Strip Is Born

Contrary to King Features' announcement on the launching of the strip, there weren't many big cheers for *Beetle* in the beginning. It started September 4, 1950, in only twelve papers, and it moved very slowly. After six months it had signed on only twenty-five clients. Strips are typically not considered to be on solid ground unless they are sold to at least a hundred papers.

King Features Syndicate publicity, 1950

We decided not to run this strip and never to show Beetle's eyes (to help identify him).
He sleeps with his hat on—even takes showers—and everyone accepts it.

The First Step

1950

A journey of a thousand miles begins with the first step, they say, but watch out for that first step—it's a biggie. Starting a comic strip is like stepping out into darkness. Who knows where it will lead you? I didn't. Few people remember that *Beetle Bailey* began as a comic strip about college life. The original Beetle also had eyes (closed). Few people remember, because the strip appeared in so few papers.

As a practical matter of survival, the strip was soon given a military theme. All the original characters (except Beetle) were discarded and new ones created. That's what's fun about doing a comic strip: You're not stuck with your first mistake, you're free to make new mistakes at any time.

1951

For instance, Sarge originally had a wife and kids. When that theme became cumbersome, I conveniently forgot his family and left them out in limbo somewhere.

I've always subscribed to the saying "When something doesn't work, try something else." Going down with the ship is for dead heroes. Over the years new characters have been introduced, found boring, and given the gate. Sarge's tooth traveled all around his mouth till it found a home in the rear of his lower jaw.

1952

Then

Sarge's shape changed from slim to fat and Beetle expanded to a normal size and weight from a lanky string bean. Camp Swampy went through several attempts to give it more character and ended up an amorphous mess, forgotten and ignored by the Pentagon. Nobody can criticize Camp Swampy for being inaccurate when it comes to modern military procedures because it's in a world all its own, disowned by the army, civilian life, and time itself.

1960

The strip has been through many turmoils—banned by the army, censored by editors, and attacked by special-interest groups—but it's a survivor. Someone said a diamond is just a piece of coal that stuck with the job. To me, the strip is a diamond. I never knew where that first step would take me and there were many rocky times, but a certain amount of fame and fortune was my reward for keeping at it.

I've enjoyed every moment. There have been so many wonderful people I've met along the way, some important, but mostly just good people who like to laugh. And it's been my joy to think I've added to the humor of the past fifty years.

1970

1980

Now

The first strip

No one knew why the college theme didn't go over. Maybe it wasn't typical of the experience of most readers. Anyway, King Features (unbeknownst to me) was considering dropping it after a year's contract was up. In the meantime I was blithely scratching away, loving my work and happy to make the royal sum of $150 a week that King was paying me.

These first strips have never been republished or seen by more than a handful of readers, so it seemed a selection of them would be of interest.

Beetle's character began to emerge. His motto is: "Whenever the urge to work comes over me, I lie down until it goes away." But in his classes he always manages to scrape through by the skin of someone else's teeth. ❖

College Days Are Over

When the Korean War heated up, college boys began being drafted right and left. Since I had painted Beetle as the campus clown, he was destined to get his hiking papers. I thought he should bumble right into uniform, rather than wait for the draft. Fate was kind. The army theme was just what a failing strip needed. It quickly added a hundred papers and never stopped growing. In spite of this, my King Features editor, Sylvan Byck, said, "If you'd brought us an army strip in the first place, we never would have bought it."

After the Korean War was over, the brass felt they needed to tighten up discipline. In combat, staying clean is not as important as staying alive. But when the fighting is over, the spit-and-polish returns. Naturally there was some resistance by battle-hardened veterans. The brass felt *Beetle Bailey* wasn't helping their program. Beetle was making fun of authority and romanticizing foot-dragging. From this myopic point of view, Beetle had to go.

In December 1952 I got a letter from a friend who worked on *Pacific Stars and Stripes* informing me that they were dropping *Beetle* from the comic page and replacing it with *Joe Palooka*. A new major had been put in charge of the paper, and he was afraid of offending his superior officers. All cartoons now had to "be in good taste, must be funny, must not poke fun at any officer, must not poke fun at any unit or branch of the service, must be liked by the majors, the colonels, and the generals throughout the Far East"—a really big order.

It was a mistake on their part. It only revealed what everyone knew all along: Military bigwigs don't have a sense of humor. A sense of humor is a sign of maturity; a person with intelligence and confidence can laugh at himself. At least that's what all the news stories and broadcasts said. They made the brass look petty and ridiculous.

Probably the best favor the army officers did for me after my discharge was to ban me from *Stars and Stripes*. It became a tempest in a teapot, and the ensuing publicity rocketed *Beetle*'s circulation to another hundred papers overnight. I thank them again for their steady supply of funny material. ❖

Journal NEW YORK American

TRUTH, JUSTICE   PUBLIC SERVICE

THURSDAY, JANUARY 14, 1954   ★

Beetle Bailey Ban

MOMENTOUS military decisions of the past week give indication to thinkers that the Pentagon is not expecting another war.

The first is an order that Navy officers must wear swords again.

The second is a ban on "Beetle Bailey" in the Tokyo edition of Stars and Stripes, the GI newspaper.

Both orders are designed to increase, or at least protect, the prestige of officers.

Return of the swords starts with the top brass and goes thence down the line, presumably in direct proportion to the need for enhanced dignity.

For the benefit of the few, if any, who didn't know, "Beetle Bailey" is Mort Walker's delightful comic strip, carried in the Journal-American, which gently kids an "eagle colonel" as freely as a yardbird. Apparently Beetle has offended someone's dignity.

The reason that we think these orders are harbingers of peace is that if an appreciable number of reservists were called back to active duty, on threat of war, they would laugh both rulings right out of existence.

Newspaper articles about the Stars and Stripes *ban, 1954*

Sarge
(Orville P. Snorkel)

When Beetle joined the army, he needed someone to keep him in line. Sarge was the result. Sarge is probably my favorite character to draw. Not only does he look funny in all positions, but he takes up a lot of space, which saves me from drawing a lot of backgrounds. He's garrulous, profane, ecstatic, rough, sentimental, voracious . . . he does everything to an extreme. At first his only characteristic was meanness. He was much leaner, and I couldn't decide how many fangs a proper sergeant should have. But he gradually took shape like a blimp in full bloom. He beats up on his boys at one moment and takes them out for a beer the next, and it all seems natural.

1952   **1953**   **1963**   **Today**

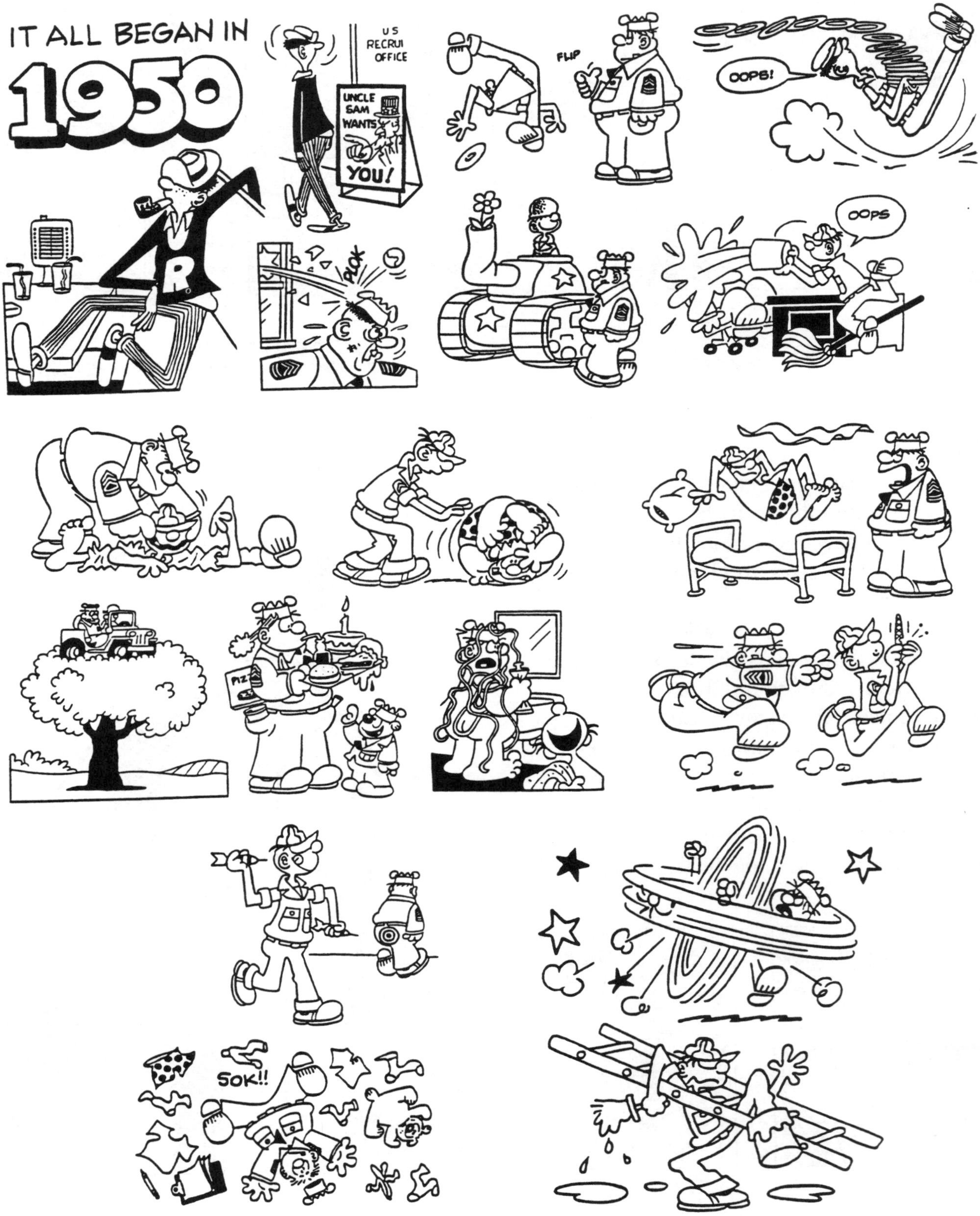
IT ALL BEGAN IN
1950
US
RECRUI
OFFICE
UNCLE
SAM
WANTS
YOU!
FLIP
OOPS!
R
PLOK
OOPS
PIZ
SOK!!

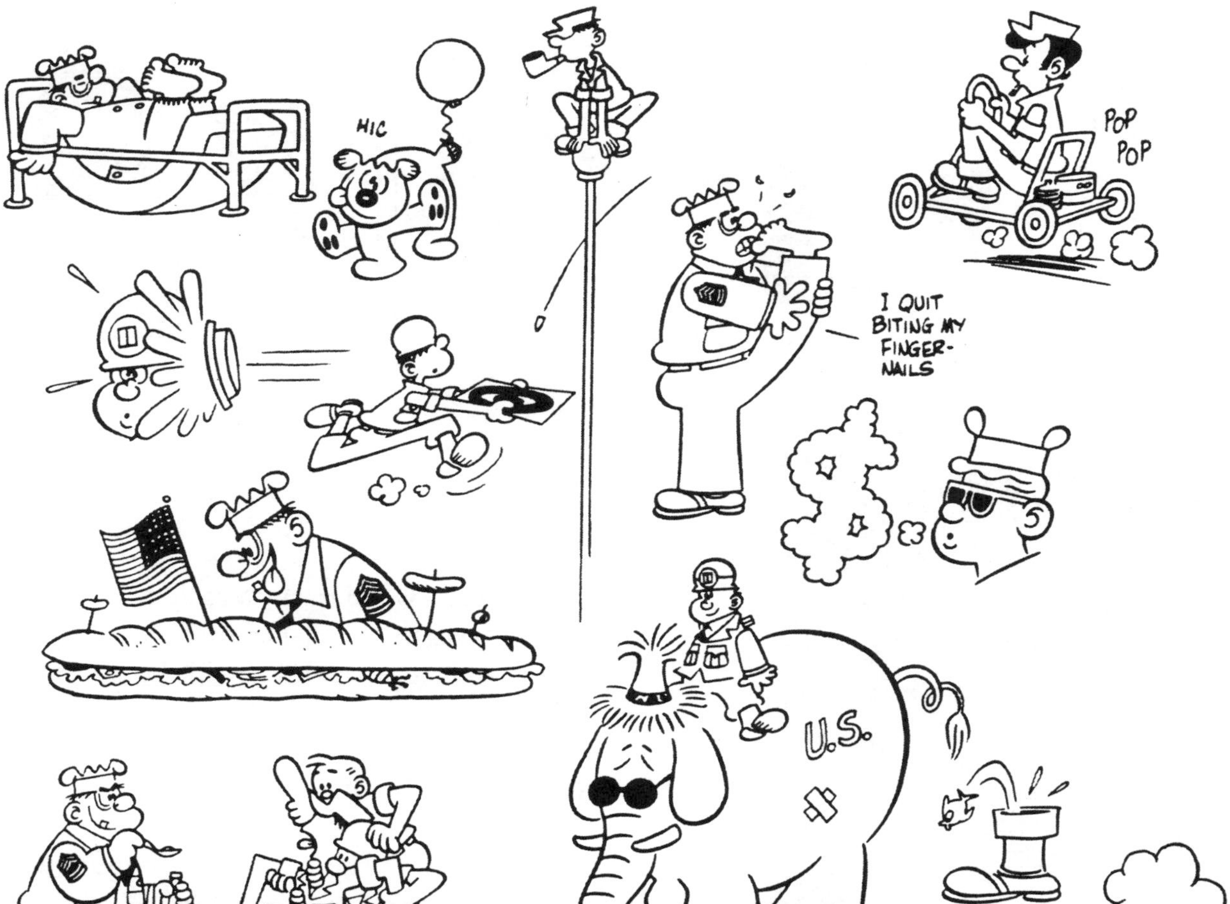
HIC
POP
POP
I QUIT BITING MY FINGER-NAILS
U.S.

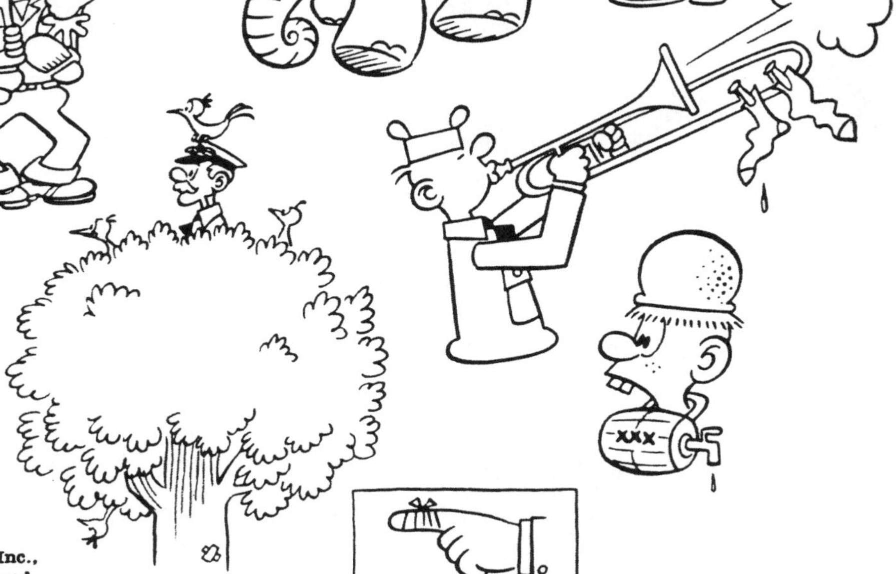
XXX
HOSPITAL

Many people wonder why a military strip like *Beetle* appeals to a civilian audience. The truth is, it isn't a military strip. It's a strip about a bunch of funny guys. They could be policemen, factory workers, college students, whatever. The army is just a convenient setting that everyone understands. The pecking order doesn't have to be explained, and the role of the poor guy at the bottom of the ladder is a classic everywhere. ❖

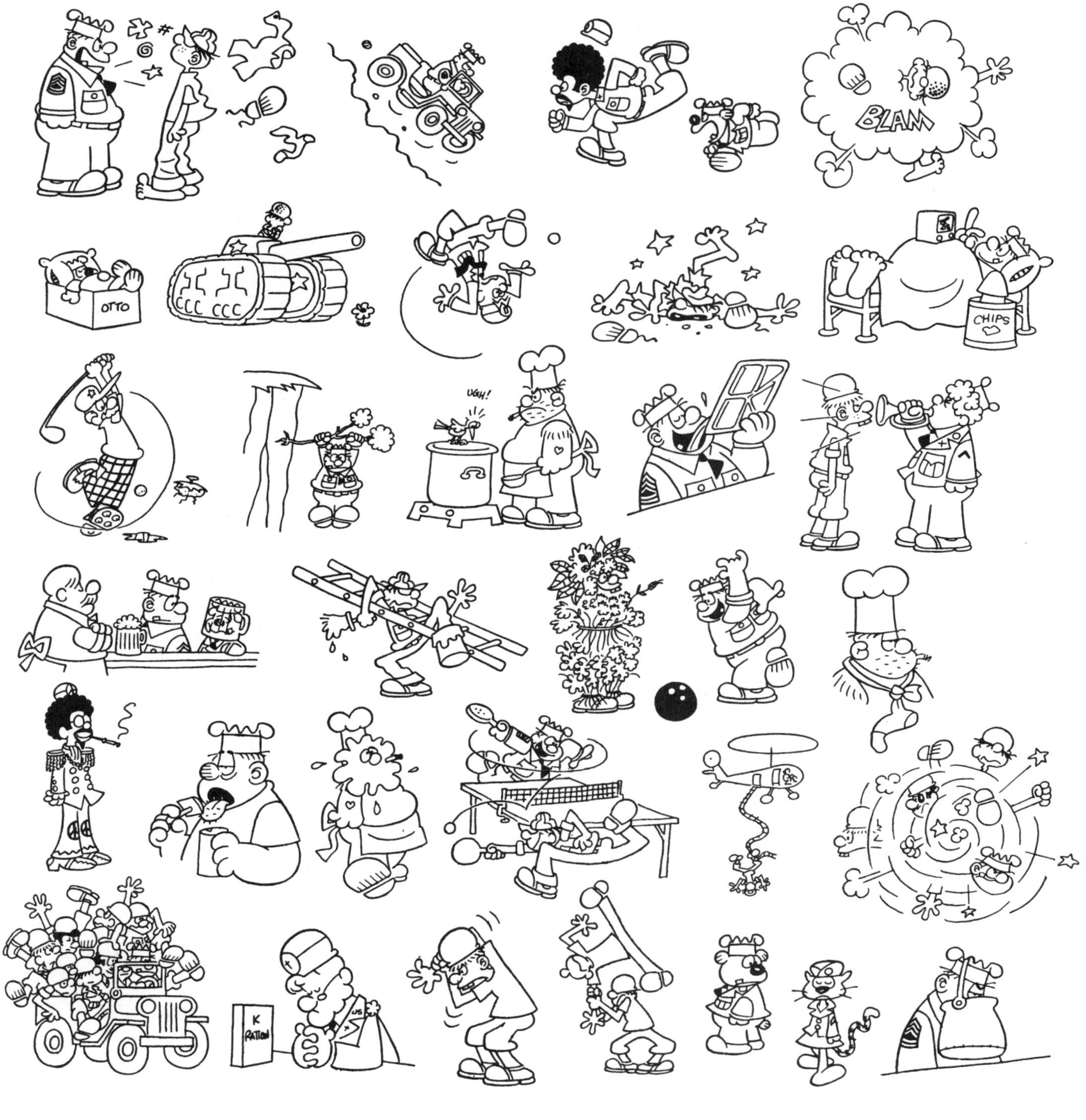
BLAM
OTTO
CHIPS
UGH!
K RATION

Lieutenant Flap

I attended a meeting around 1970 where I met several of the editors of *Ebony* magazine. They immediately jumped on me for having a "dishonest" army. "Your army is all white; it doesn't truly reflect the makeup of the real army today, with its large percentage of blacks."

I thought about it for almost a year and couldn't come up with a solution. If I put in a black that was as lazy as Beetle, I'd get criticism. If he was dumb like Zero, it would be worse. I made sketch after sketch and wasn't satisfied.

One night I dreamed of a perfect guy: an *officer*. He's black and proud of it, a strong personality with an Afro. I saw him drawn in all his glory and woke up. I lay there for about an hour and thought up six gags to launch the first week. So I wouldn't forget them, I even gave each one a name and made it into a sentence.

In the morning I rushed into my studio before breakfast and sketched him for a full week. I was overjoyed at my creation, but the syndicate wasn't sold. They said *Beetle* was one of the top strips in the country and why risk ruining it? "Because I have to," I replied. They took me to lunch at the 21 Club and tried to talk me out of it. I held fast. Finally, at the end of the lunch, the King Features president said, "Okay, if you really feel that strongly about it, go ahead."

There had been many blacks in strips in the past, but they were all subservient, lazy, and unacceptable in today's enlightened society. Mine was the first honest approach: to draw blacks in the comics as equals . . . even leaders. There was some shock when the first strips appeared. Several newspapers refused to run them. Angry blacks accused me of stereotyping; angry whites accused me of proselytizing. I got hate mail from everywhere for the first few weeks, until the readers saw I meant no harm. The papers that had canceled came back, and we added a lot of clients in the Caribbean and other South American countries. I began getting love letters, even a box of oranges from the yard of a black lady in California. I think I made the right decision. I love Lieutenant Flap.

Many people had urged me for years to put a black in my strip. The trouble was, if I made him a lazy goof-off like the regular cast, I'd get complaints. Finally I thought of creating a macho type who liked wild clothes, and Lieutenant Flap was born. There was an initial fuss from people who thought I was either propagandizing or ridiculing blacks. *Stars and Stripes* banned me again, until Senator Proxmire of Wisconsin convinced them to reinstate me. Now the flurry has died down and Lieutenant Flap is a favorite with many.

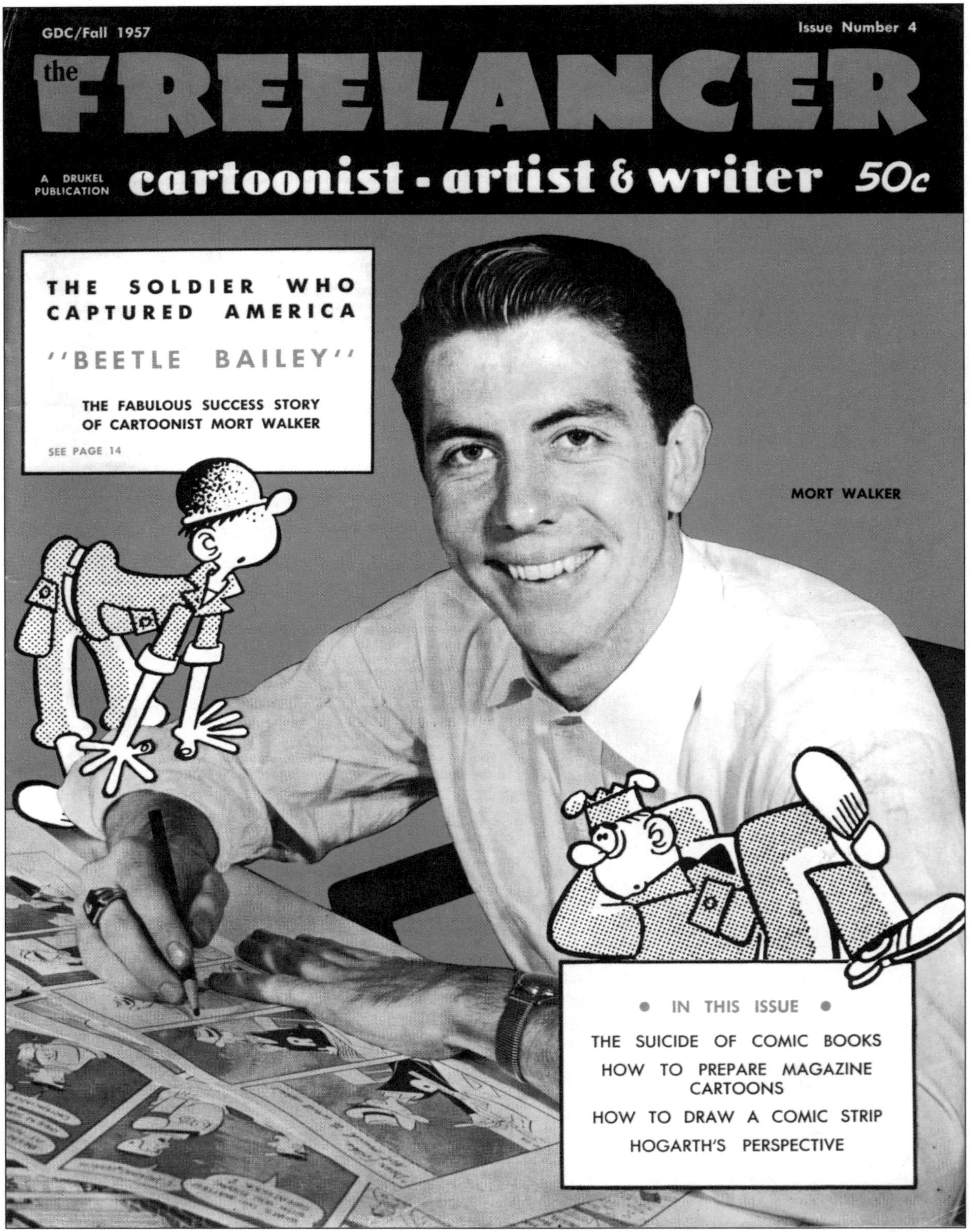
GDC/Fall 1957
Issue Number 4
the FREELANCER
A DRUKEL PUBLICATION
cartoonist - artist & writer
50c
THE SOLDIER WHO CAPTURED AMERICA
''BEETLE BAILEY''
THE FABULOUS SUCCESS STORY OF CARTOONIST MORT WALKER
SEE PAGE 14
MORT WALKER
• IN THIS ISSUE •
THE SUICIDE OF COMIC BOOKS
HOW TO PREPARE MAGAZINE CARTOONS
HOW TO DRAW A COMIC STRIP
HOGARTH'S PERSPECTIVE

Cover boy

"WELL, WE GOT RID OF THE MICE. **NOW** WHAT?"

Beetle Bailey has been studied by sociologists for the way authority is represented. As a general rule, Americans feel that authority should be questioned, not blindly followed, and people in authority in this country accept this resistance as an inalienable right. In Europe and many Asian countries, the class system and regal sovereignty are so deeply ingrained that many citizens never question an order. In Italy, there is a soldier comic strip where the private always ends up in jail for things that Beetle does routinely. Beetle and Sarge play the game, Sarge doing his job by imposing authority and Beetle doing his by resisting it. ❖

— I Base Most of My Characters on Real People —

Beetle was patterned after my old high school and army buddy Dave Hornaday. Dave was tall and skinny and was always innocently getting into trouble.

Sergeant Snorkel was inspired by a top sergeant I once had, Sgt. Octavian Savou. He was tough as nails but thought of us as "his boys."

When I wanted a young neophyte lieutenant, I thought back on all the dumb things I did as a twenty-year-old shavetail and created Lieutenant Fuzz.

My partner Dik Browne sneaked into the strip via the brainy Plato.

Chaplain Staneglass came out of Barry Fitzgerald's performance as a priest in *Going My Way*.

Marilyn Monroe was godmother to Miss Buxley.

Jesse Wrench was an eccentric professor at M.U.

From the beginning we decided it would be a great trademark never to show Beetle's eyes. But now and then we have fun with it by having Beetle get a scare and his hat flies off, only to have another hat underneath. Sometimes when I make a speech, I tell the audience I have a special treat for them. I will draw Beetle's eyes for the first time ever. Then I draw two dots.

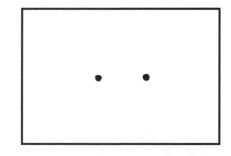

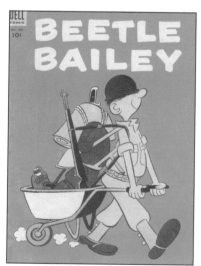

The very first comic book, Dell No. 469, 1953. The first three issues, 469, 521 (also 1953), and 552 (1954) contained art entirely by me, both covers and interiors.

The second comic book, Dell No. 521 (1953)

The first actual book compilation, containing daily strips and numerous one-panel gags, the latter created specifically for this book, 1958.

CHAPTER FIVE

Mort and Dik

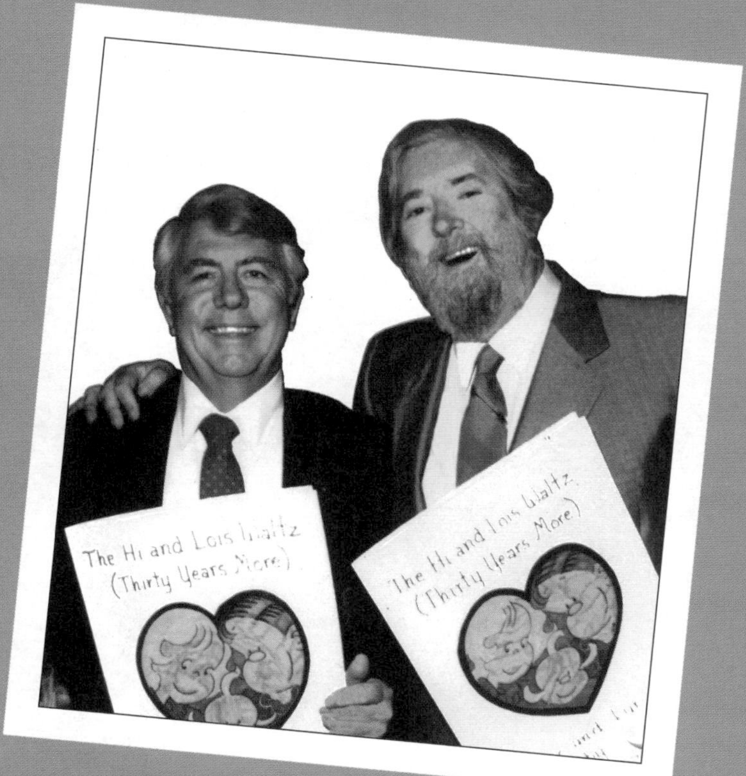
The Hi and Lois Waltz
(Thirty Years More)
The Hi and Lois Waltz
(Thirty Years More)

A cartoonist friend had sold a family-type strip to another syndicate. They suggested he get a writer, and he came to me. I asked my editor if I could write for another syndicate, and he replied that if I wanted to write a family strip, why didn't I write one for King Features? I jumped at the idea, since I was worried that *Beetle* might lose readers when the Korean War was over. In an earlier sequence, Beetle had gone home on furlough and I had introduced his sister, Lois, her husband, Hi, and their children, so I already had an unemployed family. It was easy to put them to work. Focusing on my own life, I was able to put our experiences to good use. I decided I didn't want to do the usual mean-little-kids-and-bickering-parents strip. I wanted real everyday doings with warmth and genuine feelings reflected humorously.

The syndicate liked my ideas, and we set out to find the best artist in the country to work on it. I began combing magazines and newspapers and making a list. My editor did the same and we met to compare names. To our great surprise, we both had the same guy at the top: Dik Browne. I had seen some ads he'd done and my editor had seen Dik's comic strip in *Boy's Life*.

We found out that Dik worked for an ad agency, and my editor called to see if he was interested. Dik said okay, very warily, and then went to the art department to see which one of his friends was pulling his leg. When he determined that the call was legitimate, he called the syndicate back with a resounding *yes!*

Hi and Lois began in 1954 and sold fairly well, but not what I had expected. Editors compared it to *Beetle* and didn't think it was as funny. I explained that the humor was different. *Beetle* was an army strip with slam-bang action and rough male humor. *Hi and Lois* was a nice family strip with affectionate insights into the

affairs of the average citizen. It continued to grow at a slow rate.

At a meeting with our sales manager I complained about the number of newspapers that *Hi and Lois* was sold to. He told me there were a lot of family strips out there competing with me and I should try to do something unique to make my strip more desirable. I had read a book once that revealed the thoughts of a baby who couldn't talk. I thought it was very funny and decided to use the idea on baby, Trixie. It was an immediate success. Of course, now almost every family strip has a thinking baby, so it's not unique anymore. ❖

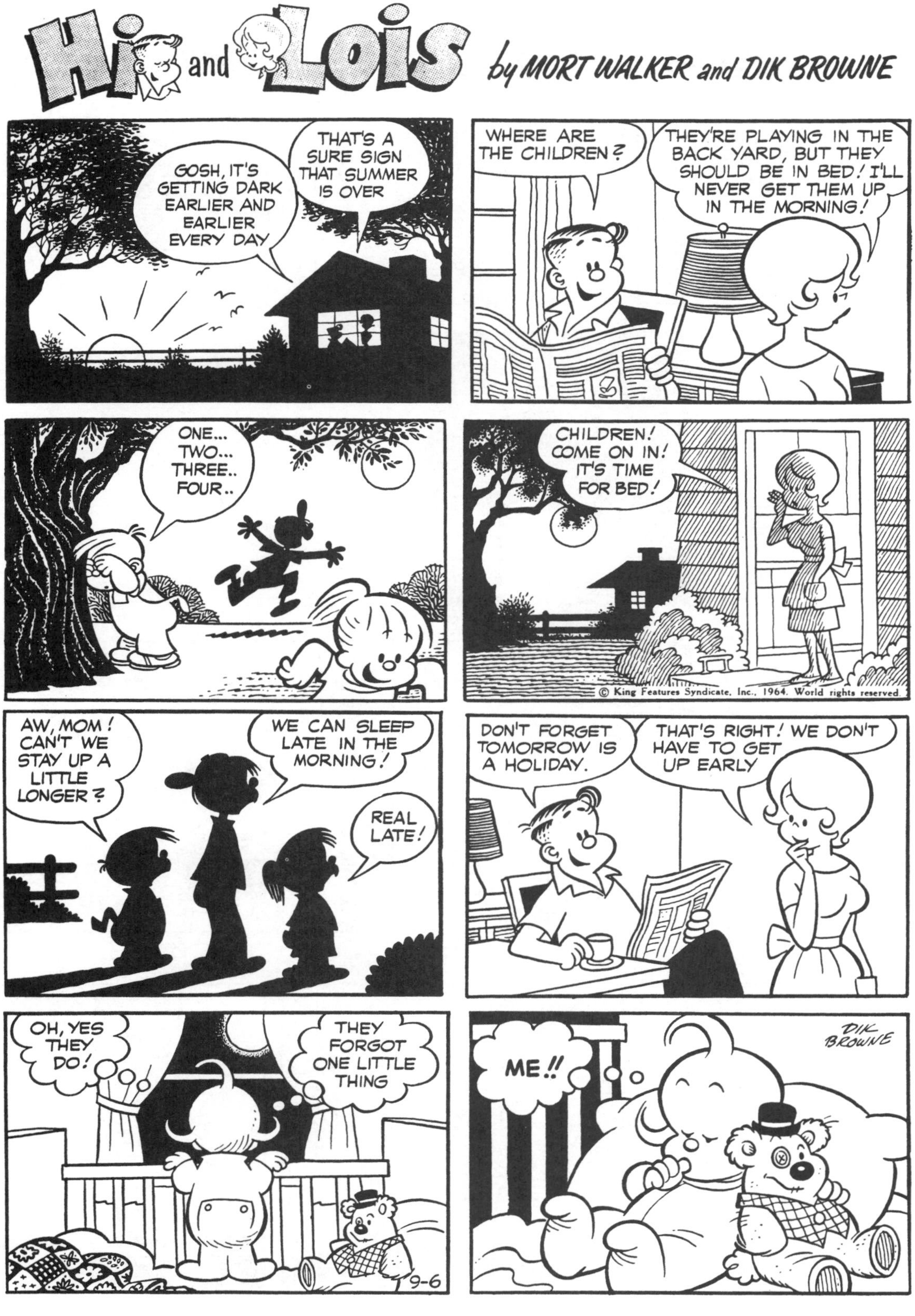
Hi and Lois
by MORT WALKER and DIK BROWNE
GOSH, IT'S GETTING DARK EARLIER AND EARLIER EVERY DAY
THAT'S A SURE SIGN THAT SUMMER IS OVER
WHERE ARE THE CHILDREN?
THEY'RE PLAYING IN THE BACK YARD, BUT THEY SHOULD BE IN BED! I'LL NEVER GET THEM UP IN THE MORNING!
ONE... TWO... THREE.. FOUR..
CHILDREN! COME ON IN! IT'S TIME FOR BED!
© King Features Syndicate, Inc., 1964. World rights reserved.
AW, MOM! CAN'T WE STAY UP A LITTLE LONGER?
WE CAN SLEEP LATE IN THE MORNING!
REAL LATE!
DON'T FORGET TOMORROW IS A HOLIDAY.
THAT'S RIGHT! WE DON'T HAVE TO GET UP EARLY
OH, YES THEY DO!
THEY FORGOT ONE LITTLE THING
9-6
DIK BROWNE
ME!!

A papier-mâché sculpture I made of Dik, about 1960

An early Hi and Lois *Sunday page shows Dik's love of detail, 1957.*

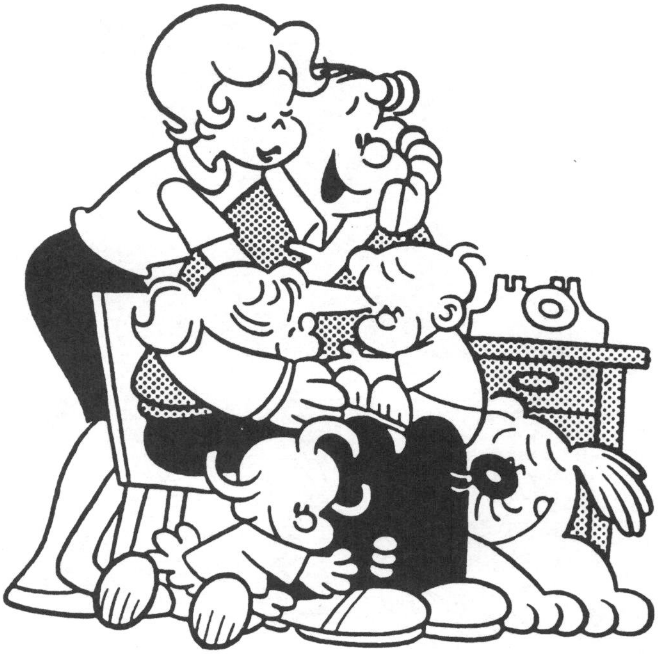

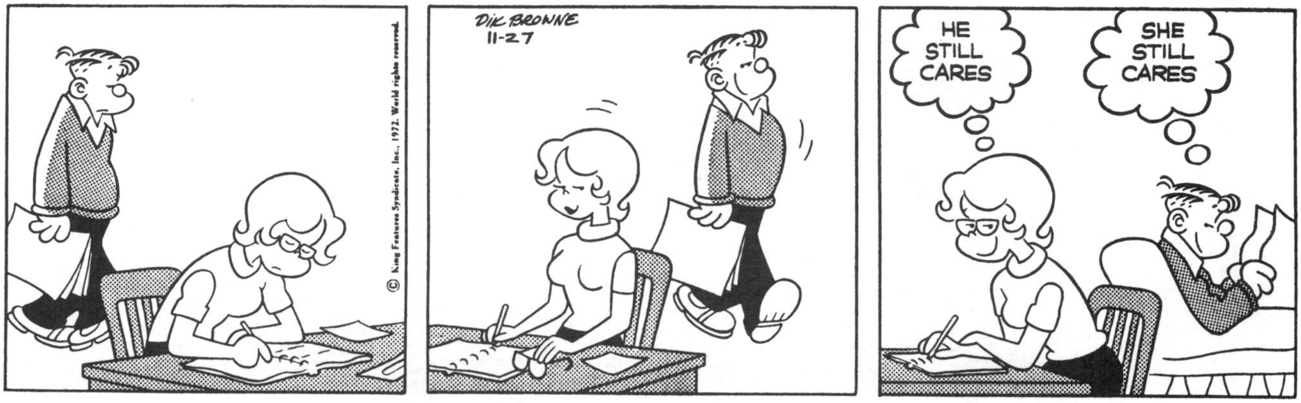
© King Features Syndicate, Inc., 1972. World rights reserved.
DIK BROWNE
11-27
HE STILL CARES
SHE STILL CARES

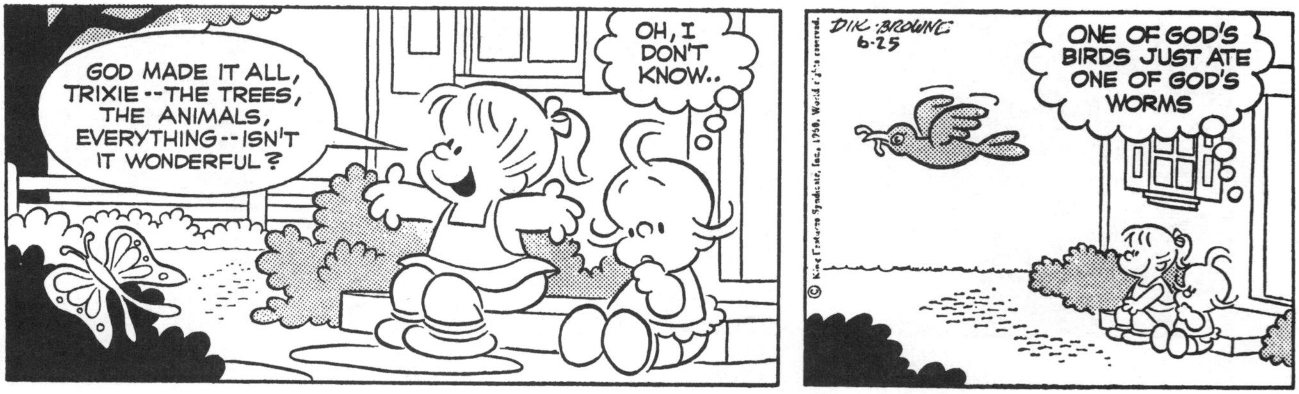
GOD MADE IT ALL, TRIXIE--THE TREES, THE ANIMALS, EVERYTHING--ISN'T IT WONDERFUL?
OH, I DON'T KNOW..
DIK BROWNE
6-25
ONE OF GOD'S BIRDS JUST ATE ONE OF GOD'S WORMS

—— I Don't Enjoy Being Banned, But... ——

Dik Browne was as warm and fuzzy as a person can get. He had a great sense of humor and a fabulous mind. We were partners for over thirty years with no contract except lots of handshakes. Everyone loved the guy. Dik Browne was the cartoonist's cartoonist; he *looked* like he drew funny pictures for a

living. I once described Dik as "a big bearded bear of a man—five years overdue at the barbershop, shirttail out, buttons open, pants drooping—he appears to be melting."

Dik's sons, Bob and Chris, are real practical jokers and were always preying on their gullible dad. Dik was an easy target. Here are a few classics: Dik was sitting with friends in his kitchen once when the phone rang. It was a woman from the neighborhood who had been bugging him to do some drawings. He answered her very briefly, "Yes . . . uh-

huh . . . yeah . . . okay . . . good-bye." He hung up and said, "That woman is driving me nuts. She's such a pest!" As he was saying this, Bob walked through the kitchen into the family room. The phone rang again. It was the woman's voice. "I heard that," she said. "You called me a pest." Dik's face turned red. "No, I didn't," he swore, protesting his innocence. It wasn't until he hung up and regained his composure that he realized the impossibility of her hearing him. His son the mimic had fooled him again.

I used to sketch up the ideas for *Hi and Lois* on typing paper and send them to Dik, who used them to draw up the finished strips. A package of ideas arrived at Dik's studio one morning, and Bob and Chris waylaid the sketches before Dik came to work. They took a six-panel Sunday page idea sketch and deftly altered Hi's face so that he gradually looked more and more like a dog. In the last panel he had grown floppy ears and had a black nose. He was saying, *Wuf! Wuf!* They forged a note from me that said, "Dear Dik, I've been studying the new trend in comic strips. It seems that dogs are in these days. There are a lot of dog strips on the market gaining great popularity. I won-

der if we shouldn't cash in on the fad and convert the whole *Hi and Lois* family into dogs. Here is an example of how it could be done gradually, Mort." Bob and Chris resealed the envelope and put it on Dik's desk. He arrived, opened the package, read it, paused, reread it, paused, reached for the phone, paused, reread the letter, reached for the phone again, paused, and repeated this act until his sons broke up.

Dik was always inviting people to visit him and then would forget all about it. The phone rang one morning when Dik and Joan were still asleep. Dik fumbled for the phone and answered it. A foreign voice

said, "Hallo, Deek? Ees Pablo here. Remember Pablo from Brazeel? You know you say come see you anytime. Well, I am here at train station with wife and kids." Dik was flustered but tried to be friendly. Joan, also awake, said, "Who are you inviting? The house is a mess. We can't entertain anyone today." Dik put his hand over the mouthpiece and said, "I'll make some coffee. I'm sure they like coffee. I'll keep

them out by the pool." Just then, Bob burst into the room and said, "Let me handle this, Dad." He took the phone from Dik and yelled into it, "Who do you people think you are, showing up here and expecting to be entertained? My father is a busy man!" He slammed down the receiver. Dik fell back in bed clutching his heart and gasping from embarrassment until he saw Bob chuckling in triumph, having taken Pop again.

Dik was the first to admit he didn't have any fashion sense, but one day he outdid himself. As he headed for the door in a horrendously clashing ensemble, his wife, Joan, eyed him incredulously. "I hope you get lost," she said, "so I can describe you to the police."

One windy day, Dik was trying unsuccessfully to light a cigarette on the golf course. "Hit the ball, Dik," yelled his partners impatiently. He put the cigarette in his pocket, hit his ball, and was striding down the fairway when someone in the distance called, "Hey! You're on fire!" "No, I just got a lucky shot," Dik called back. Billows of yellow smoke trailed behind him. His buddies ran over, ripped the jacket off his back, and stomped on it. Unshaken, he put his jacket on again and felt in the pocket. "Darn it!" he said. "You mashed my Tootsie Roll."

Dik's pockets were always filled with the day's residue. One time he was held up on a New York street by a mugger with a 45-caliber handgun. He began digging for money. Up came matches, cigarettes, keys, gum, Tums, candy, notes, a pencil stub, and rubber bands. "Oh, forget it!" the mugger said.

Dik woke out of a deep sleep one morning to find Bill Yates,

comics editor of King Features Syndicate, on the phone. He said a subscribing newspaper had discovered that Dik had repeated a *Hagar* gag, word for word. A reporter had called for a comment on the mistake, and Bill wondered if Dik had an explanation. Dik said apologetically, "As we go through life we learn that there are three things that tend to repeat themselves: history, sauerkraut, and old cartoonists."

We were on the seventh hole at the Silvermine golf

course when a car filled with cartoonists drove up. Jerry Marcus was at the wheel. He stopped and yelled out the window to Dik, "How do you get to Silvermine?" "Practice," Dik said wryly.

The seventeenth hole at Silvermine has a big lake in front of the green. Dik's shot failed to get across; he tried again and again without success. Disgusted, he threw his club in his bag just as the course superintendent drove by in his cart. "Aren't you going to finish the hole?" he asked. "No," Dik replied. "I have a man who comes in Thursdays who does it for me."

A woman friend drove by one day and stopped to wave to Dik. He thought he'd be cute and respond in French. *"Je vous adore!"* he called out. She got out, looked at her car door, and said, "Oh, it's just a little scratch."

Dik always had a hard time keeping his pants up around his ample waist. On Ladies' Day at the club he was lifting his bag out of his trunk when his pants fell to his ankles. As he tried to put his bag back he yelled, "Don't look, ladies, don't look!" Of course, nobody looked.

There was a power outage in the area where Dik and Joan lived. After a few days, the laundry began to pile up and Joan suggested they find a Laundromat. She dropped Dik off with the clothes while she went to get candles and ice and a few other necessities, telling Dik to watch for her and she'd try to pull up right in front of the Laundromat. He did the laundry and was in the process of putting everything through the drying cycle when he thought he saw Joan drive up. It was raining and hard to see, but he ran out to the car and yelled at the lady in the driver's seat, "My shorts are still wet!" The woman sped off. "That wasn't our car," Dik observed, as the car disappeared.

Dik's definition of golf:
"An obscene act indulged in by consenting adults."

Dik's definition of philosophy:
"Looking for a black cat in a dark room when there is no cat."

Dik's definition of religion:
"When you think you have found the black cat."

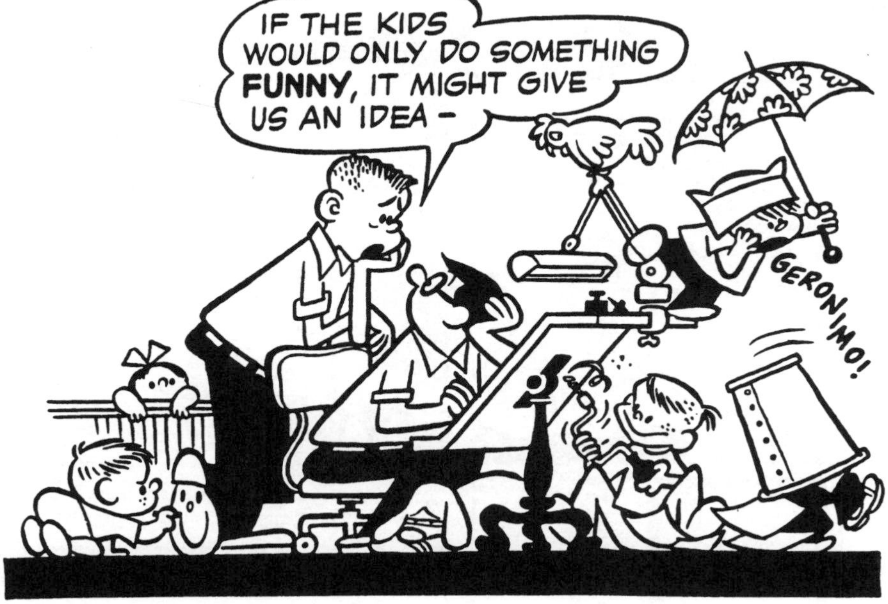
IF THE KIDS WOULD ONLY DO SOMETHING **FUNNY**, IT MIGHT GIVE US AN IDEA –
GERONIMO!

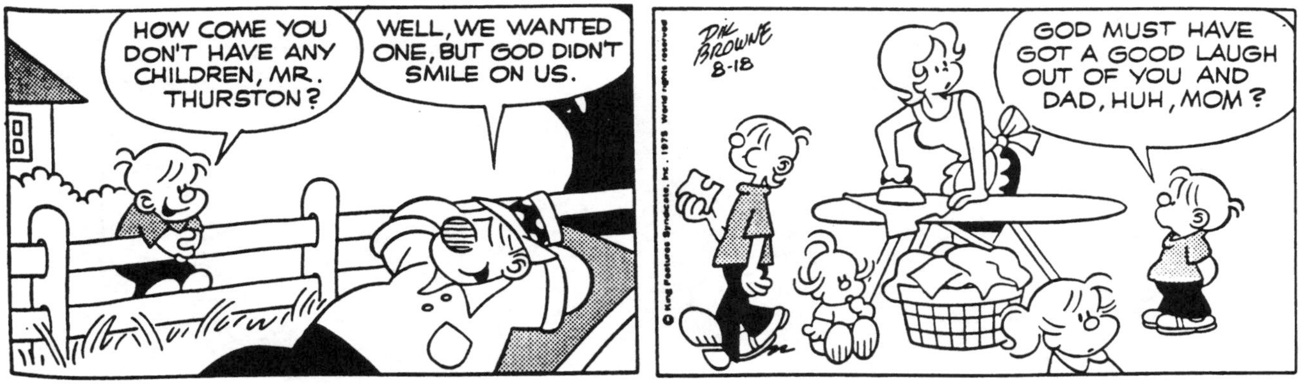
HOW COME YOU DON'T HAVE ANY CHILDREN, MR. THURSTON?
WELL, WE WANTED ONE, BUT GOD DIDN'T SMILE ON US.
DIK BROWNE 8-18
© King Features Syndicate, Inc. 1978 World rights reserved
GOD MUST HAVE GOT A GOOD LAUGH OUT OF YOU AND DAD, HUH, MOM?

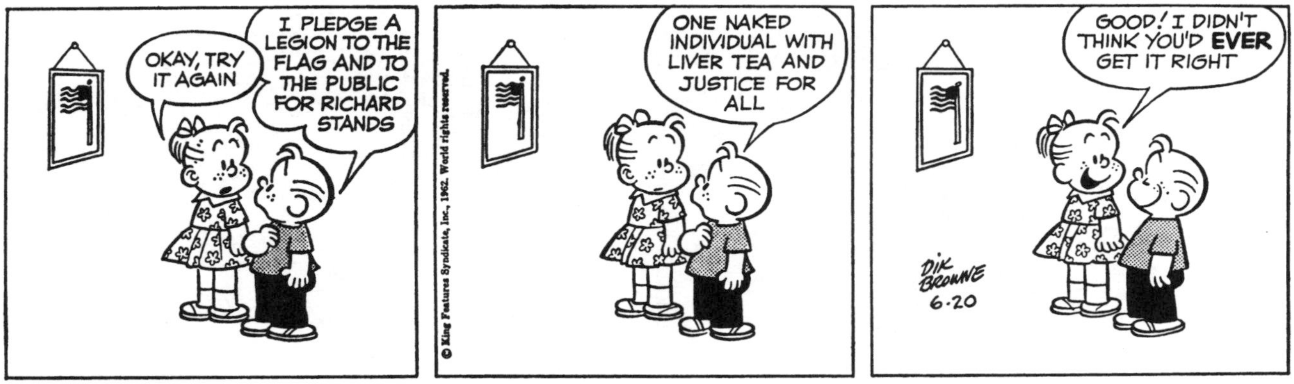
OKAY, TRY IT AGAIN
I PLEDGE A LEGION TO THE FLAG AND TO THE PUBLIC FOR RICHARD STANDS
© King Features Syndicate, Inc., 1962. World rights reserved.
ONE NAKED INDIVIDUAL WITH LIVER TEA AND JUSTICE FOR ALL
GOOD! I DIDN'T THINK YOU'D **EVER** GET IT RIGHT
DIK BROWNE 6·20

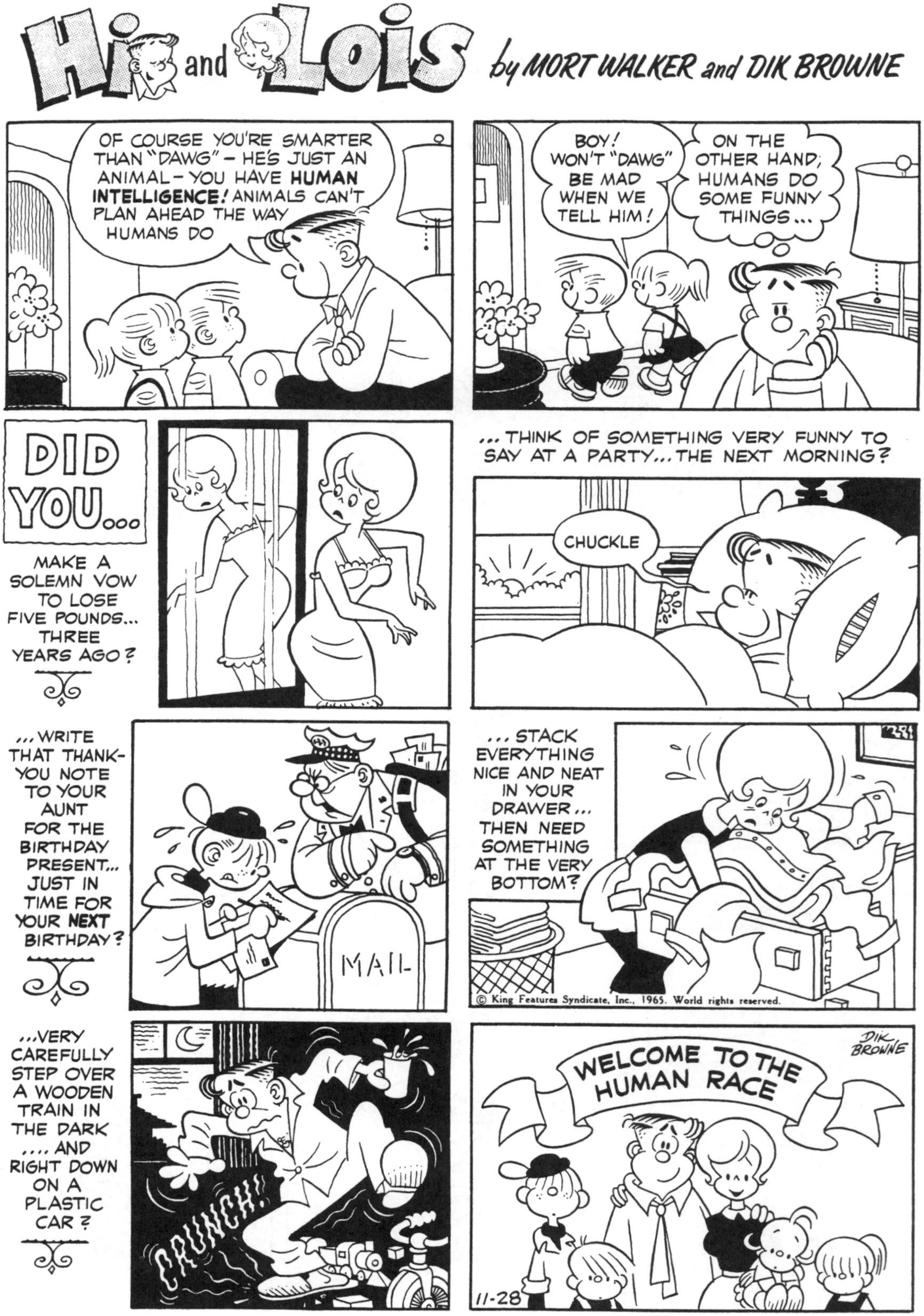
Hi and Lois
by MORT WALKER and DIK BROWNE
OF COURSE YOU'RE SMARTER THAN "DAWG" – HE'S JUST AN ANIMAL – YOU HAVE **HUMAN INTELLIGENCE!** ANIMALS CAN'T PLAN AHEAD THE WAY HUMANS DO
BOY! WON'T "DAWG" BE MAD WHEN WE TELL HIM!
ON THE OTHER HAND, HUMANS DO SOME FUNNY THINGS...
DID YOU...
MAKE A SOLEMN VOW TO LOSE FIVE POUNDS... THREE YEARS AGO?
...THINK OF SOMETHING VERY FUNNY TO SAY AT A PARTY... THE NEXT MORNING?
CHUCKLE
...WRITE THAT THANK-YOU NOTE TO YOUR AUNT FOR THE BIRTHDAY PRESENT... JUST IN TIME FOR YOUR **NEXT** BIRTHDAY?
MAIL
...STACK EVERYTHING NICE AND NEAT IN YOUR DRAWER... THEN NEED SOMETHING AT THE VERY BOTTOM?
© King Features Syndicate, Inc., 1965. World rights reserved.
...VERY CAREFULLY STEP OVER A WOODEN TRAIN IN THE DARK .... AND RIGHT DOWN ON A PLASTIC CAR?
CRUNCH!
DIK BROWNE
WELCOME TO THE HUMAN RACE
11-28

Dik was talking to my former wife one day, and she said jokingly, "You better be nice to me, because when Mort is gone, you'll have to deal with me." He thought about this for a few months and then created *Hagar the Horrible*. ❖

FOR GOSH SAKE, HELGA! LET'S TALK ABOUT IT LATER — CAN'T YOU SEE I'M BUSY?!

DIK BROWNE 2·7

WHAT IS THE KEY TO HAPPINESS?

ABSTINENCE, POVERTY, FASTING AND CELIBACY

IS THERE SOMEONE ELSE UP THERE I COULD TALK TO?

2·7 DIK BROWNE

CHAPTER SIX

The Funny Factory

Mort "Working"

Mort Walker sits in his lounge chair to think up ideas.

Where do you get your ideas? is the question most often asked of cartoonists. Mort Walker answers that, although he gets many from reading the newspaper, watching television, or going to movies, most of his material comes from observing people. "The main ingredient in humor is the revelation of human nature—its frailties, its reasoning power—and the interrelationships between characters," Mort explains. "You can't have a good story unless you have conflict. You can have violent conflict as in an adventure story, or you can have the conflict of ideas. Mostly, what we do in *Hi and Lois* is focus on the conflicts

between the different family members due to their age differences. You can get a lot of gags out of the way people reason and do things. It's human nature you're after." Mort claims that what he tries to do is to reveal to the readers truths about their daily lives that perhaps they hadn't seen before. Mort gets a lot of satisfaction out of the process of writing a daily comic strip like *Hi and Lois*. "To create an idea out of thin air, to think of a situation in your mind that becomes a good story line that someone is going to enjoy, is an absolute thrill," he claims. "The amazing thing is that a thought you put down on paper might live for-

ever by being quoted, and that's something to be proud of." *Hi and Lois* has been quoted many times in *Reader's Digest*, among other places. "I think some great ideas are expressed in comic strips," he continues. "They should be observed and studied and preserved because they are a chronicle of everyday life, and there's some great philosophy in them." Mort obviously takes the humor business very seriously and gives his creative role a great deal of thought. That single-minded sense of purpose is one secret of his tremendous success.

—From *The Best of "Hi and Lois"*

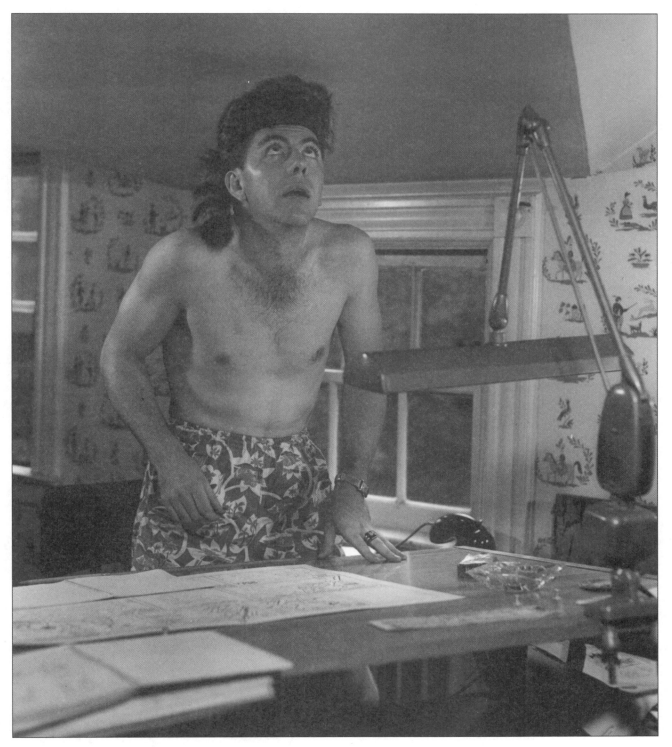

*My early studio in Greenwich, Connecticut, was on the third floor of my house.
It was so hot I worked only in my shorts. The ceiling was slanted and I hit
my head every time I stood up, so I wore a coonskin hat to protect me.*

Photograph from a 1960 newspaper story

I was ecstatic to have my own comic strip and be able to work at home. No more commuting to my magazine job in New York City. The awful crush of the subways, the waiting for buses in the rain, the waste of time—these were other people's problems now.

But soon I discovered a new set of concerns. I was completely on my own. I would sink or swim depending on my own ability to paddle. It's tough to discipline yourself to get up in the morning, start to work (rather than read newspapers till noon), and stick to it, resisting the many temptations for fun. It's tough to discipline the family, too. Isn't Daddy available for play, baby-sitting, shopping, conversation? Even neighbors get in on the act when they see male power around to help carry things, fix cars, or draw posters. Surely if you're not in New York, you can't be *working*.

I used to work in a barn behind my house. It was a wonderful place to get things done, except for the family of raccoons who lived in the attic. Their noises didn't usually bother me much, but once I was working on a very large drawing of about fifty figures. I'd been working several days on it when I came in one morning and found my drawing board covered with plaster and urine all over the drawing. They had broken through the ceiling and ruined my work. Or maybe it was an editorial comment. The ASPCA suggested that I throw mothballs up there to drive them away; they just came out and gave me dirty looks and went back in. At least I found out how they got in and out: through the cupola. I watched one day to see them leave and had the carpenter put on a plywood door. They simply opened the door and went inside. Next time I tried chicken wire and it worked. For a long time they would come up to my window and glare at me or hang out in the tree to face me as I came out my door. Eventually they left for someone else's attic—and I missed them.

BEETLE, YOU'LL NEVER BECOME A LEADER LYING IN THE SACK

LISTEN TO THIS...

"20 ROMAN EMPERORS WERE ASSASSINATED..." "4 PRESIDENTS, AND 70 WORLD LEADERS SINCE WORLD WAR ONE."

AND HE WANTS ME TO BE A LEADER!

People always ask me if I was in the war. "Yes," I answer. "I don't claim that I won the war. But I was in it and we didn't lose it."

When I draw my comic strip, I rule the world. I can make my characters do whatever I want and say whatever I want, and there's no back talk. I'm in complete control. I lose it all when I lay down my pencil and deal with my wife and family. ❖

I like to call cartoons "our art" because of their universal appeal to the young, the old, all genders, all ages, all religions, and all nationalities. People everywhere enjoy cartoons every day, from comic strips in the morning papers to editorial cartoons, advertising, animation on TV and in the movies, in magazines, and on T-shirts, cereal boxes, toys, and other products. Cartoons are always in our lives.

Why? Because they make people feel good. They entertain us, excite us, and make us think. It's a happy art, usually.

Cartoons create friends for people, whether it's good old Dagwood in trouble again or Donald Duck losing his temper, Superman saving the world or Snoopy and his dreams of glory. We all respond to the basic human nature in these characters and embrace them.

We don't need a college course on cartoon appreciation to enjoy these drawings; they are instantly understandable. Cartoonists design them that way, analyzing universal experiences and condensing them into an immediately recognizable form. It requires a

collection of skills: illustration, writing, character creation, and an ability to interpret events. It gets into every part of our lives. It is truly "our art."

beetle bailey®
the all-american musical

In 1982 a songwriting team, Neil and Gretchen Gould, came to me with the idea of doing a *Beetle Bailey* musical for the stage. I liked their approach and agreed to do a script. After much work we got a presentation together and invited some Broadway producers to come and look at it in a room we rented in New York. One producer was interested, but he wanted some changes to make it more dramatic; then he disappeared. We went to a number of theaters without any luck and finally found one that agreed to put it on the stage, the Candlewood Theater in Connecticut.

We hired a director and held our auditions in New York and saw some great talent. The toughest part to cast was Sarge. We didn't find him until the last minute. We rented a dormitory for the cast to live in during rehearsals and the show. I was constantly rewriting as the cast and the director invented new

Sarge (Joe Paparone, at right) offers words of dubious wisdom to Beetle (Greg Whalen) in Beetle Bailey.

lines and scenes. We threw out the first scene, and a scene in the middle that the producer had insisted on, and were left with two extra actors we had to pay for the duration.

Opening night was as exciting as having a new baby or sending a child off to college. Buses of important people came from New York. I felt it

was a good show, but the critics didn't all agree. Several of them thought the scenes with Miss Buxley and General Halftrack were too sexist.

Since then we've had some interest in it and I've rewritten it many times. I hope someday it will find a home. ❖

Poll Crowns 'Potentates' Of Comics

Philip H. Love, feature editor of the *Washington* (D. C.) *Star*, reported several "surprises" in the Newspaper Comics Week poll he ran to see how the Star's 34 cartoon strips and panels rate with readers.

The top 10 were:

1. Beetle Bailey.
2. Hi and Lois.
3. Wizard of Id.
4. B. C.
5. Mr. Tweedy.
6. On Stage.
7. Juliet Jones.
8. Kerry Drake.
9. Freddy.
10. Buz Sawyer.

In his report on the poll, Love said:

* * *

There's no surprise in the fact that Beetle Bailey placed first, with 4,702 points and only four nominations for oblivion, a net score of 4,698. This otherwise hapless GI has been No. 1 in the Star for 10 of the last 11 years.

There's no surprise, either, in the fact that Hi and Lois finished second. It did that last year.

It is surprising, however, to find the Wizard of Id in third place, a jump from 13th, and B. C. up from 10th to fourth.

This makes Mort Walker and Johnny Hart the potentates of the Star's comic pages. Mort draws Beetle and writes Hi and Lois, and Johnny does the same jobs on the Wizard and B. C. Hi and Lois is drawn by Dik Browne and the Wizard by Brant Parker.

Other surprises—to me at least—were the advances of On Stage and Juliet Jones to the No. 1 and No. 2 spots among story strips, leaping over both Kerry Drake and Buz Sawyer, which came third and fourth in this category. Last year's top story strip was Gil Thorp, now No. 5.

Ballots were tabulated by scoring 10 points for each first-choice vote, nine for second, eight for third, and so on. Nominations for oblivion were subtracted from the totals to determine the final scores.

Bailey achieved the most first-choice points (1,340), with B. C. second (940) and the Wizard third (910). Hi & Lois garnered only 540 first-choice points, but this was offset by the fact that only seven readers nominated it for oblivion. In contrast, B. C. got 121 of these nasty nominations and the Wizard 97.

But 97 and even 121 are modest anti-scores in comparison with 170—which is what Wayout collected. This strip has been replaced by Batman.

Among the nine week-day comics, the best scores were made by Mr. Tweedy, Marmaduke and Gil Thorp, in that order, while the leaders of the half-dozen features appearing only on Sundays were Mandrake the Magician and Walt Disney's Classic Tales. Tweedy had 19 oblivions, Marmaduke 64, Thorp 44, Mandrake 84 and Disney 38.

Reading over the foregoing, it occurred to me that I may have given the impression that I'm less than enthusiastic about the increased popularity of On Stage and Juliet Jones. On the contrary, these strips have always been favorites of mine, and I'm delighted to see them win greater recognition.

What surprised me was to see them soar from 18th and 24th places in the over-all ratings last year to sixth and seventh this year. Have they really improved that much—or is it just that more readers have come to appreciate Leonard Starr and Stan Drake for the superb artists and story-tellers that they are?

Washington Star

Comic Election Results

Favorite	Percentage	Least Liked	Percentage
1. Hi & Lois	57	Seckatary Hawkins	58
2. Beetle Bailey	45	Dick Tracy	45
3. Blondie	41	Crock	42
4. B.C.	40	Judge Parker	30
5. Wizard of Id	38	Mary Worth	29
6. Apartment 3-G	37	Wizard of Id	27
7. Mary Worth	30	Steve Canyon	27
8. Snuffy Smith	28	Donald Duck	27
9. Judge Parker	27	Apartment 3-G	26
10. Tiger	27	Buz Sawyer	26
11. Steve Canyon	20	Flintstones	23
12. Gasoline Alley	19	B.C.	21
13. Crock	15	Gasoline Alley	19
14. Buz Sawyer	15	Archie	18
15. Dick Tracy	14	Tiger	16
16. Archie	14	Snuffy Smith	12
17. Flintstones	9	Blondie	5
18. Donald Duck	8	Beetle Bailey	5
19. Seckatary Hawkins	5	Hi & Lois	4

PANELS

Favorite	Percentage	Least Liked	Percentage
1. Dennis The Menace	74	Big George	49
2. Marmaduke	53	Charmers	45
3. Hazel	39	Lockhorns	41
4. Brother Juniper	32	Girls	29
5. Lockhorns	30	Brother Juniper	27
6. Girls	29	Marmaduke	23
7. Big George	22	Hazel	21
8. Charmers	10	Dennis The Menace	7

Cincinnati Enquirer

Most major newspapers include questions about the comic page in their periodic surveys of readers, and that, too, can be a guide in decision-making. The Chicago *Tribune* has dropped eight strips in the last 18 months because they ran poorly in reader surveys.

Editors also consult independent national comics surveys — the best-known is the Nelson Ratings — but these, like newspapers' own surveys, have a common and critical shortcoming: they measure only what percentage of readers look at a given comic; they do not measure the intensity of interest those readers have.

Peanuts does not appear among the top half-dozen or so "most popular" strips in at least two recent Nelson Ratings, for example, and yet most editors would agree that it is the one comic they would be most afraid to discontinue.

Doonesbury does not even appear in the top 25 in those two Nelson Ratings, but its fans are also fearsome in their fidelity.

Most comics that do well in the surveys are mass appeal comics like *Hagar the Horrible* and *Beetle Bailey*, but editors realize they must carry some comics that deliberately appeal to a more narrow audience, simply to attract that audience

Los Angeles Times

Beetle in Bronze

The University of Missouri approached me to do a sculpture of Beetle for the campus, since I was a graduate. I used to hang out at the Shack, the local watering hole. It had just burned down and the spot was available. (I could never figure out how a place so beer-soaked could ever burn.) I loved the idea.

I had seen a sculpture by Gutzon Borglum (the Mount Rushmore creator) of Lincoln seated on a bench with space beside him. I had watched kids climb up to sit with Lincoln and get their pictures taken. So I adapted (stole) the idea and designed Beetle sitting in a booth at the Shack with room beside him. People used to carve their names on tables, walls, seat backs, ceilings, everywhere. We financed the sculpture by selling two-inch sections for people to have their initials "carved" forever in the bronze for $250 a section.

My son Neal did the model in our garage, the casting was done in Bridgeport, and we had a party in the truck as the completed sculpture was shipped to M.U.

The unveiling took place during Homecoming. There was a parade that ended at the sculpture. Speeches were made, many pictures were taken, and it has become one of the most photographed spots on the campus. ❖

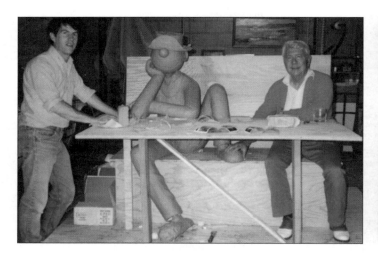

Neal, above, doing sculpture in our garage with Joe D'Angelo watching

David Hornaday, my high school and college buddy and model for Beetle Bailey, poses with his bronze counterpart.

WOW! SIXTY THOUSAND DOLLARS JUST TO MOVE ME... I MUST BE LAZIER THAN I THOUGHT!

In 1999 they had to move the statue to a new site. It took $60,000 to do the job, twice as much as the cost of the original sculpture.

— Beetle Gets a Makeover for Licensing —

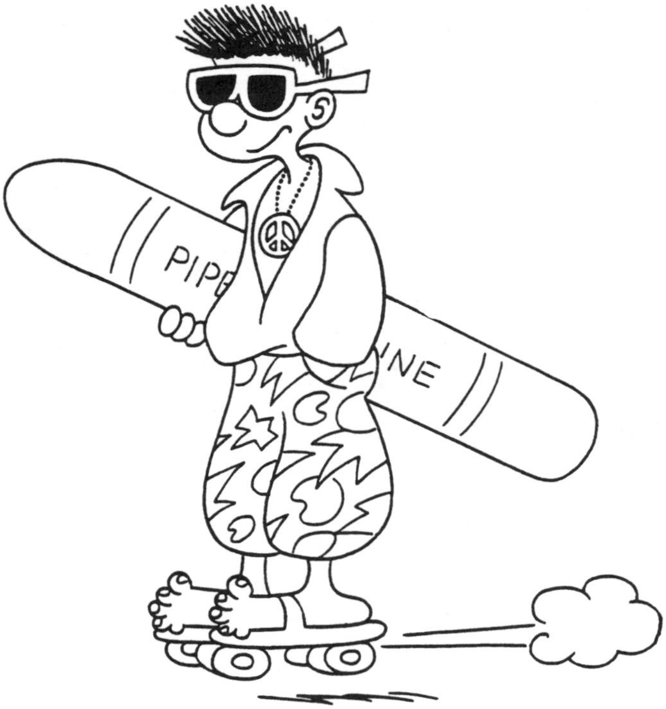
PIPE
INE

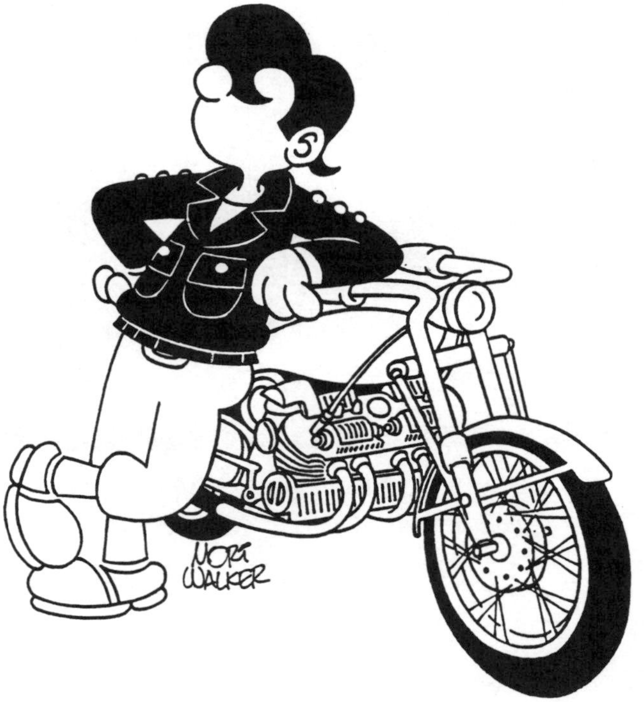
MORT WALKER

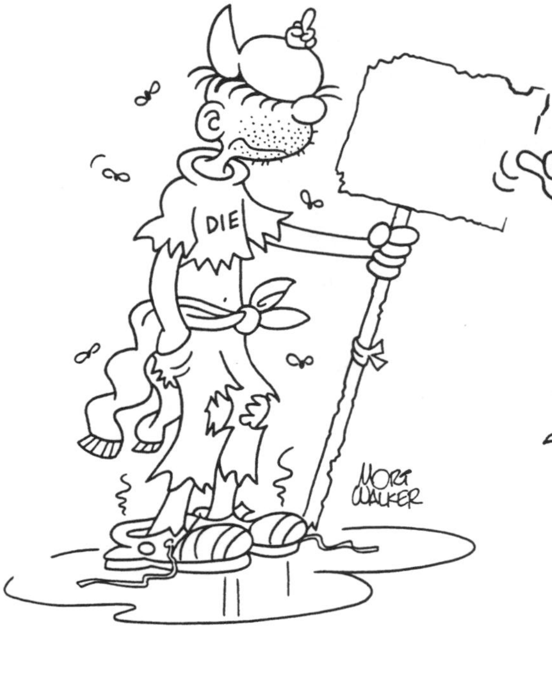
DIE
MORT WALKER

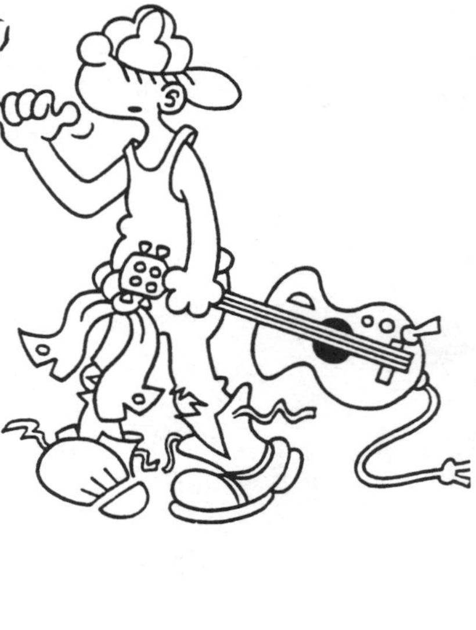

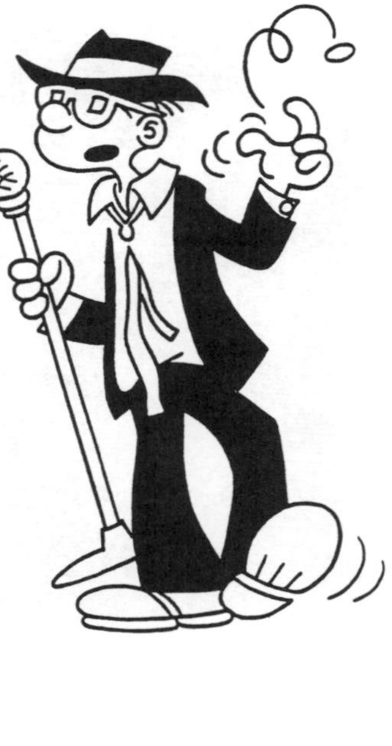

Beetle Bailey's 40th Birthday Party — September 4, 1990

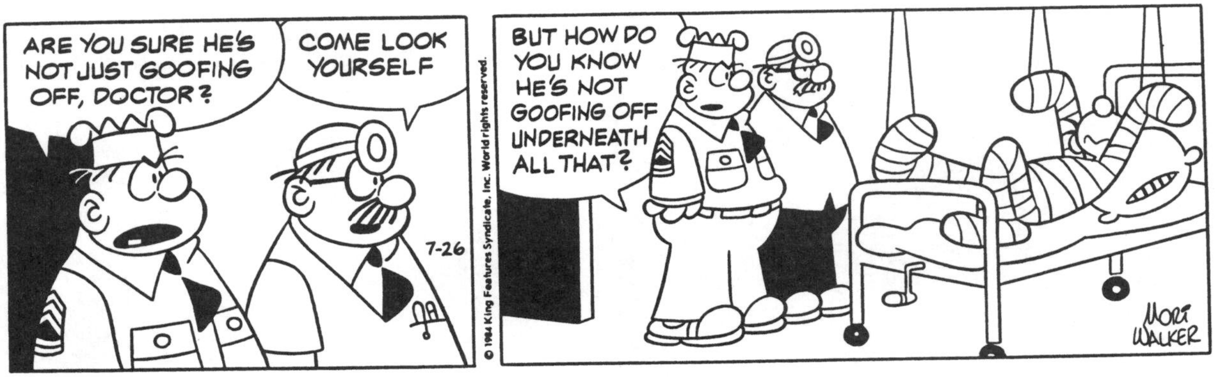
ARE YOU SURE HE'S NOT JUST GOOFING OFF, DOCTOR?
COME LOOK YOURSELF
7-26
© 1984 King Features Syndicate, Inc. World rights reserved.
BUT HOW DO YOU KNOW HE'S NOT GOOFING OFF UNDERNEATH ALL THAT?
MORT WALKER

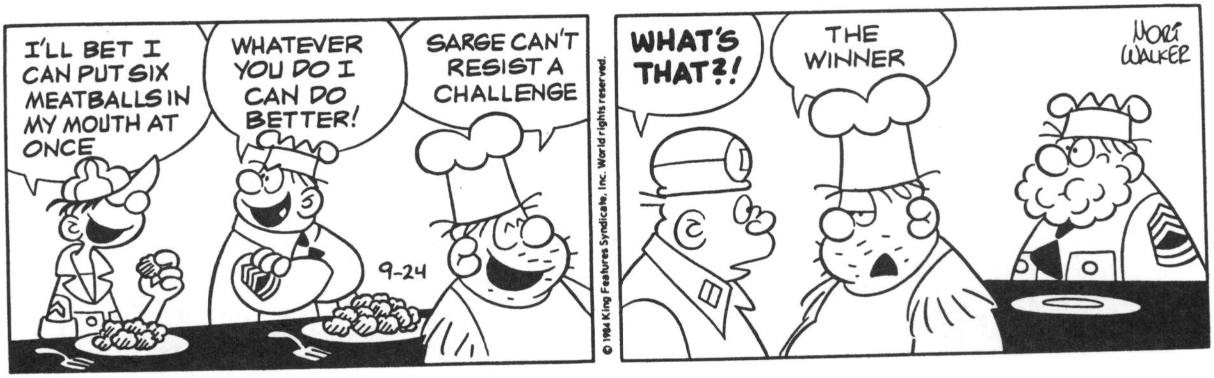
I'LL BET I CAN PUT SIX MEATBALLS IN MY MOUTH AT ONCE
WHATEVER YOU DO I CAN DO BETTER!
SARGE CAN'T RESIST A CHALLENGE
9-24
© 1984 King Features Syndicate, Inc. World rights reserved.
WHAT'S THAT?!
THE WINNER
MORT WALKER

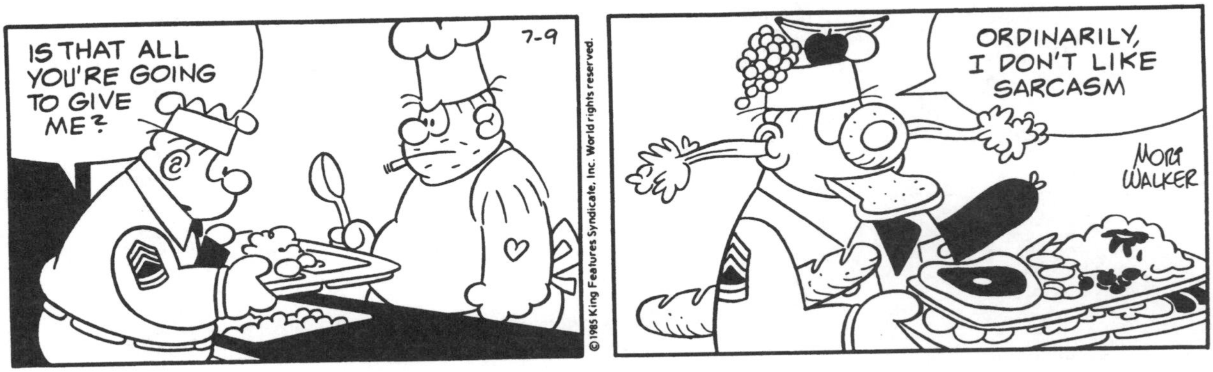
IS THAT ALL YOU'RE GOING TO GIVE ME?
7-9
© 1985 King Features Syndicate, Inc. World rights reserved.
ORDINARILY, I DON'T LIKE SARCASM
MORT WALKER

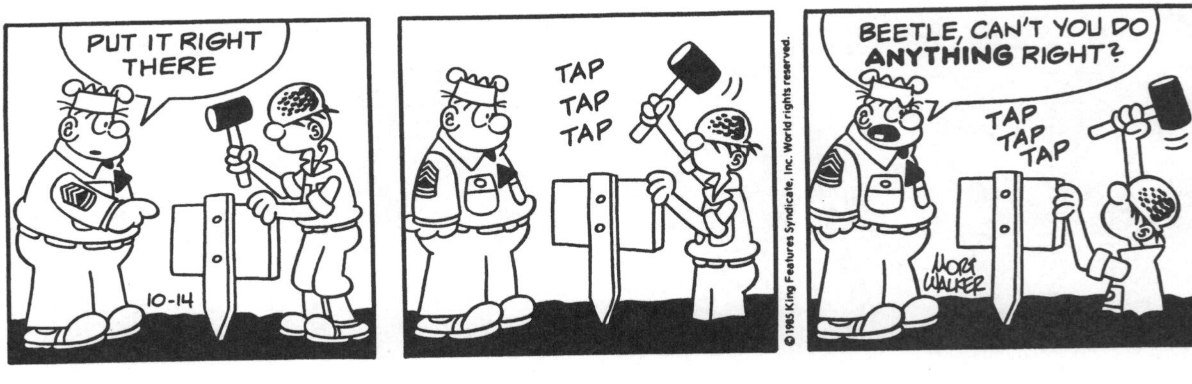
PUT IT RIGHT THERE
10-14
TAP TAP TAP
© 1985 King Features Syndicate, Inc. World rights reserved.
BEETLE, CAN'T YOU DO ANYTHING RIGHT?
TAP TAP TAP
MORT WALKER

Every cartoonist has his or her own way of working. Some just sit down every day with a sheet of drawing paper, wait till an idea comes, and then draw. Some sketch out on tracing paper and use a light board to get it on the drawing paper. Some use computers. There is no right or wrong way. I take a sheet of typing paper and line off six sections. I sit down and think of ideas and fill up each section—usually, fifty ideas at a sitting. Then I choose the best ideas and draw each of them on separate sheets of typing paper. I take them to my staff meeting, where all our ideas are voted on. The best ideas are put in a vault and sorted every six months. I lay them out on the floor of my vast studio in rows of weeks. They go back into the vault until I'm ready to draw. I do each week in pencil and give them to my son Greg, who inks them. We must have 100,000 gag sketches in our attic that we haven't used. ❖

Gag sketch

Finished drawing

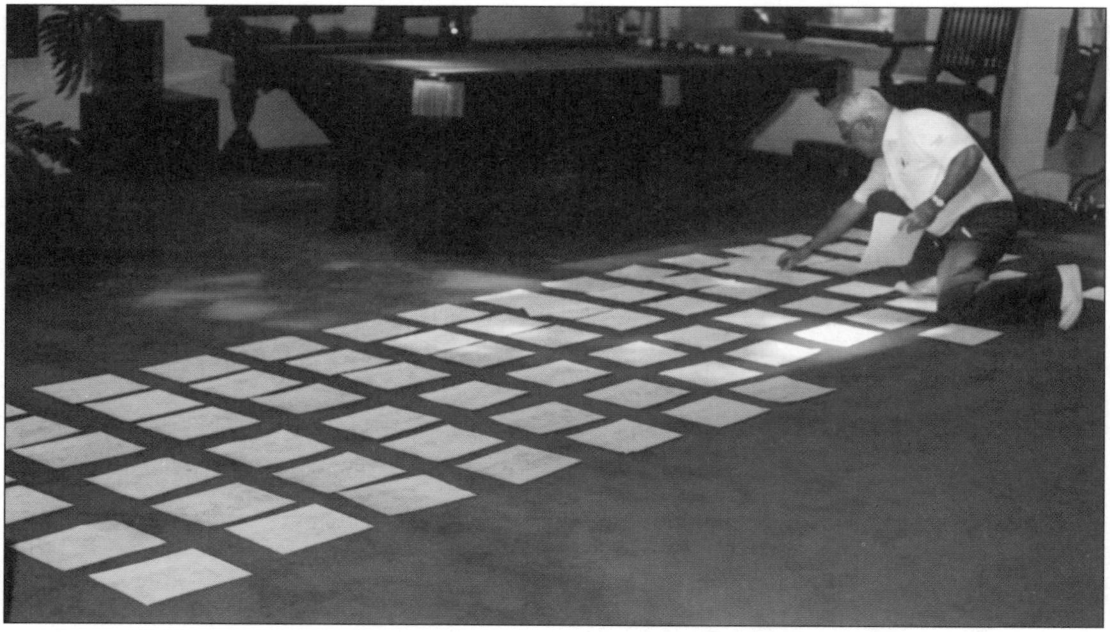

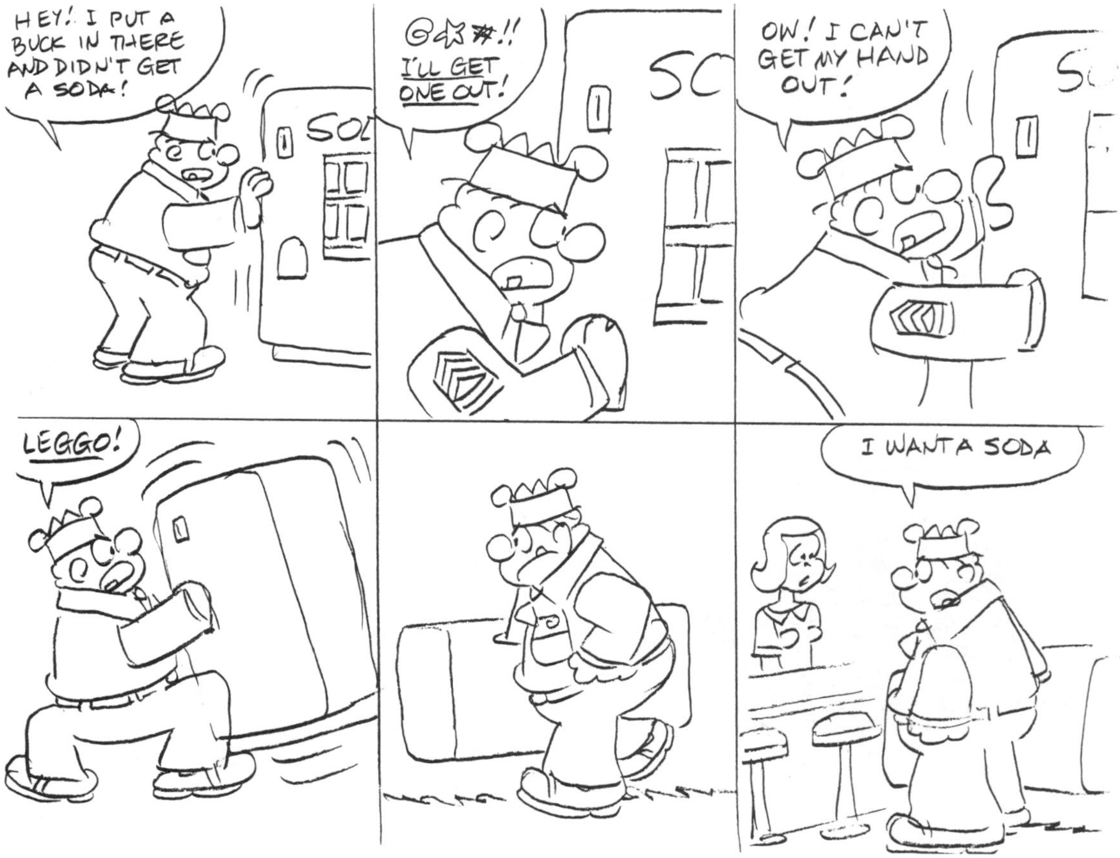
HEY! I PUT A BUCK IN THERE AND DIDN'T GET A SODA!
SO
I'LL GET ONE OUT!
SC
OW! I CAN'T GET MY HAND OUT!
LEGGO!
I WANT A SODA

Gag sketch

A PRETTY GIRL
IS LIKE A MELODY

THERE ARE TWO THINGS
THAT MAKE ME HAPPY

We started a greeting card company around 1980 with a line of *Beetle* cards, a line of public domain characters from the museum, and a line drawn by my son Neal. We had booths at stationery shows and signed up reps, but they never lasted long. We finally quit.

What Say, Joe?

Translations can be tricky sometimes. When General Halftrack looks at Miss Buxley and sighs, the Swedish translation has him saying, "Suck." Garfield says, "I knew a dog that was so ugly, cars chased him," and the translation in one country has Garfield saying, "I once knew a dog with unfortunate looks, so unfortunate, in fact, that he was pursued in traffic by vehicles." *Peanuts* in another country is called *Radishes.* ❖

Beetle in Other Countries

Our strips are used in many countries to teach people to read English.

Beetle *in Japan*

「ハンバーグ係よ、ビートルは、午後ずっと

軍曹の命令で」 「気の毒ねえ！」

「大丈夫、ビートル？」 「少々

焼け過ぎました」　'98. 9. 9

Hi and Lois *in Sweden*

Boner's Ark *in Italy*

Universal Studios' Islands of Adventure in Orlando has created a cartoon area called *Toon Lagoon*. *Beetle Bailey* has a gift shop and costumed characters greeting the crowds.

Gift shop

Beetle and Zero clown around.

Other characters join in.

The best ideas come from personal experience, as in the above strip. The bulletin board at Camp Luis Obispo, California, said there were ten openings for Officer Candidate School, and I asked permission to take the test. My sergeant thought it was humorous that a mere private should have such lofty ambitions. When his laughter subsided, he gave me permission. Four hundred applicants showed up. I took one look and recognized it as a test I'd taken before. I breezed through it and was on the train for OCS that night.

The monster on every cartoonist's shoulder is deadlines. That space on the comic page must be filled every single day, in sickness or in health, drunk or sober, inspired or clueless. We're all wedded to deadlines like drool on a tie. One friend keeps drawing as his cousin races him in the car to the syndicate. I've seen guys finish their work in the syndicate lobby. Jerry Dumas once arrived after the office closed and slid his week's work under the door. The cleaning lady found it on the floor next to the wastebasket and threw it out. Stan Drake would get behind and work several days at a stretch to catch up. To keep from falling asleep he soaked one foot in cold water, the other in hot. At the end of a long session he dozed off, hitting his head on his drawing board and causing a nosebleed. He called his editor the next day to explain why he was late. The editor cried, "You didn't get any blood on the drawings, did you?"

John Portman has written a book, *When Bad Things Happen to Other People.* In it he proposes the delight that can be taken in "the real misfortunes and pain of others." He notes that "to behold suffering gives pleasure," like seeing someone slipping on a banana peel. The Germans even have a name for it, *Schadenfreud.*

Perhaps this explains the appeal of comic strips. When Charlie Brown misses the football and falls flat on his back, when Dagwood gets kicked by his boss, when Beetle gets beat to a pulp by Sarge—these are just a few examples of the hilarious mayhem in the comics. It wouldn't be funny if it happened to *us*, but when the *other* guy gets it, what a laugh! ❖

It's important to learn how to speak correctly and communicate your thoughts. In fact, it is vital. For example, when Lizzie Borden went to her father and said, "Dad, can I go out tonight?" and he said, "I dunno. Ax your mother," he made a fatal mistake.

My Other Strips

Mrs. Fitz's Flats (1957–72). I thought a strip about a little old lady who ran an apartment building full of crazy characters would be fun. I worked on it first and then my former assistant, Frank Roberge, took over until he died and we canceled it.

Sam's Strip (1961–63). Sam was a character who was trying to establish his own strip by hiring characters from other strips. We spoofed a lot of comic clichés and drawing devices. We loved doing it, and the other cartoonists thought it was a howl, but the average reader simply didn't get it. Our satire was over their heads. Jerry Dumas did most of the drawing and I switched roles, becoming his assistant and doing the lettering. We shared the writing chores and very reluctantly gave it up because it wasn't selling.

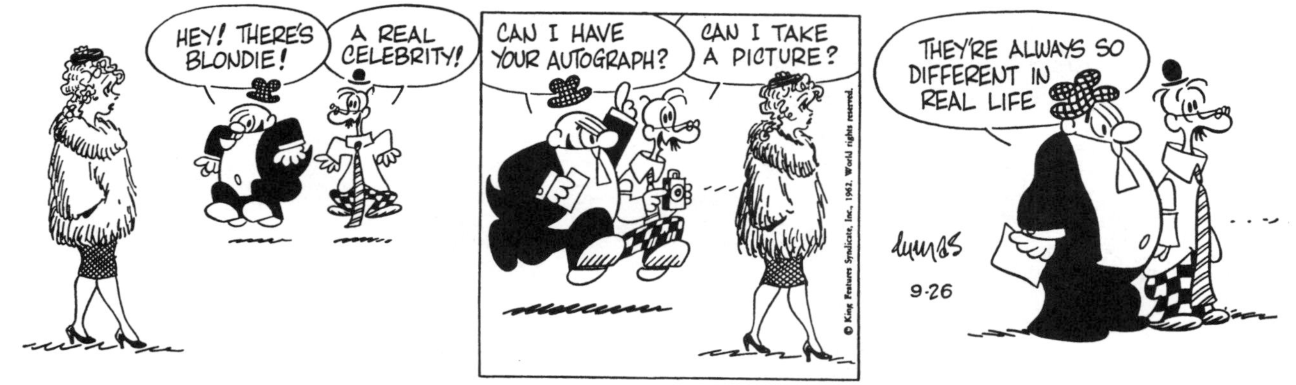
HEY! THERE'S BLONDIE!
A REAL CELEBRITY!
CAN I HAVE YOUR AUTOGRAPH?
CAN I TAKE A PICTURE?
© King Features Syndicate, Inc., 1962. World rights reserved.
THEY'RE ALWAYS SO DIFFERENT IN REAL LIFE
dumas
9-26

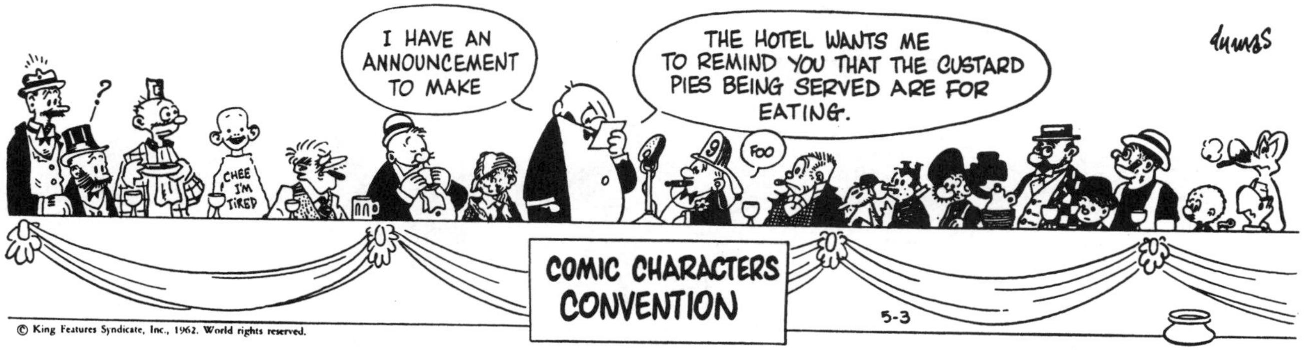
I HAVE AN ANNOUNCEMENT TO MAKE
THE HOTEL WANTS ME TO REMIND YOU THAT THE CUSTARD PIES BEING SERVED ARE FOR EATING.
dumas
?
CHEE I'M TIRED
FOO
COMIC CHARACTERS CONVENTION
5-3
© King Features Syndicate, Inc., 1962. World rights reserved.

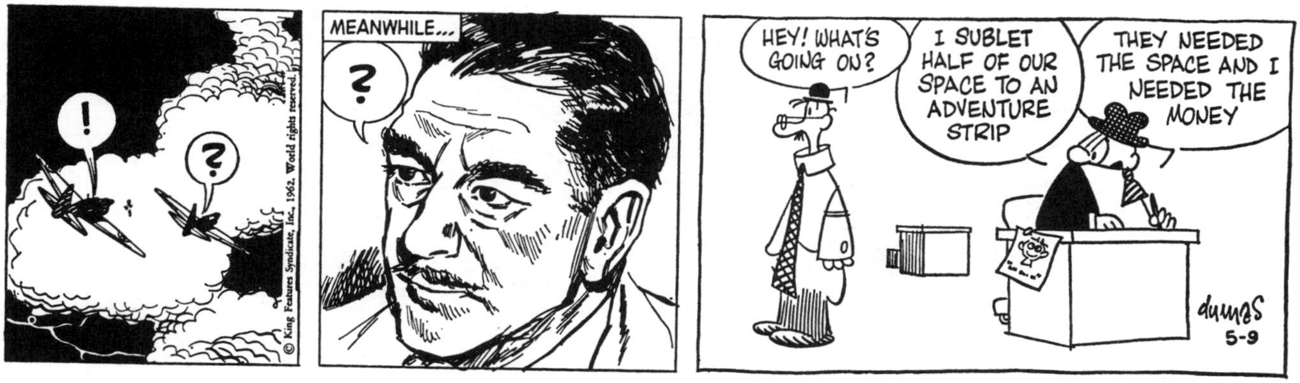
!
?
© King Features Syndicate, Inc., 1962. World rights reserved.
MEANWHILE...
?
HEY! WHAT'S GOING ON?
I SUBLET HALF OF OUR SPACE TO AN ADVENTURE STRIP
THEY NEEDED THE SPACE AND I NEEDED THE MONEY
dumas
5-9

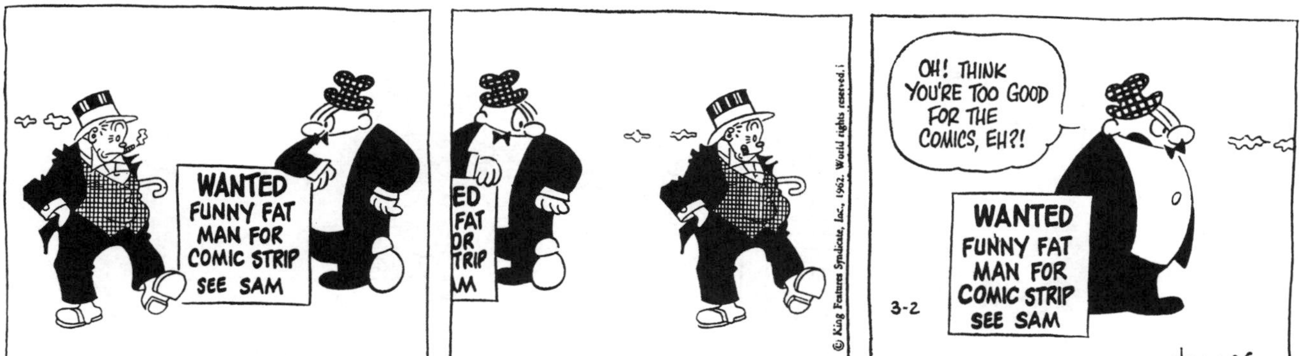
WANTED FUNNY FAT MAN FOR COMIC STRIP SEE SAM
© King Features Syndicate, Inc., 1962. World rights reserved.
OH! THINK YOU'RE TOO GOOD FOR THE COMICS, EH?!
WANTED FUNNY FAT MAN FOR COMIC STRIP SEE SAM
3-2
dumas

Boner's Ark (1968–2000). This involved a
dumb captain who built his ark out of knotty
pine and only brought one of each species. I did
all the drawing in the beginning and then turned
it over to Frank Johnson.

Sam and Silo

(1977–). This is a spinoff of *Sam's Strip* using the same characters in a different setting. Another syndicate had wanted to revive *Sam's Strip*, but King didn't want that and suggested this change. I worked on it at first, but Jerry Dumas does it now.

The Evermores (1982–86). The original title was *The Same Couple,* and Johnny Sajem was the artist. Designed to show that people everywhere had the same problems, it showed the same family in ever-changing locations.

Betty Boop and Felix (1984–88). I was reading an animation book one day and saw pictures of Betty Boop and Felix. I thought they were such great graphic characters that they should be revived. King Features agreed, and I got four of my sons to write and draw it.

Gamin and Patches (1987–88). I drew this for United Features. My theory was that a plucky little street urchin was a classic character that would charm everyone, but readers saw only a poor little homeless boy on the street and couldn't see the humor. I signed it with my first name, Addison, with a little "walker" after it.

Each strip we create has to be promoted in a new way. Gamin and Patches *got its boost with photos in my studio (right).*

Betty Boop and Felix *was launched as a family effort, produced by me and four of my sons (below): Brian, Morgan, Neal, and Greg, with me in the driver's seat. (Priscilla is playing Betty Boop.)*

In the Boner's Ark *strip we had a little koala bear character with no name. We decided to have a contest to name him. We received over 50,000 letters, so many we never could read all of them. The winning name was Cubcake. My daughter Polly here is helping me get unburied from the stack of mail.*

Advertising Campaigns

I've done a number of advertising campaigns with good results. Some have lasted for several years, and a few have won awards. Beetle lends himself to any labor-saving product. Sarge is good for anything strong, tough, or edible. General Halftrack can be used for absolute authority. And of course Miss Buxley is the ultimate sex symbol. Here are a few ads. ❖

Tabasco used all the characters to illustrate each page in a cookbook.

I did a series of ads for Chef-Foil.

Ralston used our cartoons on boxes of Morning Funnies.

I created a family of giraffes for a series of Sprite ads.

Federal Express

I was appointed with four of my sons
to represent the Creative Family for
a year-long campaign for Crayola.
We did posters and many interviews.

Protective Life Insurance

General Electric Company

Army Preserve Rust Remover

beetle bailey
by mort walker

U-Haul

beetle bailey

Vicks products

Animation

In 1963, King Features produced fifty *Beetle Bailey* animated shorts done by Paramount Studios. Comedian Howie Morris did the voices for Beetle and General Halftrack. They were seen on Saturday morning TV and in movie theaters overseas and are available at Blockbuster and other video stores now. ❖

Comicana, Inc.

In 1979, I created a corporation employing all seven children in various capacities. We've printed books and greeting cards, sold licensing, and created products. Our main concern is writing and drawing comic strips and comic books. We enjoy working together. ❖

Licensing

Hundreds of *Beetle* products were produced over the twenty-five years we sold comic books in this country, until the superheroes began to dominate the market. But our comics are still big in many foreign countries. We've had dolls, clothing, greeting cards, games, stationery, bank checks, toys, cels, prints, and countless other stuff licensed. ❖

Beetle Bailey (*Knasen*) is the second favorite comic book in Scandinavia, after *Donald Duck*. I was invited to appear at the book fair in Gothenburg a few years ago and ran into crowds blocking the doorways and aisles. When I got to my booth, I found the lines were for me. They had been waiting for hours for me to sign their books. The manager of the fair came to us and said the other booths were complaining that our lines were blocking them and we'd have to move upstairs to a bare hallway. I went up the escalator with the line following me and signed books for a solid three hours before they dragged me away to a press conference. I never saw the people at the end of my line, and I felt bad about leaving them. ❖

The book-signing line at the Swedish book fair

Surviving in the comic strip business is not easy. King Features Syndicate gets about 5,000 new strips submitted every year; they usually take on one or two. The top seven other syndicates do the same. That means that up to twenty new strips can appear every year to try and knock you off.

In my fifty years I've had to fight off a thousand hopefuls for that precious space on the comic page in order to stay alive, to buy food, and pay tuitions and greens fees.

Greg Walker

To stay alive in this business you have to give something to the readers each day to keep their interest, keep them coming back. It's tough. The ideas, the gags, are the most important in my strip. I try to make people laugh every day, either with a good idea that strikes home or a funny visual picture that catches the eye and cracks people up.

I used to write all my own gags, but I soon realized it would be better to bounce gags off someone who would appraise my ideas, and bring in new thoughts. Over the years, Fred Rhoads, Frank Roberge, Bob Gustafson, Frank Johnson, and Bud Jones have worked with me. In 1956, Jerry Dumas appeared in my driveway and we hit it off.

Jerry is a prize-winning artist and photographer, the author of several books, a newspaper and magazine columnist, a *New Yorker* cartoonist, a tennis player, and New England handball champion. He's also great company, a raconteur who can recall every movie ever made and every book ever written. In other words, he's never boring. And he's a great help with the strip.

Along with Jerry, my two oldest sons help with the writing chores. I want to make sure

*Jerry Dumas,
the Renaissance Man*

they are well prepared to carry on after I'm gone (God forbid). Greg was a newspaper editor and worked in the Hearst film department before coming to draw and write for *Beetle*. Brian helped establish the Museum of

Brian Walker

Cartoon Art and has created most of the exhibits for the past twenty-five years. He's produced many books and is currently editor in chief of *Collectors Showcase* magazine.

These are my staff. We meet once a month, and each brings in his quota of ideas sketched up on typing paper. Several hundred gags are passed around and silently appraised. We mark on the back a #1 if it's good and a #2 if it's rejected. Of course, there are many notes for improvements. Then we gather to see the results and add more thoughts and suggestions. The session lasts about two hours. It's a very creative and cooperative time. The whole point is to keep up the quality of the strip. Then we go to lunch and play golf.

When I'm out golfing or working at the museum in Florida, the office is run by

my assistant, Bill Janocha, and my daughter Cathy Jr.

My role is that of final critic. When no one's around, I select the best ideas to work with. Out of a hundred, I may choose thirty. I rewrite most of them to reflect my point of view, so they are in *my* voice, and I reduce the number of words. Hours of work are involved for the reader to enjoy my strip in under seven seconds.

Our staff is pictured, above, in front of one of the walls of book covers that decorate my office: Bill Janocha, my all-around assistant; Greg Walker, inking and ideas; me; Jerry Dumas, ideas; and Brian Walker, ideas. This is how we assemble every month to judge one another's work. It's fun but very professional. No one is allowed to laugh, because that might influence the others. There are usually about 150 gags sketched out. When everyone has voted, we put the sketches on my old army footlocker and review the votes and opinions. No one is allowed to defend an idea of his that has been vetoed. Being funny is a serious business. No campaigning.

In a separate operation, *Hi and Lois* is produced in Brian's studio. Jerry, Bob Gustafson, and I used to write *Hi and Lois,* and Dik Browne drew it. When Dik died, his son, Chance (Bob), took over the drawing and I felt it was time for the next generation to take control. Greg and Brian do all the writing now and meet with Chance to discuss the work. They've done a good job. *Hi and Lois* is one of the top strips in the business, with over 1,100 papers worldwide. ❖

An editor called me one day and said he wanted me to write some children's books. His theory was that comic strip artists have the ability to create characters and tell stories in an appealing way, which is needed for the juvenile market.

THE LAND OF LOST THINGS

by Mort Walker and Dik Browne

The Land of Lost Things

An illustration of Priscilla's for Coconut Crew

Dik Browne and I did two children's books together, *Most* and *The Land of Lost Things*. The latter got great reviews, was translated into many languages, and sold all over the world.

by **Mort Walker and Dik Browne**

Written by Mort Walker
Illustrated by Priscilla M. Prentice

I also wrote a book for the Breakers Hotel in Palm Beach, *Coconut Crew*. The head of the gift shops there had asked me if I knew someone who could write a book for them about the parrots on their property. A legend had developed about how the birds came to be there. I said I would write it, and I asked my daughter Priscilla to illustrate it. It has been very popular. They sell T-shirts and other products now, using the drawings.

My adult nonfiction books are *Backstage at the Strips* and *The Lexicon of Comicana* (see chapter 9).

There have been many books written about the comics business, and they're all dull as . . . catalogs. How can you write about funny people doing funny cartoons and not be funny? I decided to do a book about the business that truly reflected what I knew and saw. I put together all the funny stories I knew about the cartoonists I loved and the

humorous things in the business and called my collection *Backstage at the Strips*. About two months after publication, the publisher went bankrupt and the copies were remaindered. The book never got the wide distribution it deserved, but I still receive letters from people who find a copy somewhere and love it. Out-of-print editions are now available on the Web.

In addition to hundreds of paperback collections of our strips, we have published a number of large books of our own and other artists' strips. Brian is in charge of our book division. He will go to a large chain like Barnes and Noble and present an idea and cover art for a book. If they approve, they will usually guarantee at least three books for each of their thousand stores, which covers our production costs. Brian has created a format for these books that has been adapted by other publishers. Instead of just reprinting comic strips, as was originally done, he will include some background information and break up the space with funny pictures. This provides the feeling of a biography in a very entertaining way. ❖

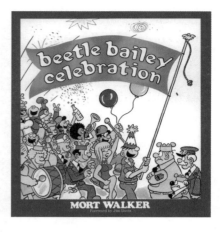

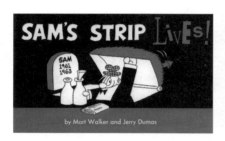

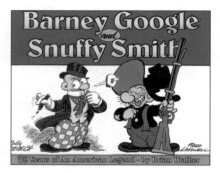

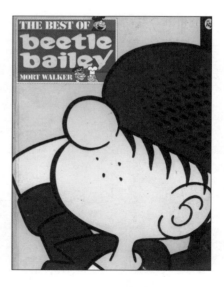

Censored

Comic strips in America are probably the cleanest form of literature in print. Even when the front pages of the newspapers are revealing every sordid detail of the president's affairs, on the comic page all Dagwood gets is a peck on the cheek from Blondie. Even in children's literature, vile things happen. What could be worse than the parents who deliberately lose Hansel and Gretel in the woods and the witch who tries to shove them in the oven? But death, divorce, blood, and infidelity are still no-no's in the comics. Magazines, movies, and television shows are full of sex, but Charlie Brown never even played doctor with Lucy.

This repression of natural urges sometimes breaks down when we are thinking up gags. Risqué ideas come to us even though we know we can't use them. One day my comic-book editor from Sweden was visiting and saw some of the censored pencil sketches we'd done. He was ecstatic; he had to have them for his magazine.

We weren't sure it was a good idea, but he insisted and we gave in. It proved to be one of the most popular things we've ever done in Europe. Newspapers run them on the front page, and they've been published in book form. I was interviewed by a pretty young female reporter in Sweden a few years ago. "Oh, Mr. Walker, we just love your censored gags over here! It shows you have a warm heart!"

When I was young, I was taught that sex was dirty and bad. When I grew up, I found that sex was dirty and good!

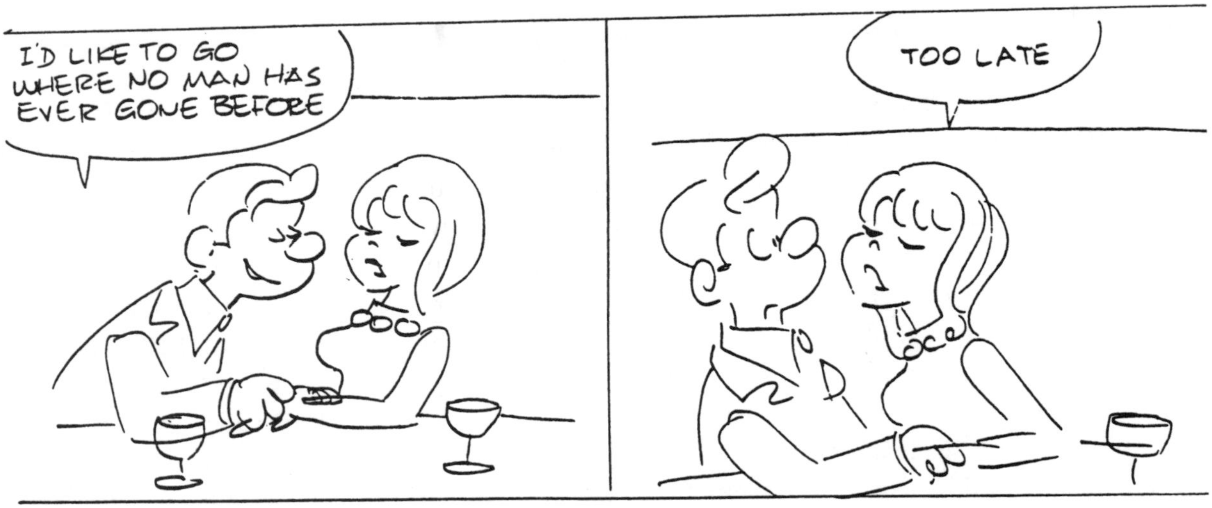
I'D LIKE TO GO WHERE NO MAN HAS EVER GONE BEFORE
TOO LATE

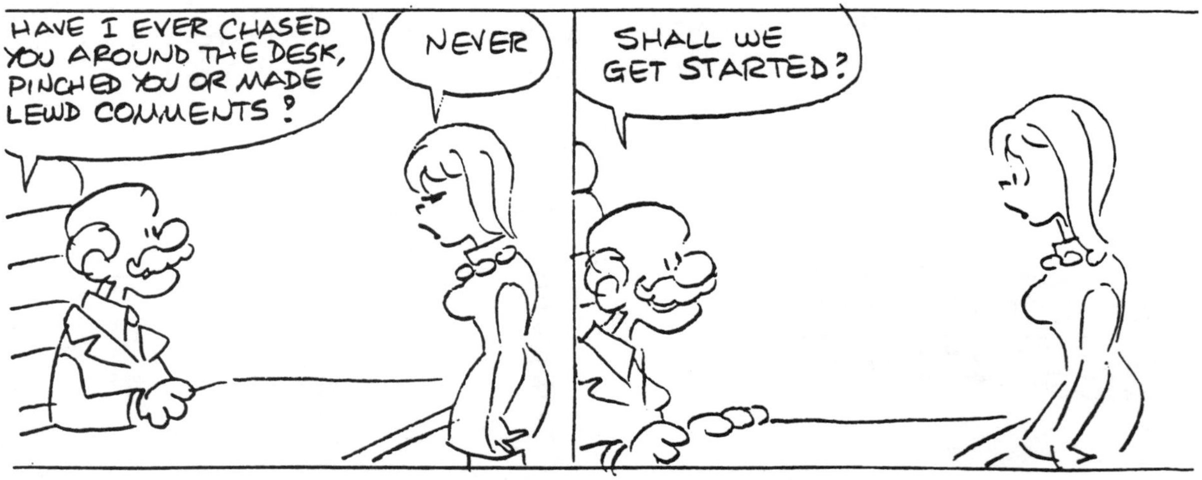
HAVE I EVER CHASED YOU AROUND THE DESK, PINCHED YOU OR MADE LEWD COMMENTS?
NEVER
SHALL WE GET STARTED?

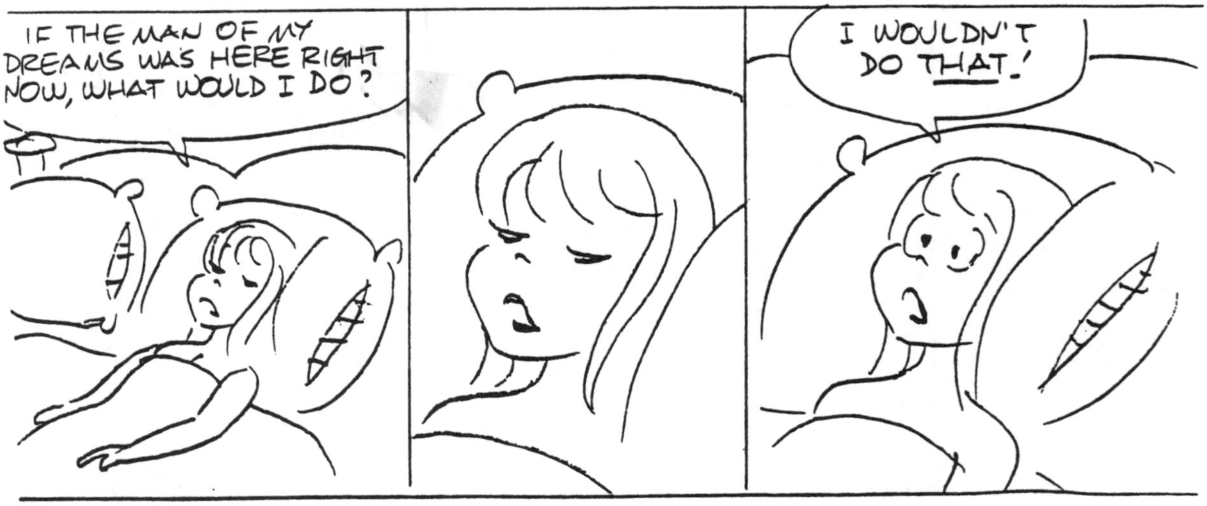
IF THE MAN OF MY DREAMS WAS HERE RIGHT NOW, WHAT WOULD I DO?
I WOULDN'T DO THAT!

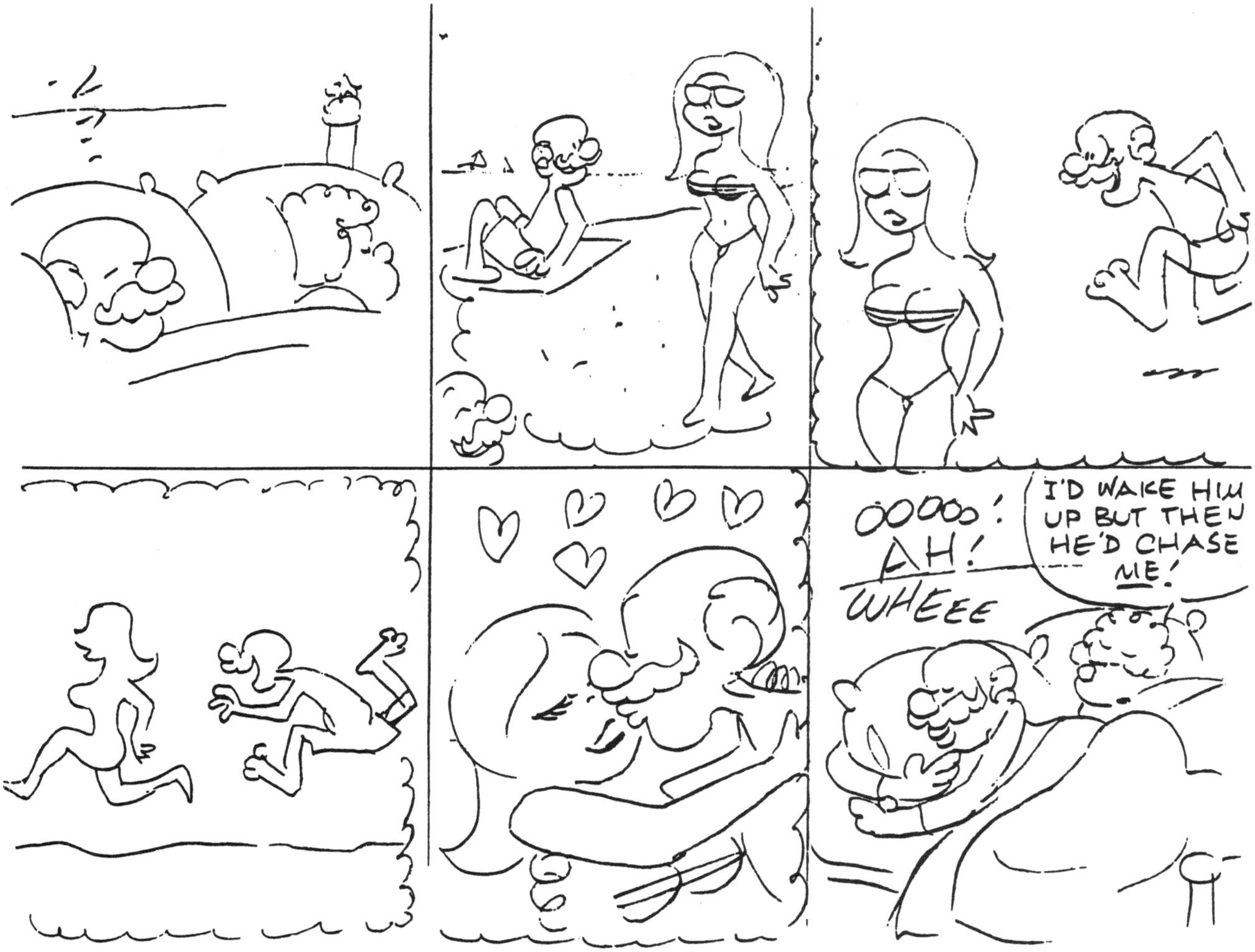
OOOOO! AH! WHEEE
I'D WAKE HIM UP BUT THEN HE'D CHASE ME!

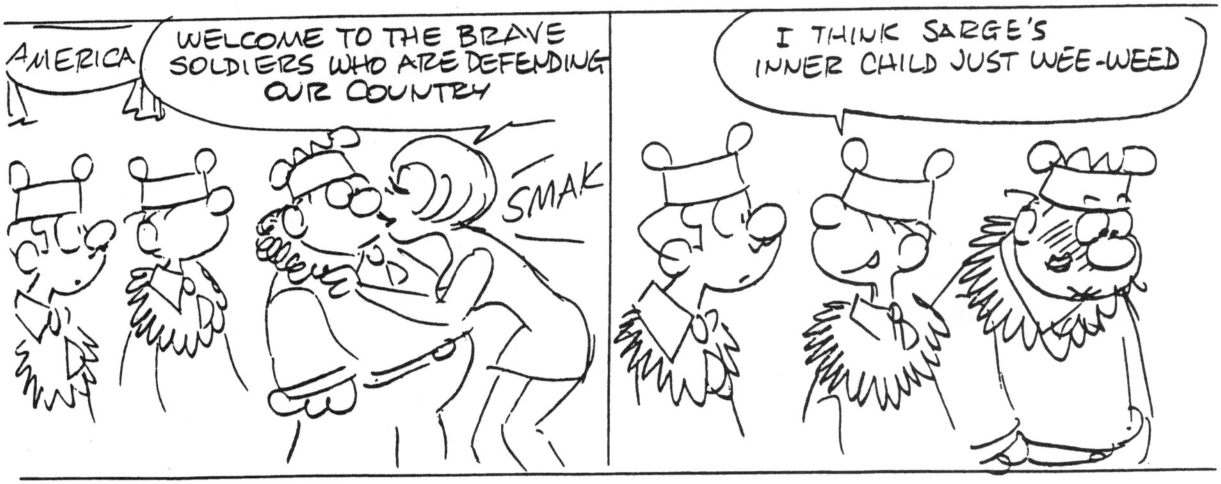
AMERICA
WELCOME TO THE BRAVE SOLDIERS WHO ARE DEFENDING OUR COUNTRY
SMAK
I THINK SARGE'S INNER CHILD JUST WEE-WEED

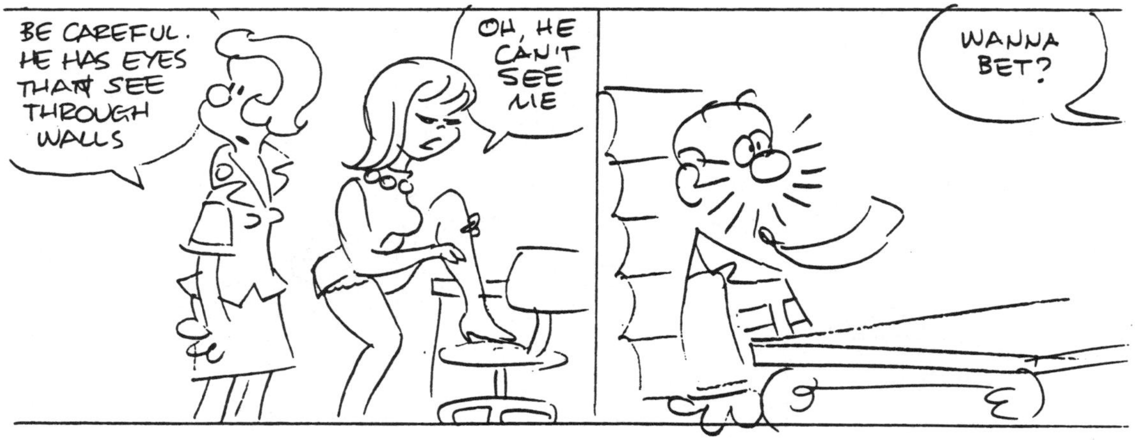
BE CAREFUL. HE HAS EYES THAT SEE THROUGH WALLS
OH, HE CAN'T SEE ME
WANNA BET?

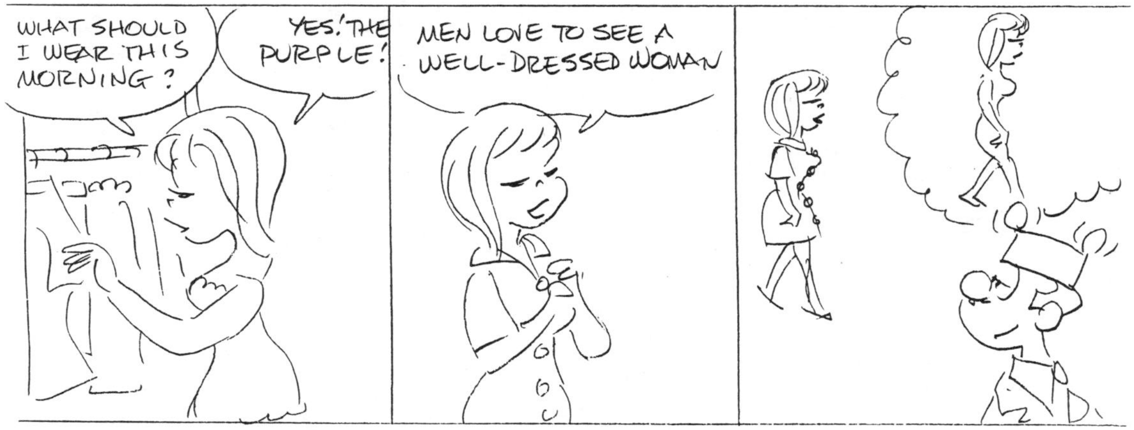
WHAT SHOULD I WEAR THIS MORNING?
YES! THE PURPLE!
MEN LOVE TO SEE A WELL-DRESSED WOMAN

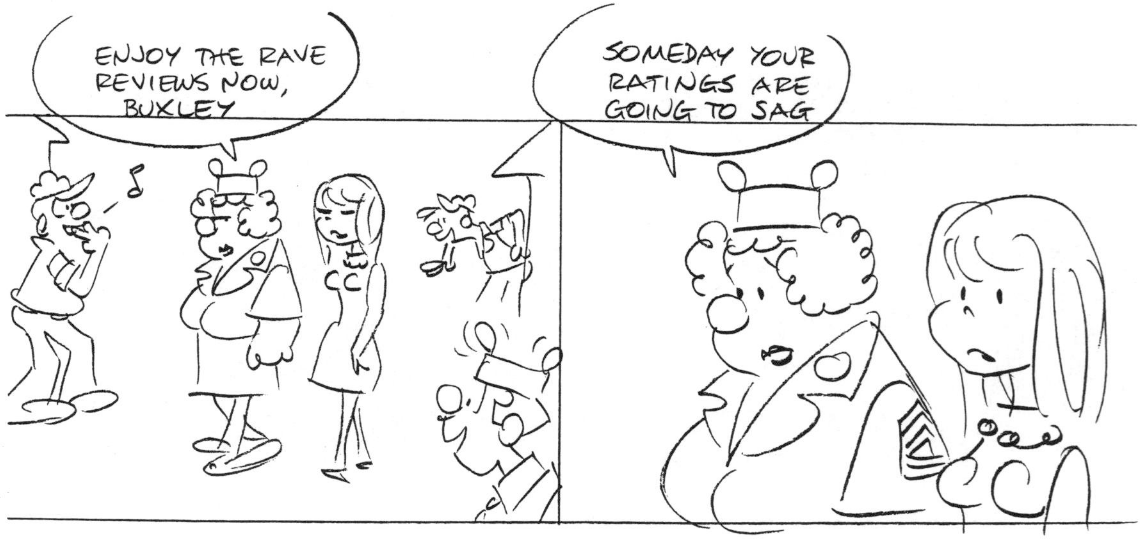
ENJOY THE RAVE REVIEWS NOW, BUXLEY
SOMEDAY YOUR RATINGS ARE GOING TO SAG

Newspaper editors often censor strips without
notifying us and they usually do a very crude job of it.

Original version

Cleveland Plain Dealer

Original version

Arab News

Sex Rears Its Beautiful Head

I discovered the charms of women at an early age and assumed the illicit role of "doctor" at five. During an "examination" an older girl discovered us and proclaimed that we would burn in hell. But it was worth it.

I didn't get into the real stuff until I was thirteen and found myself alone in the house with a girl who was known as Round Heels.

I suavely chased her around the dining table with what I felt was a reasonable request, but she kept eluding me. "Come on," I pleaded. "You let all the other guys do it." "No," she said, "you're too nice a boy." "I am not! I'm not nice at all," I countered. I might have been successful with this line of reasoning had not my parents arrived to protect my virginity. ❖

The editor of my Swedish comic book asked me to do a center spread of Miss Buxley, which I enjoyed drawing. An American publisher saw it and asked if he could make a limited-edition print. It sold out.

New Freedoms, Old Taboos

When I got into this business, the taboos were awesome. You couldn't draw snakes, skunks, dirty socks, alcohol, nudity, divorce, cleavage, toilets—the list went on and on. My big contribution to progress was the navel. Whenever I put one on a girl in a bathing suit, the editors would cut it off the drawing with a razor blade. One day I visited our syndicate office and saw a box on the editor's desk labeled BEETLE BAILEY'S BELLY BUTTON BOX. In it were piles of little black dots—the offensive navels! Since the editor seemed to enjoy this exercise, I began giving my girls several navels, with spare ones in the margins. One day I drew Cookie receiving a big shipment of navel oranges, navels all over the place. The editor gave up the battle. Now I can draw my girls with everything they were born with.

Comics are still our cleanest form of literature. Editors believe that comics are for kids, which they're not. A few cartoonists, like Garry Trudeau, have cut a path into the present, but the rest of us are limping along, carrying our load of Victorian taboos and making just enough progress to keep from slipping back into the Dark Ages. ❖

BELLY BUTTONS

CLEAN RECESSED DIRTY OLD TIRED HAIRY BIG UGLY

CHAPTER SEVEN

Family (and Lots of It)

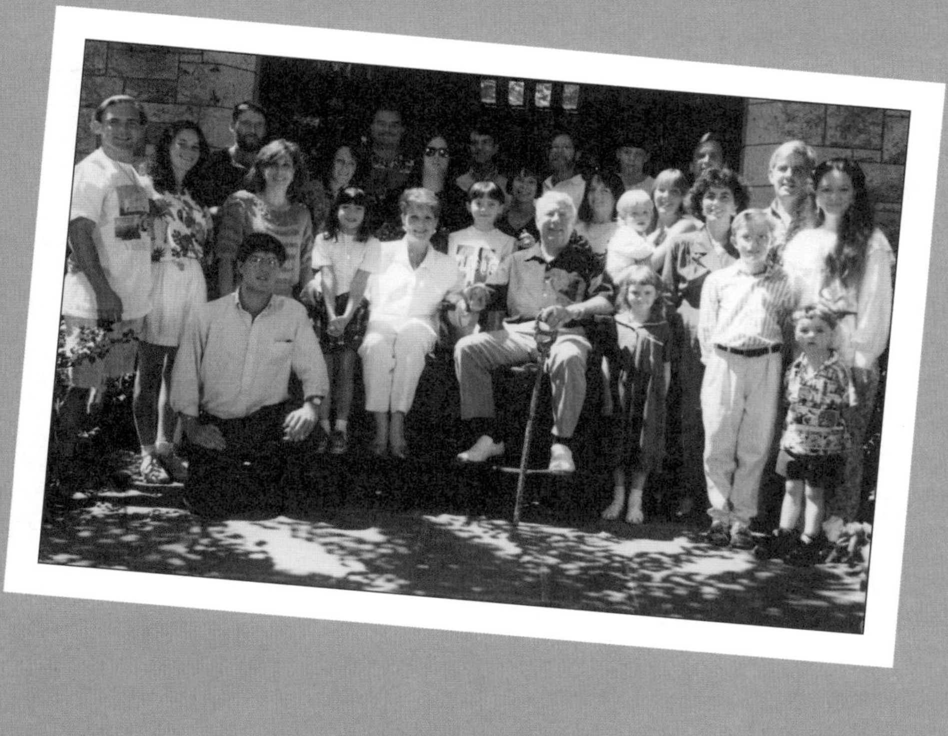

The End and a New Beginning

It was Saturday morning, September 16, 1978. I had finished getting my list together—in my first marriage I did all the weekly shopping—and was ready to go. My regular routine for over thirty years was to take one or more of my seven children to town with me while I did the marketing and family errands: groceries, cleaners, hardware, liquor store—whatever needed to be done.

"Let's go, Roger," I called.

Roger was the youngest, at eleven, and the last to accompany me on my Saturday rounds. It was almost a social event. I'd start at the top of the avenue and work my way down, store by store, stopping to visit with friends along the way. Most of the owners knew my kids by name. "Hi, Roger, want to help me stack some cans?" They'd give him a lollipop or a dime. It was a pleasant excursion.

"I'm not going today, Dad, I have something else to do," Roger called back.

I should have expected this to happen eventually—all the kids dropped off around this age—but there was always another one to take instead. This was the end of the line.

I didn't anticipate the impact this would have. I was alone for the first time in three decades. I left to do my errands with a heavy heart. I felt lonely and abandoned. My marriage had already turned sour. Suddenly I realized I'd been depending on my children for my own emotional needs, which was wrong. They needed to have their own lives, with friends and lovers. It would be against all my hopes and plans for them to try and hold on to the children for *my* needs.

That was the beginning of the end of my first marriage. Five years later I found someone who loved me and gave me the affection I could return: Cathy. And the joy in my life was restored.

I was married in 1949 to Jean Suffill of Kansas City. We had dated a lot at the University of Missouri. I was editor of the school magazine, the *Showme,* and she was the advertising director. She did some cartooning and humorous writing, and I felt we had a lot in common. We came back from the honeymoon pregnant. Within four years we had three children, and they kept coming until we had seven in all. Our relationship became more of a partnership than a love affair. We worked hard raising the children and they all did well, but there was something wrong. Despite our respect for each other, we both knew a lot was missing from our lives. We were both dedicated to marriage and believed in our vows, but after thirty-six years of trying desperately to make our marriage work, I told her I couldn't go on and she agreed. We spent a year in counseling and finally went to court and got a divorce. ❖

During my wartime service in Italy I saw many operas. Cathy and I were discussing them one day.

CATHY: *"What is your favorite opera?"*

ME: *"The one where the girl drives the Cadillac."*

CATHY: *"A girl drives a Cadillac? What opera is that?"*

ME: *"Barbara Seville."*

Cathy

Cathy grew up in New York City on West 108th Street across from Central Park, where she played. Her parents, the Cartys, were both from Ireland. She was married for twenty-six years to an artist, John Prentice.

She was intelligent and beautiful, had great taste, and was very successful. At nineteen she had been head of the personnel department at Flower Hospital. Later, after marrying,

Cathy Carty (Prentice) when I first met her. We married twenty-six years later, in 1985.

she did secretarial work at Richardson-Vicks. I was vice president of the Newspaper Features Council, made up of top cartoonists, columnists, syndicate presidents, and newspaper executives, a distinguished national group. I was given the job of finding a new executive director to organize meetings, exhibits, speakers, and all of the council's activities, and I immediately thought of Cathy. She took the job. She had an office in the turret of the Cartoon Museum, and we began to work closer and closer and closer. . . .

Cathy and I pose with our combined family of ten children and ten grandchildren.

When Cathy and I left our first marriages, we also left behind most of our possessions: pots and pans, books, artwork. We had to start over. I asked her what kind of art she liked and she said, "Illustration."

I agreed, and we set about acquiring a whole new collection of illustrations. There were many illustrators in the area, and we were able to deal with them directly. An old friend had a large collection and eventually opened a gallery in New York called Illustration House. We ended up with one of the best collections in the country and were written up in *Architectural Digest*.

When Cathy and I first got together, she would describe some of her favorite recipes. I guess she was trying to tell me what a great life we would have. One of her most favorite dishes was paella, a Spanish combination of different kinds of fish. She described it in such glowing terms that I couldn't wait to taste it.

But as time went on she never got past the stage of description. As our wedding date approached I told her I wanted it to be part of our vows, that she would promise to "love,

honor, and paella me." We've been married now for sixteen years and I still have never seen a paella. Yesterday we were having lunch with my son Neal, who does a lot of cooking. Cathy launched into her paella recitation, how succulent and moist it was, "not *seca* or dry."

When she was through, I said to Neal, "It's come down to this. She describes paella to me, and I describe sex to her.

"Not *seca*," I added. ❖

Above is one wall with a Lyendecker, a Dean Cornwell, a Norman Rockwell . . . and one of my own characters horning in.

A portion of our cartoon collection

Portraits by Stan Drake and Ward Brackett

Cathy was in the closet putting something in the safe and knocked some papers off the back. I came in as she was lying over the safe to retrieve the papers. "What is this?" I asked. "Safe sex?"

Reading my Swedish comic book

Our home in Connecticut was the former studio of Gutzon Borglum, who sculpted the presidents' heads on Mt. Rushmore. A number of artists owned it and added rooms. We did it over completely, adding several buildings, a guest house, and a three-car garage.

The Architect

When I was in my teens, I would occasionally help my father with his architectural plans. I'd visit his jobs with him and sometimes assist with construction. All the time he would be telling me he didn't want me to be an architect and starve like he did. But some of it stuck.

An assignment in one of my college courses was right up my alley. We were supposed to design our dream home. Since I had worked for my father in his architecture firm, I felt I had an inside track. I enthusiastically dove into the job, knowing that I had an easy A on this one. My father dove in with me and made sure that everything I planned was architecturally correct. It was a U-shaped building with four bedrooms and two baths. I was excited when I turned my plans in and couldn't wait for the approval from my professor. I was shocked when I received a C and went to her for an explanation. She said, "Oh, Morton, you're such a dreamer. Your plans were not realistic. You'll never have a house like that." I wish she could see my house today.

Later on I got an engineering diploma at Washington University specializing in architecture.

The knowledge I gleaned from those days has come in handy. I designed a wing on my house in Old Greenwich, Connecticut; converted a stable in Greenwich into a beautiful gift shop; redesigned our whole house, garage, and guest house in Stamford; and contributed designs for the International Museum of Cartoon Art in Boca Raton, Florida. All around my house are tables, cabinets, and other furniture I created, as well as an elaborate mailbox I did for our four-house community. But Dad was right. I never made a penny on architecture.

We live on a river with a number of small islands in it. I was cleaning up my studio one day and came across a very old, yellowed piece of paper and was inspired. I found a little velvet bag from a jewelry drawer and put a bunch of coins in it left over from our European travels. I waded out to a nearby island and buried the bag near a tree. Then I drew a map on the old paper. At the next family gathering I showed the map to my two oldest grandsons, ten and twelve at the time. I told them some workers on our property were digging a ditch and had found it. "It looks like a treasure map!" they yelled. "Yeah,"

I replied, "and that looks like the island in our stream."

We ran and got shovels, waded out, and found the rock that was ten feet from the X on the map. We paced it off and excitedly started digging. When they found the velvet bag, they began screaming and jumping up and down. They looked at one coin. "Ten thousand lire! We're *rich!*" They ran around showing everyone their loot until the younger one went to Cathy and said, "There's something strange about this. If this is old pirate

treasure, why does this coin say 1991?" I hate it when kids are so smart. ❖

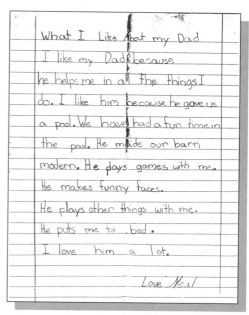

An essay Neal wrote in third grade

Brian (left) and Neal (right) and me on the Crayola promotional campaign

Married Again

Cathy and I were married in our fireplace. Daughter Cathy Jr. is at right.

Neil and Gretchen Gould performed the original tribute "Go with the Future."

Brother Bob toasts us from the balcony.

Brothers

As we took our vows in the fireplace, cartoonist friends commented variously, "There he goes, marrying his old flame"; "I hope he doesn't make an ash of himself"; and "Aw, it's like falling off a log."

John Cullen Murphy (Prince Valiant) at my Mt. Rushmore bar

Priscilla and I share popcorn.

I share laughs with Ted Coyer and with Chuck Saxon of The New Yorker.

Popcorn instead of rice

We honeymooned in Paris, Frankfurt, and Venice and traveled through the Italian countryside.

Me and the kids: Morgan, Brian, and Roger in back, Polly, Margie, Greg, and Neal in front

Cathy and her family: Cathy Jr., Whitney, Priscilla, and mother Anna

My birthplace, Eldorado, Kansas, invited us to a Walker Day celebration.

We were presented with the cornerstone from a school our father had built.

The Ages of Man

When my grandchildren arrive, I immediately revert to childhood. I drag out toys, get out my puppets, walk on the pool table, make faces and odd noises, act silly, and really have fun while the other adults sit around engaged in serious conversation. Is there something wrong with them? ❖

Cathy and I had gone to New York for the weekend and were staying at the Riga Hotel. We checked into our room and Cathy turned on the TV to listen to the news. "Mort, it's December seventh!" she yelled to me. "Pearl Harbor Day and we're in a Japanese hotel! What do we do?" "Let's go down to the bar and get bombed," I said.

Family (and Lots of It) ❖ **171**

Priscilla

When you get a divorce and have to try and blend ten children in two families, there are bound to be some glitches.

Priscilla, Cathy's youngest daughter, came to live with us. At first she seemed a little resentful of me. I'd say something and she'd bark back, "Mort, that's stupid." I tried a humorous ploy. I'd say, "Priscilla, you have more imagination than that. Don't say stupid. Say, 'Mort, you're not playing with a full deck,' or 'Mort, you're a two-story elevator in a ten-story building.'"

Soon she was coming back with jibes like "Mort, when they passed out the brains, you must have been behind the door" or "Mort, the lights are on, but nobody's home."

We started to laugh together and be playful. She'd try to style my hair like Michael Jackson's and I'd show her how to draw cartoons. I helped her design a Christmas card for her school, which they used as their official card. We became great friends through humor, and my greatest joy was walking her down the aisle at her costume wedding, me dressed like a skunk and she like a white peacock. ❖

TO PRISCILLA AND DAVID
MAY 28, 1999
THEIR WEDDING DAY

THEY BLENDED TOGETHER LIKE ICE CREAM AND CAKE
THE VERY FIRST TIME THAT THEY MET.
THEY THOUGHT ALIKE, LAUGHED ALIKE AND LOVED ALIKE
AS ALIKE AS ANY TWO PEOPLE CAN GET.

AT RISDI ENVIRONMENT WAS DAVID'S STRONG SUIT,
BUT THEY BOTH EXCELLED IN THEIR ART.
IT SOON WAS APPARENT TO ALL OF THEIR FRIENDS.
THAT THEY'D NEVER, NO NEVER, WOULD PART.

THEN THE CYBERWORLD BECKONED AND DAVID CAME RUNNING,
AND HIS PUNCH WORLD BEGAN TO LOOK BRIGHT.
HE FELL TO HIS KNEES WITH A KISS AND A SQUEEZE.
AND ASKED PRISSIE TO SHARE HIS WEBSITE.

MORT WALKER
BARD FOR A DAY

Priscilla's wedding. *Dressed as a skunk, I walk Priscilla down the aisle (top left). The men were lizards and the ladies were butterflies (top right). Cathy, in flowers, was escorted by her son, Whitney, dressed as a buccaneer (above left). Rev. Zeman wore a cardinal's costume (above). Priscilla and her husband, David Campbell, were white and blue peacocks (left). The attendees were rabbits, gorillas, zebras, flowers, bees, and other forms of nature in keeping with the setting, the New York Botanical Gardens.*

ABOUT FACE!

Cartoonist Mort Walker brings *Beetle Bailey* into the '90s with an apology by General Halftrack

> I'M BEING SENT FOR SENSITIVITY TRAINING!

▲ "I can't get on a soapbox," says Walker (with wife Catherine in his Boca Raton, Fla., studio). "I've got to entertain people."

> I SURE ENJOY WATCHING MISS BUXLEY WALK

> SO DOES THE GENERAL

▲ Modeled after Marilyn Monroe, Miss Buxley made her *Beetle Bailey* debut in 1971.

HE JUST DIDN'T GET IT. BUT LUCKI-ly for him, comic-strip charac-ters don't have to answer to ethics committees, only to read-ers—which means that after a quarter century of shameless ogling, double entendres, single entendres and blatant sexism toward his secretary, Gen. Amos Halftrack is getting off easy.

For years *Beetle Bailey* creator Mort Walker, 73, stood up to feminists who complained that the doddering sol-dier's passes at the shapely Miss Bux-ley were less than humorous. Then came the recent slew of Army sex scandals. "I began to worry about peo-ple linking my strip to what's happen-ing in the military today," says Walker. After considering retiring the general, Walker opted for a more '90s solution: Send him to sensitivity training.

Walker's wife, Catherine, 64, insists the cartoonist is no sexist but thinks he would benefit from such a course. "It would give him a different perspec-tive," says Catherine, who told him that the general's behavior reflected "an attitude that was not acceptable to people anymore." Rumblings that some papers were considering pulling the strip—which Walker, a World War II veteran, created in 1950—accentu-ated her opinion. "I hope I'll make a point," says Walker of Halftrack's July 10 apology to Miss Buxley.

But without the sexual innuendo, will the general be able to get a laugh? Walker promises that Halftrack will still be a bad golfer, a hopeless tippler and an inattentive husband. And that's the whole point. "He has a lot of the weaknesses that many people have," says Catherine. "And the way Mort portrays him, it allows people to laugh at themselves." ∎

Photograph by Bill Frakes

People magazine, July 14, 1997

"BEEN WAITING LONG?"

"AND STOP SAYING, 'OOPS!'"

Each year my siblings get together somewhere in the country to catch up on each other, since we're scattered across the continent. Left to right, Bob and Peggy Harman, Ed and M. L. White, me, Cathy, and Ramona and Bob Walker.

We held the thirtieth birthday party for Hi and Lois in my studio.

Many cutout figures dotted the lawn and inside.

My son Brian had my sixtieth birthday party in his driveway. His wife, Abby, made funny hats for everyone out of comic pages. Bill Yates blessed me with a belly dancer.

My children at Margie's wedding in 1983: left to right,
Greg, Brian, Neal, Margie, Morgan, Polly, and Roger

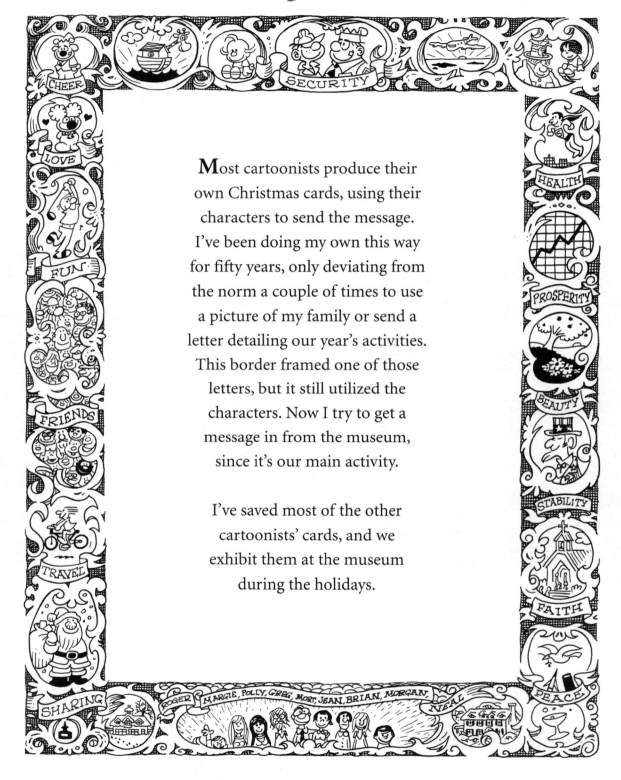

Most cartoonists produce their
own Christmas cards, using their
characters to send the message.
I've been doing my own this way
for fifty years, only deviating from
the norm a couple of times to use
a picture of my family or send a
letter detailing our year's activities.
This border framed one of those
letters, but it still utilized the
characters. Now I try to get a
message in from the museum,
since it's our main activity.

I've saved most of the other
cartoonists' cards, and we
exhibit them at the museum
during the holidays.

and litters of Good Wishes for the Coming Year!

Roger is expected.

Roger arrives.

We moved away from Greenwich and moved back.

_1968_

_1969_

_1970_

The kids grew and got involved in activities that I tried to update on our Christmas cards each year.

A **M**ERRY CHRISTMAS is HAVING YOUR CARDS ALL MAILED, etc.

MERRY CHRISTMAS IS LOSING THE F.A.O. SCHWARZ CATALOG

MERRY CHRISTMAS IS FINDING A TREE THAT ISN'T SCRAGGLY ON ONE SIDE IN A $2 LOT.

MERRY CHRISTMAS IS KNOWING YOU WON'T HEAR RUDOLPH THE RED NOSE REINDEER FOR AT LEAST 300 DAYS

MERRY CHRISTMAS IS HAVING ALL THE FLASHBULBS WORK

MERRY CHRISTMAS IS BUYING EVERYTHING ALREADY GIFTWRAPPED

MERRY CHRISTMAS IS GETTING THROUGH THE HOLIDAYS WITHOUT HAVING TO EAT A SINGLE PIECE OF FRUIT CAKE

MERRY CHRISTMAS IS GETTING LOTS OF MONEY...AND NO SOCKS OR UNDERWEAR

MERRY CHRISTMAS IS FINALLY FINISHING YOUR THANK-YOU NOTE TO GRANDMOTHER

MERRY CHRISTMAS IS GETTING A GOOD SANTA WHO DOESN'T SMELL OF BEER

MERRY CHRISTMAS IS NOT GETTING SICK ON CHRISTMAS CANDY UNTIL THE MORNING SCHOOL STARTS

MERRY CHRISTMAS IS KNOWING ALL OUR FRIENDS ARE HAVING A MERRY CHRISTMAS (AND A HAPPY NEW YEAR)

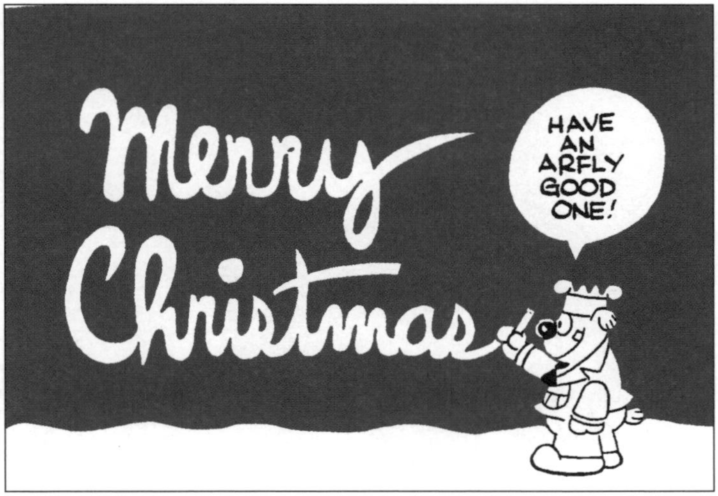
Merry Christmas
HAVE AN ARFLY GOOD ONE!

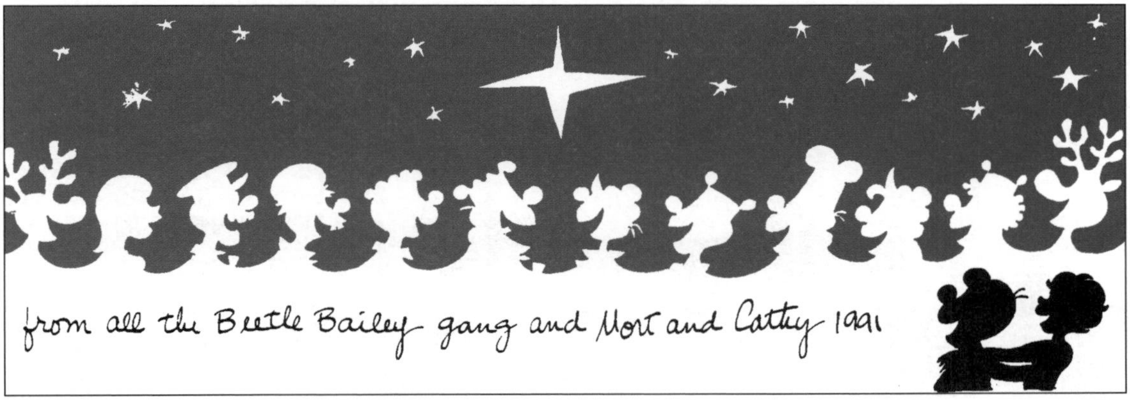
from all the Beetle Bailey gang and Mort and Cathy 1991

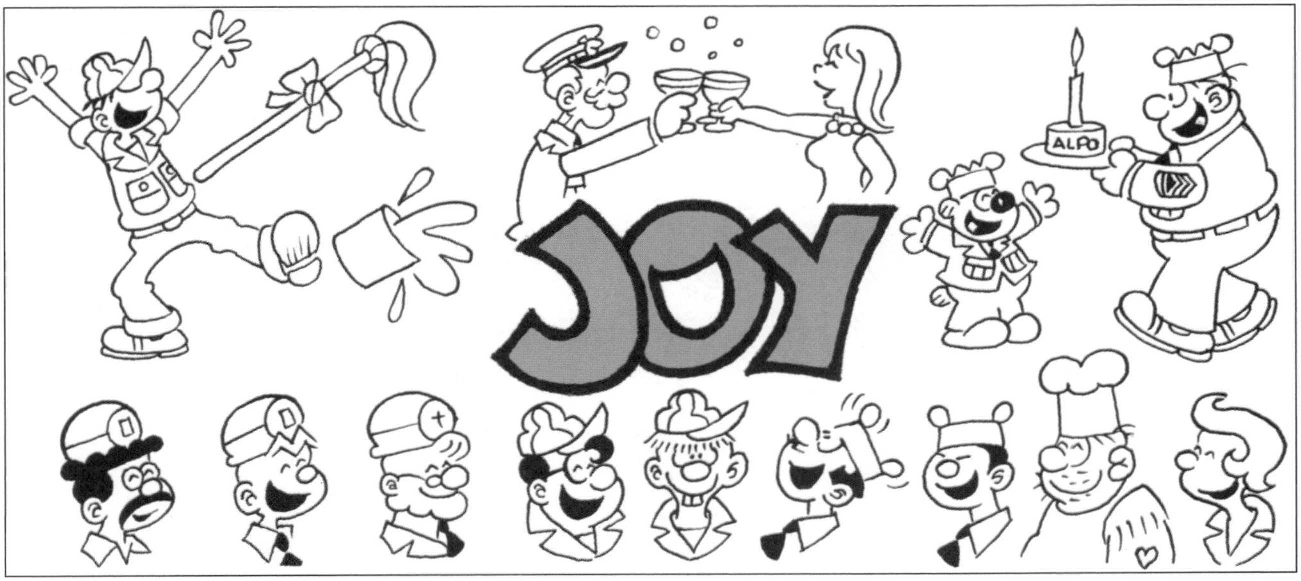
ALPO
JOY

Toot if you like Christmas

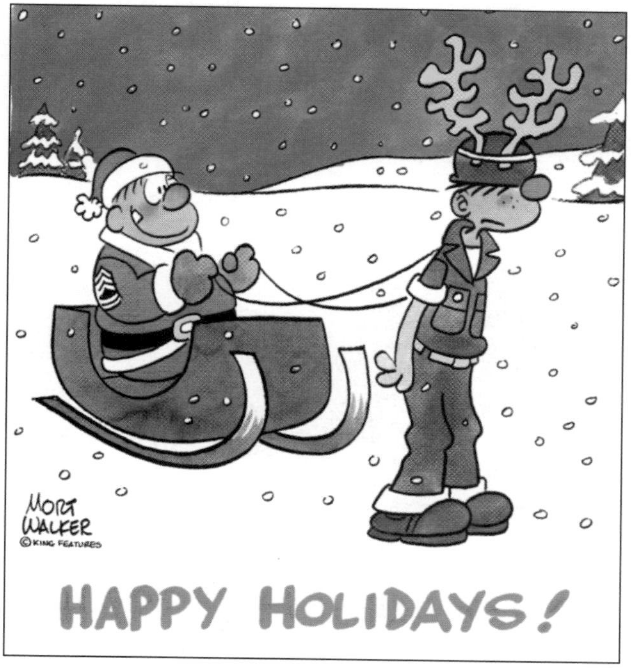
MORT WALKER
©KING FEATURES
HAPPY HOLIDAYS!

My card for 1998

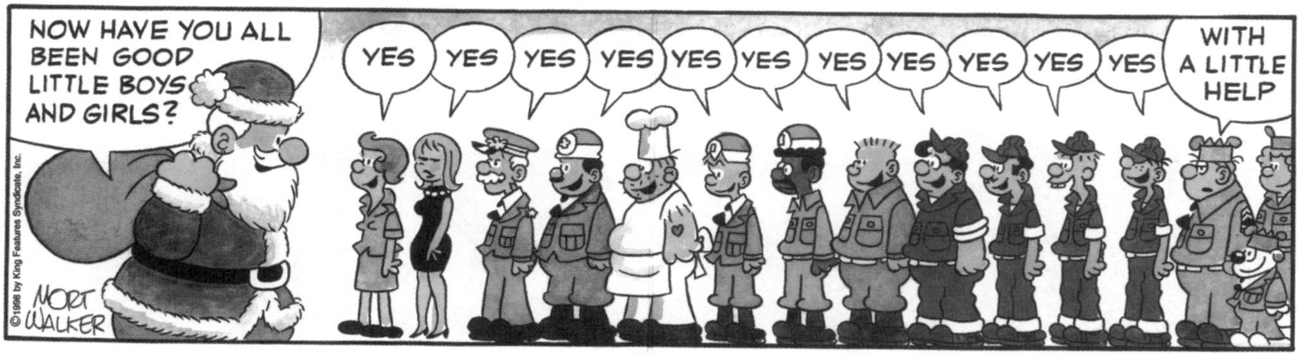
NOW HAVE YOU ALL BEEN GOOD LITTLE BOYS AND GIRLS?
YES
YES
YES
YES
YES
YES
YES
YES
YES
YES
YES
WITH A LITTLE HELP
MORT WALKER

1999

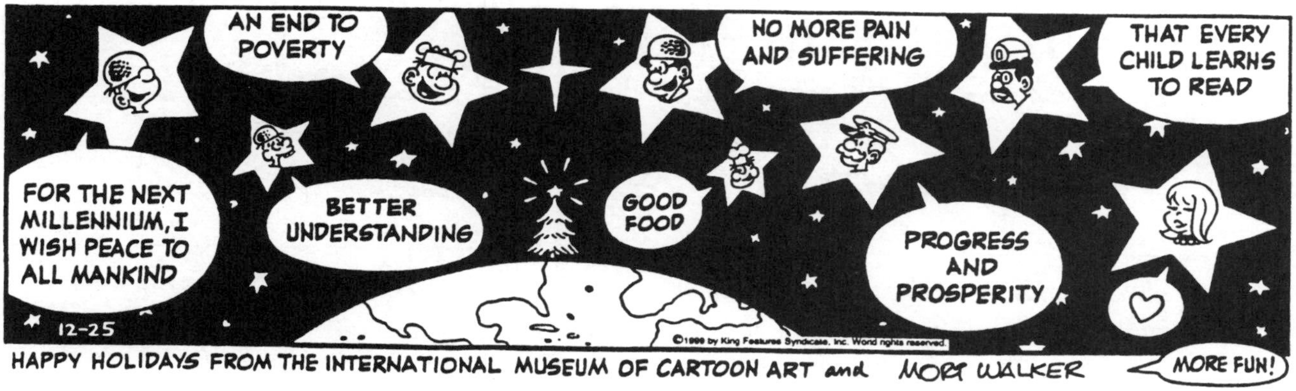
FOR THE NEXT MILLENNIUM, I WISH PEACE TO ALL MANKIND
AN END TO POVERTY
BETTER UNDERSTANDING
GOOD FOOD
NO MORE PAIN AND SUFFERING
PROGRESS AND PROSPERITY
THAT EVERY CHILD LEARNS TO READ
12-25
HAPPY HOLIDAYS FROM THE INTERNATIONAL MUSEUM OF CARTOON ART and MORT WALKER
MORE FUN!

SEASON'S GREETINGS
TO THE ARMED FORCES OVERSEAS
from BEETLE BAILEY and *Mort Walker*

AREN'T **YOU** SUPPOSED TO SAY THAT, SARGE?

© KFS

Happy Father's Day – June 1944

DR. MORTON

I've always made my own cards for special occasions. This one for Father's Day shows my sister Marilou; my sister-in-law, Ramona; my brother, Bob; my mother, Carolyn; my father, Robin; my sister Peggy; her husband, Bob; my nephew Bobby; me; and my nephew Dick.

CHAPTER EIGHT

Friends

In 1951 a friend wrote that there was a young cartoonist in Minneapolis who didn't know any other cartoonists and would like to meet some. He had just started a strip called *Peanuts* and it wasn't doing well. I started corresponding with him and invited him to come up and visit us. We threw a party for him, took him out to dinner, and had a friend put him up. He was a very nice guy and everyone liked him and felt a little sorry for him. I sponsored him for membership in the National Cartoonists Society and they turned him down. I went to Otto Soglow, a *New Yorker* cartoonist and the membership chairman, and complained. I said, "Otto, you can't reject him; he's syndicated and appearing in the *New York World*." Otto finally agreed to let him in. Little did we know that he would become one of the most famous cartoonists in history.

The death of Charles Schulz on February 12, 2000, and the resulting display of affection, was a poignant example of the love of cartoons. The outpouring of lament from all over the world went on for months. We had all lost an important piece of our lives. Something we enjoyed and loved was gone.

Charles Schulz sent me this original after I had won the Reuben Award and
he had come in tenth. I have it hanging on my wall to remind me that
good guys usually win in the long run if you give them a chance.

We used to have fabulous parties in New York. This was a group called "the Banshees," which met four times a year. We had top entertainment from Broadway, attracting famous stars like Jack Benny, Bing Crosby, Marilyn Monroe, and Phil Silvers, and the audience was just as glamorous. Here's one of the tables, which includes William Randolph Hearst Jr., Bob Considine, J. Edgar Hoover, Herbert Hoover, the Duke of Windsor, and Henry Cabot Lodge. Times changed and the Banshees disappeared.

We put on this skit at a banquet at the Waldorf. It was a live enactment of a Rube Goldberg invention. Stan Drake, Otto Soglow, Jimmy Hatlo, and Milton Caniff sang a sad song, making Fred Laswell weep into a flowerpot, causing the flower to grow. It hits a bathing beauty, pushing her down the slide, awakening the bugler (me). Bob Dunn in his skivvies is chilled by the blast from the bugle and has a fit of sneezing, which activates the turbine, which finally lifts off the rocket.

A group of us went to Cape Cod to stay with Jim Berry, who draws Berry's World, *and played golf for a week. The day we were leaving, Jim called up to tell us to bring our sheets down to the laundry. We draped the sheets over us and went outside to take a picture, causing a stir in the neighborhood.*

Receiving our honorary doctorates from William Penn College. Bil Keane (Family Circus), Charles Saxon (The New Yorker), Bill Hoest (The Lockhorns), an unidentified man, me, and Paul Szep (Boston Globe editorials).

Thirty-five miles up the coast from New York City lies Fairfield County, Connecticut, home to most of the country's top cartoonists and illustrators. They live there because they are only forty-five minutes from the most important syndicates, publishers, and ad agencies. The towns are called Greenwich, New Canaan, Westport, and Stamford and have pretty harbors with sailboats dancing in Long Island Sound, white colonial houses behind stone walls, red barns, and towering oaks with rolling fields. It's a great place for artists to raise children and enjoy the company of fellow artists. Hundreds of them once lived in the area, but computers, e-mail, faxes, and airplanes have allowed them to spread out to other parts of the country. Oh, but it was a glorious period of parties and camaraderie and the exchanging of information! There are plenty of us left. When my son Brian, who is in charge of the National Cartoonists Society regional chapter, schedules a dinner, about a hundred show up. A recent exhibit in Westport of just that town's cartoonists had over a hundred entries.

My fortieth birthday party. I'm top center, wearing the hat Dik Browne made for me. He's directly below me. Others include Jack Tippit (Amy), Bill Yates (Redeye), Frank Roberge (Mrs. Fitz), Tony DiPreta (Dr. Rex Morgan), Jack Murphy (Prince Valiant), Gill Fox (Side Glances), Bud Jones (Mr. Abernathy), Frank Johnson (Bringing Up Father), Orlando Busino, Jerry Dumas (Sam and Silo), Jerry Marcus (Trudy), Dick Cavalli (Winthrop), Bob Weber (Moose), and John Fischetti (editorial cartoons).

All my life I had people all around me—family, friends, and fellow soldiers. When I first went to New York to start my career, I had no one, only me. I worked all day in my little room and ate at a diner all by myself. It was terrifying. I'd never want to go through anything like that again.

During the sixties a group of friends thought it would be fun to get together and dance. We usually went to square dances, but when the Latin rhythms became popular, we decided to learn them. We found a former Arthur Murray instructor who got us going. It turned out that his day job was at the local grocery store. I was shopping one day when I ran into him. He asked how my dancing was going, and I told him I was still having trouble with the cha-cha. "Here, I'll show you," he said, and we proceeded to cha-cha down the aisles of the Food Mart to the astonishment of the other customers. ❖

Early in my career, when I had the strip and my comic book to do, I didn't have any assistants. I worked long hours all by myself and started having back trouble, which kept me from doing a lot of things. I found that walking helped, and I thought golf would add some interest to the walking. I talked my buddies John Cullen Murphy, who does *Prince Valiant*, and John Fischetti, a Pulitzer Prize–winning editorial cartoonist, into learning the game with me. We played every Friday and I was hooked from then on.

Soon I was playing three times a week and practicing almost every day. I got my handicap down to 7 and was shooting consistently in the 70s and sometimes in the 60s. I was winning tournaments all over the place: Pebble Beach, Disney World, Shawnee, Jamaica, Sarasota, and many places in New York and Connecticut. I now belong to eight golf courses, but I only get to play a couple of times a month. My work and the museum keep me too busy.

There are a lot of cartoonists and illustrators in our area, so we decided to have an annual golf tournament, the Connecticut Cartoonists Invitational. That was forty-two years ago, and I've been running it for most of that time. All year long I keep my eye out for good presents, so the prize table is loaded with all kinds of nice shiny things. Everyone gets at least one prize and the winner gets hit in the face with a pie. We dress him up in a robe and a pretty girl walks up and slowly grinds the pie in his face. (One year she was naked.)

THE CONNECTICUT CARTOONIST INVITATIONAL GOLF TOURNAMENT

The pie in the face from 1998, our forty-first year.

I was the first recipient of the pie. Dik Browne thought it would be funny if someone sneaked up behind me and let me have it as I was receiving the first-place trophy. That first pie was real custard, and I could smell it in my ears and nose for days. Now we use shaving cream.

Currently I am president of the Artists and Writers Association, another golfing group that dates back over seventy years. It was founded by the famous sportswriter Grantland Rice and presided over by such luminaries as Rube Goldberg and Bob Considine. We play on the greatest courses in the area. We once had a large membership of famous actors, comedians, playwrights, columnists, cartoonists, illustrators, and sports figures. Our numbers have dwindled, but we're having too much fun to quit.

At the invitation of my partner, Dik Browne, I agreed to help create the Joan Browne Cartoon Classic pro-am golf tournament in Sarasota to benefit the hospital and other charities. Many cartoonists participated with their costumed characters. Here I am with Johnny Hart and a bunch of the characters.

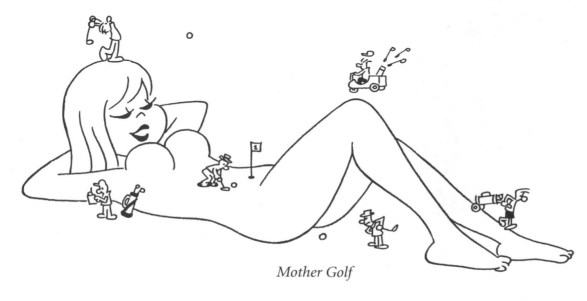

Mother Golf

I've done a number of things with *Golf Digest*. For one of the U.S. Opens I organized eighteen cartoonists to illustrate each of the holes with their characters playing with one of the pros. For the January 1970 issue, we took a bunch to Hilton Head, South Carolina, to do an article on "The World's Wackiest Tournament," where the cartoonists competed in doing what duffers do best. Some of the events were: How far can you hit it into the woods without hitting a tree? Who can take the biggest divot? How many times can you lip the cup without sinking a putt? How far can you throw a club? The events were all cartooned and printed in the magazine.

Winners of the Second Annual Joan Browne Cartoon Classic pro-am golf tournament were, from left, golf pro Mike Healy, Garfield *creator Jim Davis of United Feature Syndicate, King Features Syndicate president Joseph D'Angelo,* Blondie *writer Dean Young of King, and* Beetle Bailey/ Hi and Lois *creator Mort Walker of King. Also shown is philanthropist Marcia Rubin, who donated the silver Revere Bowl trophy.*

Event No. 5: Who Can Use the Most Swearwords in Fifteen Seconds Without Repeating?

MORT WALKER, creator of *Beetle Bailey*, won this event. "I got a little help from Sgt. Snorkel," Mort admits, "and my four years of barracks life let me see some real pros in action." Mort never swears at home but saves his energies for the water holes and blooped trap shots. "The thing that really gets me is to flub a chip shot right off the green," he says. "So, to get myself in the right frame of mind for this event, I deliberately flubbed three in a row, using a quick backswing, raising my head, and being sure not to follow through. The effect of three flubbed shots is explosive. The words come out in a torrent, bleaching overhanging leaves and sending any women on the course home where

The World's Wackiest Tournament

Golf Digest, *1970*

they should be." Mort's careful preparation paid off. He scored 23 separate swearwords in 15 seconds (not counting a "heck" and a "darn," which were thrown out for lacking body and flavor). He went on to chip in the hole and get his 8. "Gee whillikers," adds Mort. "Just as in all other professions, I think the duffer's game would improve if he developed his dingdong vocabulary."

—*Golf Digest*, 1970

Silvermine Golf Club, Norwalk, Conn.

The Better Golfer

I have an apartment in Florida overlooking a golf course. I'd see the golfers come through one by one, slicing the ball into the woods, hitting it short down the fairway, and plunking it into the lake. Then I'd turn on the TV and see the pros hitting it straight and long, going over all the lakes, and wonder what the difference is. What is the cause? They're all on the same courses, same clubs, same conditions. There must be other factors involved. Suddenly it came to me. *Skill!* That's it! The amateurs are much more skillful at slicing and hitting the ball short and into the water. The pros have never achieved the skill that the great majority of golfers have attained. I slept much better that night, knowing that I belonged to the fraternity of skillful golfers.

By Dik Browne

Happy Birthday
Joan and Dik

I have the distinct reputation of never quitting on a golf course, whatever the weather. I've played in all kinds of storms, even hurricanes. My fellow golfers will say, "I'm getting wet. Let's quit." I say, "You're already wet, and you'll get even wetter walking back to the clubhouse. Let's just play on." I don't know why they kid me about this.

My fantasy of a naked golf game

From Golf Digest

"Chi-Chi came at him doing his saber dance and the general went for his pistol."

Stan Drake *(Juliet Jones, Blondie)* was an outstanding artist, storyteller, and golfer. He shared a studio once with Dik Browne. After Stan enthused about the charms of the game, Dik decided to take the plunge. He came back after lunch and told Stan he was ready to go. He had gone out and bought a ball and a tee. Stan screeched, *"A ball and a tee? You're going to need lots of balls and tees!"* He turned out to be right. ❖

An invitation I did for an Artists and Writers banquet

— Other Cartoonists Draw My Characters —

Baby Blues

TO MORT FROM YOUR FRIENDS, THE BABY BLUES BROTHERS. RICK KIRKMAN JERRY SCOTT

Curtis

Beetle Bailey

From Mad magazine

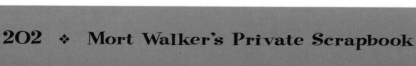

Mother Goose and Grimm

STRIP POKER

TO MORT WITH LOVE AND ADMIRATION

Zippy

"ARE WE DEBRIEFED YET?"

BILL GRIFFITH

FOR MORT--HOW 'BOUT THAT WACKY, SIX WEEK WAR, HUH? —BILL GRIFFITH

B.C.

On April Fool's Day, 1998, I drew Shoe *and Jeff MacNelly drew* Beetle.

Marvin

8/19/91 TO: MORT from YOUR BIGGEST FAN! WARMEST REGARDS, Tom ARMSTRONG

BEETLE BAILEY

From Mad *magazine*

Off the Mark   by Mark Parisi

Ziggy

To Mort...with admiration and apologies! Mark Parisi (off the mark)

SO GENERAL, WHAT BRINGS YOU TO CAMP SWAMPY?

CAMPBELL

NEWS
GENERAL CALLS CLINTON NAMES

©1993 DAYTON DAILY NEWS
TRIBUNE MEDIA SERVICES

APOLOGIES TO BEETLE AND MORT WALKER!
FROM YOUR PAL — MIKE PETERS

Beetle Bailey, 66, Dies;
Was Army's Oldest Private

Pvt. Beetle Bailey

Beetle Bailey, the only Army enlisted man to serve 47 years as a private, was pronounced dead today at 1400 hours. However, exact time of death has yet to be determined.

"I found him in his bunk unconscious, which for him was normal," said Sgt. Orville Snorkel at Camp Swampy. "I tried punching him awake, but he wouldn't come around. I figured he was faking a coma to get out of latrine duty. I got a little concerned when rigor mortis set in, but I figured he was faking that too. He could have been dead for a week, for all I know."

Bailey, who joined the Army in 1950, had a long history of service-related ailments. During the Korean War he complained of acute combat fatigue, and during the Vietnam conflict, was often hospitalized for post-traumatic stress. Following treatment for shell shock during the invasion of Grenada, he spent six months on sick leave in 1990, the result of Desert Storm syndrome.

These claims of illness remain open to question. According to Pentagon records, Bailey spent his entire Army career at Camp Swampy.

Bailey qualified for promotion to PFC on 21 occasions. Each time he refused, concerned about the strain and pressures of added responsibility.

Befitting his rank, funeral services will be private. To honor Bailey's death, all Army posts will fly their flags at full mast.

From Mad *magazine*

THE BEETLE SIDE

ROOM 521

WART MAKER

"Jenkins, I've done it! I've perfected a fool-proof star wars defense system! All my calculations are right in here, you must see them!"

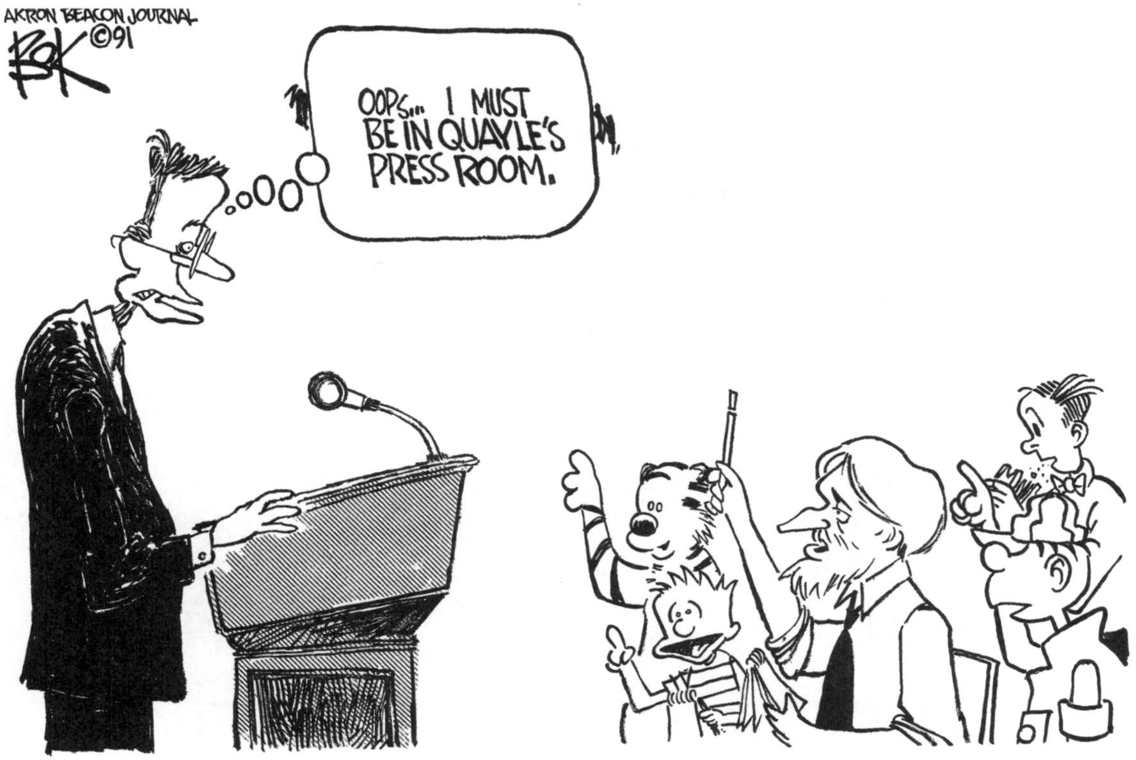
AKRON BEACON JOURNAL
BOK ©91
OOPS... I MUST BE IN QUAYLE'S PRESS ROOM.

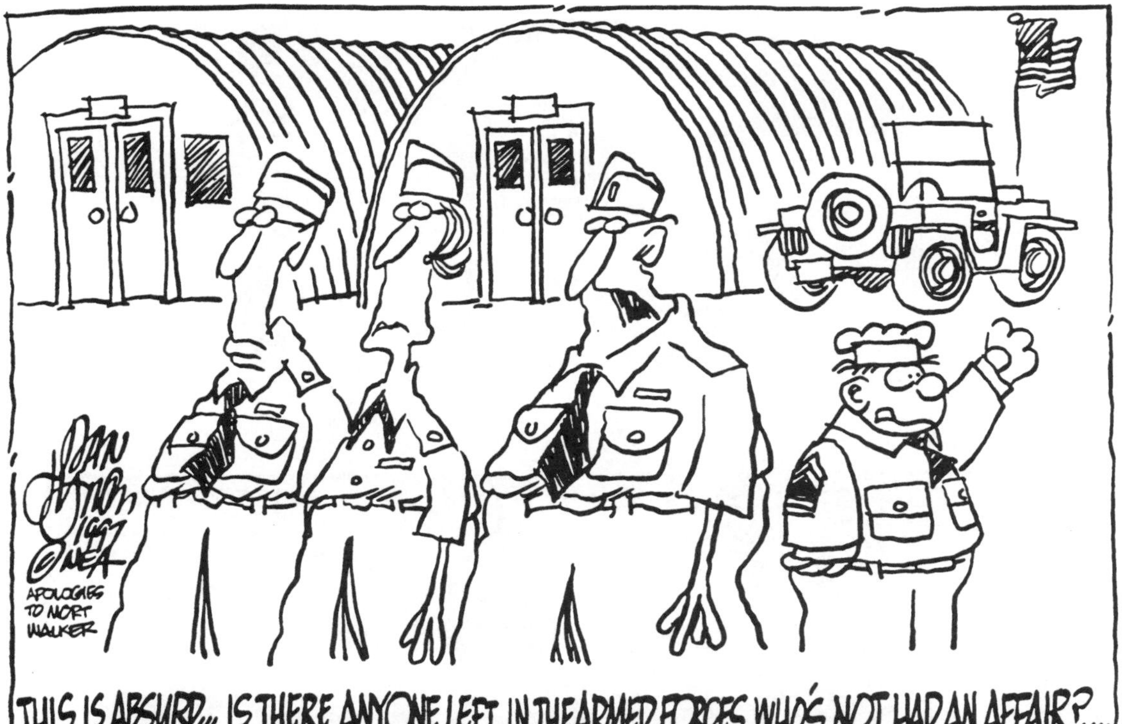
APOLOGIES TO MORT WALKER

THIS IS ABSURD... IS THERE ANYONE LEFT IN THE ARMED FORCES WHO'S NOT HAD AN AFFAIR?...

TO MORT! YOUR FRIEND, MIKE.
BEATLES REUNION '95
IT'S NOT THE SAME WITHOUT JOHN!...
THE BEATLES
MIKE LUCKOVICH ATLANTA CONSTITUTION '95 (APOLOGIES TO MORT WALKER)

john tower at the Pentagon
GENERAL HALFTRACK!! THAT'S NO WAY FOR AN OFFICER AND GENTLEMAN TO BEHAVE!!
HERE, LET A PRO SHOW YOU HOW IT'S DONE!

Mother Goose

STUNT DOUBLE? WHAT DO YOU MEAN I HAVE TO BE A STUNT DOUBLE?
WE CAN'T ALLOW OUR TOP STRIP CHARACTERS TO DO DANGEROUS STUNTS. SO YOU STAND IN FOR THEM.
BEETLE, COME HERE!
HERE HE IS SGT. SNORKLE!
THUD
POW
CRACK
EGK
GOOD, NOW HURRY UP... GARFIELD'S ABOUT TO STUFF ODIE IN A BLENDER!
4/17

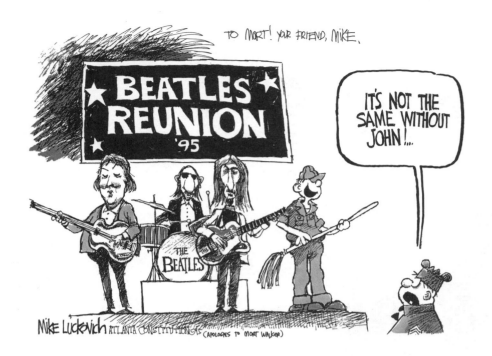

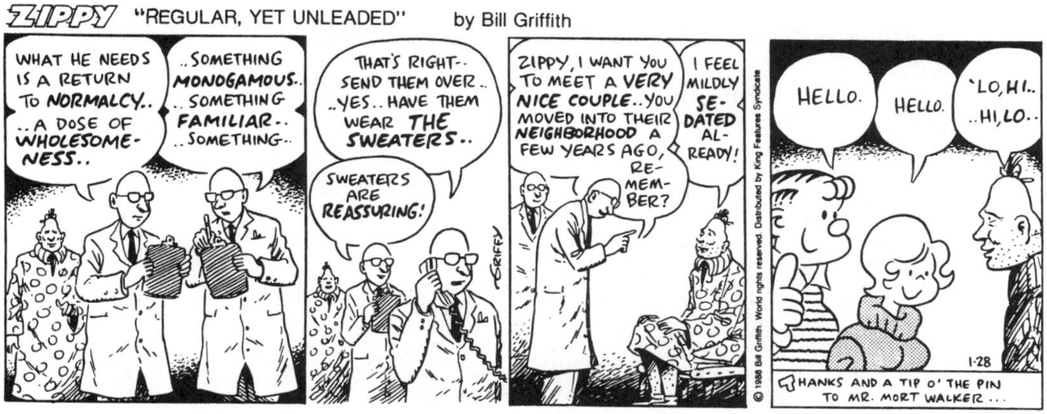
ZIPPY "REGULAR, YET UNLEADED" by Bill Griffith
WHAT HE NEEDS IS A RETURN TO NORMALCY.. ..A DOSE OF WHOLESOME-NESS..
..SOMETHING MONOGAMOUS.. ..SOMETHING FAMILIAR.. ..SOMETHING..
THAT'S RIGHT-- SEND THEM OVER.. ..YES.. HAVE THEM WEAR THE SWEATERS..
SWEATERS ARE REASSURING!
GRIFFY
ZIPPY, I WANT YOU TO MEET A VERY NICE COUPLE.. YOU MOVED INTO THEIR NEIGHBORHOOD A FEW YEARS AGO, RE-MEM-BER?
I FEEL MILDLY SE-DATED AL-READY!
© 1988 Bill Griffith. World rights reserved. Distributed by King Features Syndicate
HELLO.
HELLO.
'LO, HI.. ..HI, LO..
1·28
THANKS AND A TIP O' THE PIN TO MR. MORT WALKER...

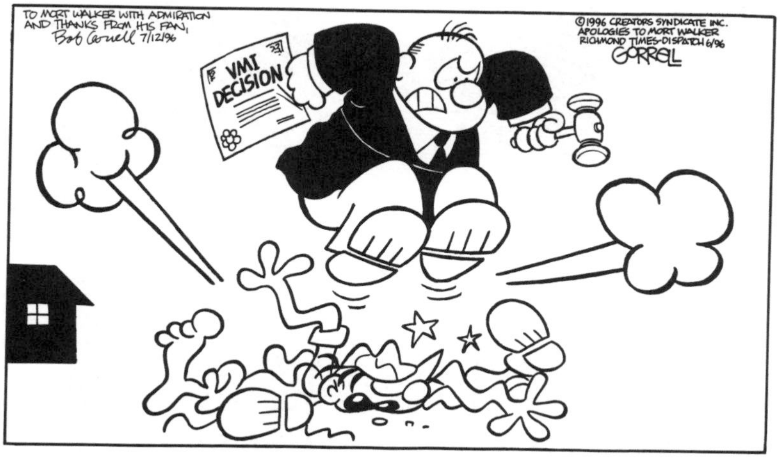
TO MORT WALKER WITH ADMIRATION AND THANKS FROM HIS FAN,
Bob Gorrell 7/12/96
©1996 CREATORS SYNDICATE INC. APOLOGIES TO MORT WALKER RICHMOND TIMES-DISPATCH 6/96
GORRELL
VMI DECISION

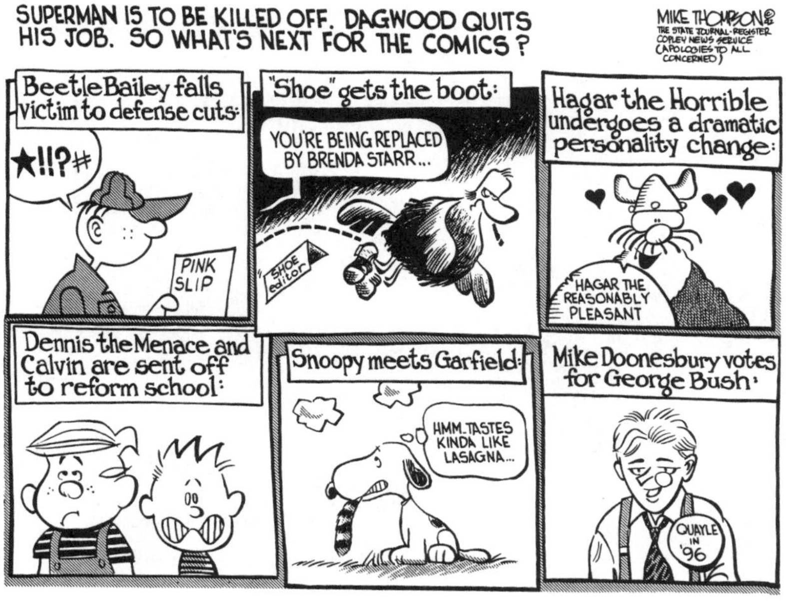
SUPERMAN IS TO BE KILLED OFF. DAGWOOD QUITS HIS JOB. SO WHAT'S NEXT FOR THE COMICS?
MIKE THOMPSON © THE STATE JOURNAL-REGISTER COPLEY NEWS SERVICE (APOLOGIES TO ALL CONCERNED)
Beetle Bailey falls victim to defense cuts:
★!!?#
PINK SLIP
"Shoe" gets the boot:
YOU'RE BEING REPLACED BY BRENDA STARR...
SHOE editor
Hagar the Horrible undergoes a dramatic personality change:
HAGAR THE REASONABLY PLEASANT
Dennis the Menace and Calvin are sent off to reform school:
Snoopy meets Garfield:
HMM..TASTES KINDA LIKE LASAGNA...
Mike Doonesbury votes for George Bush:
QUAYLE IN '96

JIM MORIN'S VIEW

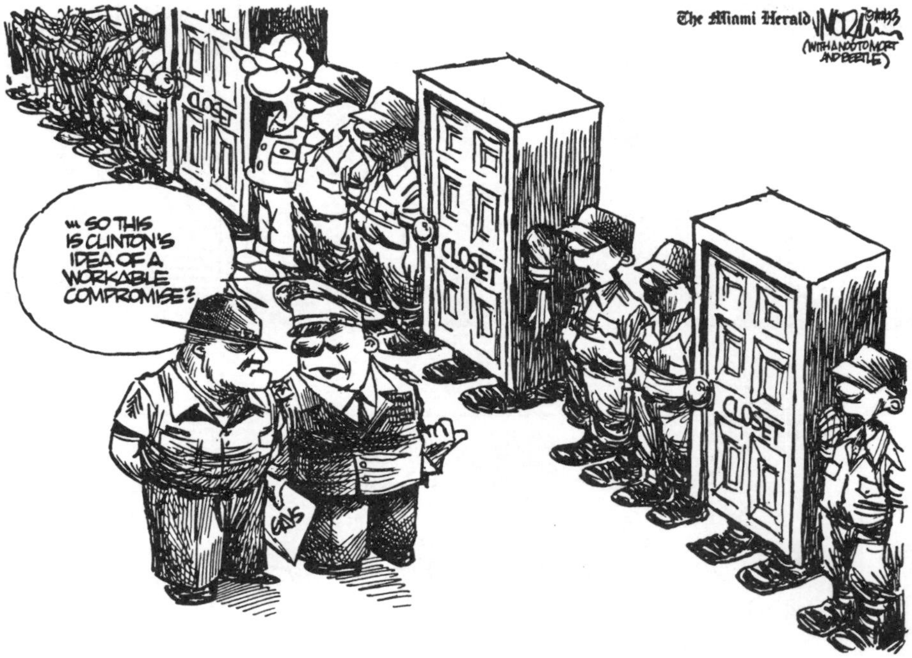
The Miami Herald
MORIN ©1993
(WITH A NOD TO MORT AND BEETLE)
... SO THIS IS CLINTON'S IDEA OF A WORKABLE COMPROMISE?
CLOSET
CLOSET
CLOSET
CLOSET
GAYS

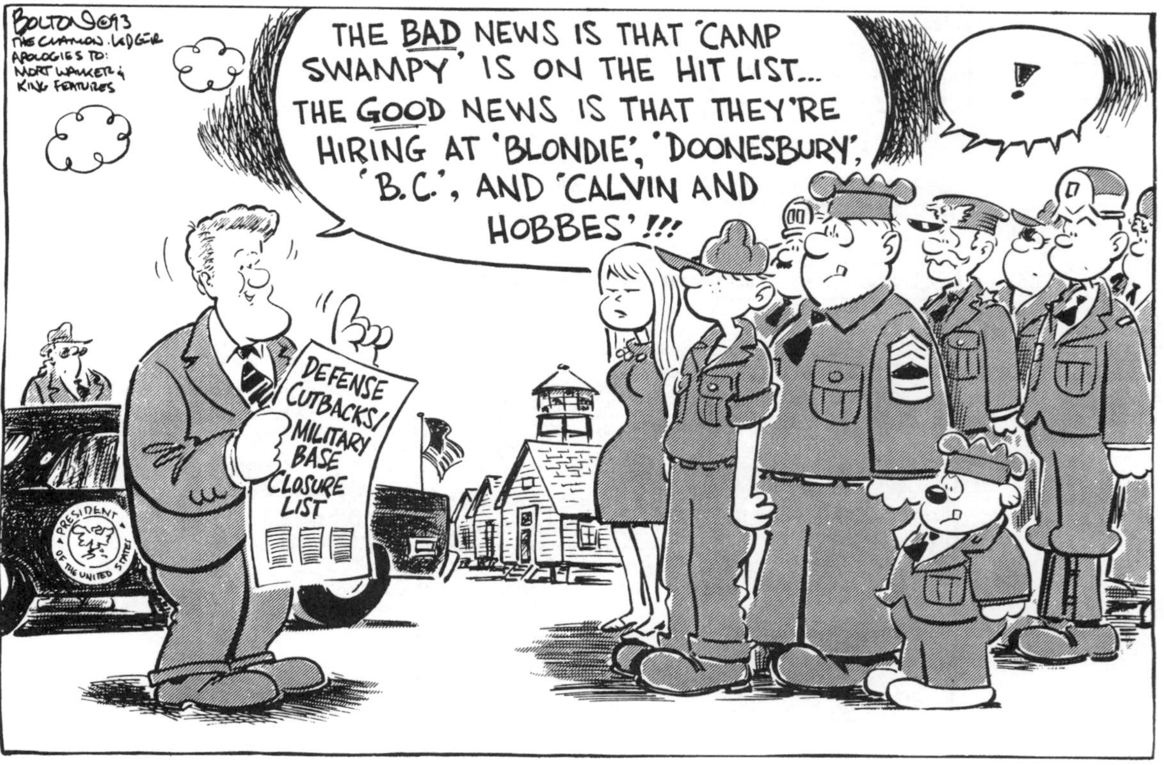
BOLTON ©93
THE CLARION-LEDGER
APOLOGIES TO: MORT WALKER & KING FEATURES
THE BAD NEWS IS THAT 'CAMP SWAMPY' IS ON THE HIT LIST... THE GOOD NEWS IS THAT THEY'RE HIRING AT 'BLONDIE', 'DOONESBURY', 'B.C.', AND 'CALVIN AND HOBBES'!!!
!
DEFENSE CUTBACKS/ MILITARY BASE CLOSURE LIST
PRESIDENT OF THE UNITED STATES

FREE FOR ALL

With apologies to Matt Groening, Mort Walker and Charles Schulz.

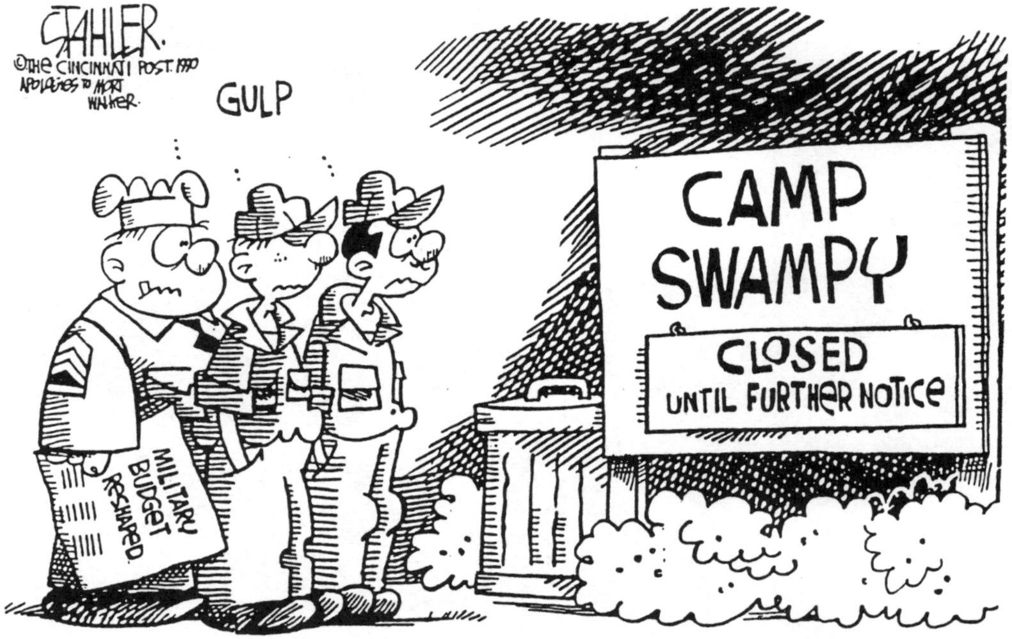
STAHLER.
©THE CINCINNATI POST. 1990
APOLOGIES TO MORT WALKER.
GULP
MILITARY BUDGET RESHAPED
CAMP SWAMPY
CLOSED
UNTIL FURTHER NOTICE

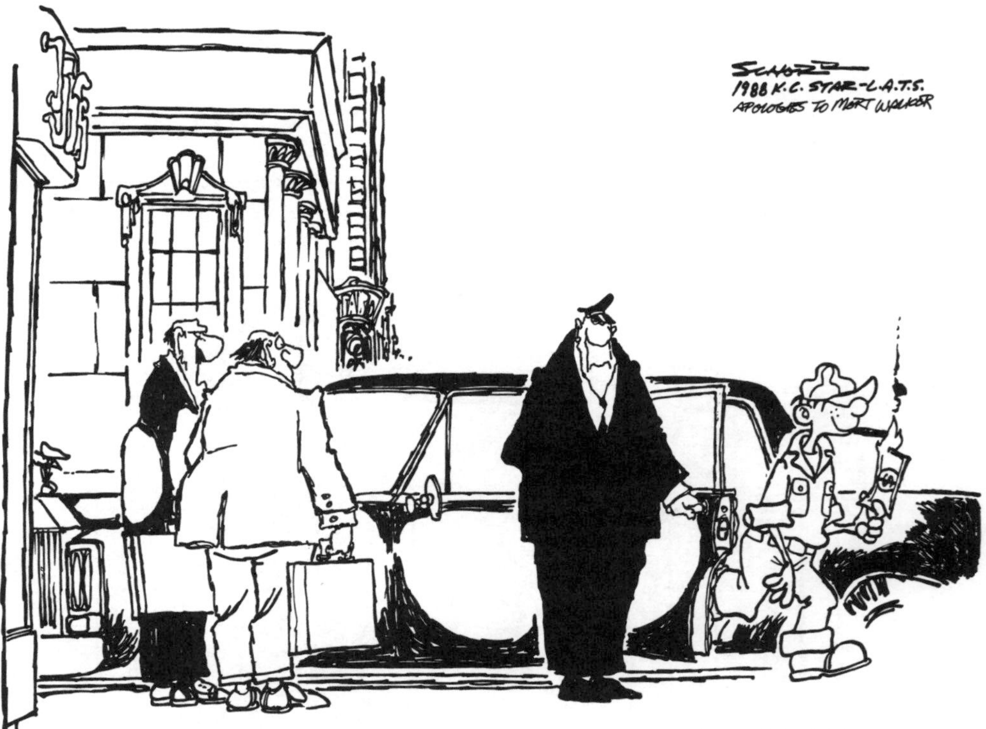
SCHORR
1988 K.C. STAR-L.A.T.S.
APOLOGIES TO MORT WALKER
"I HEAR HE WAS TRANSFERRED TO PENTAGON PROCUREMENT..."
To Mort Walker... from a big fan... Best Wishes Bill Schorr

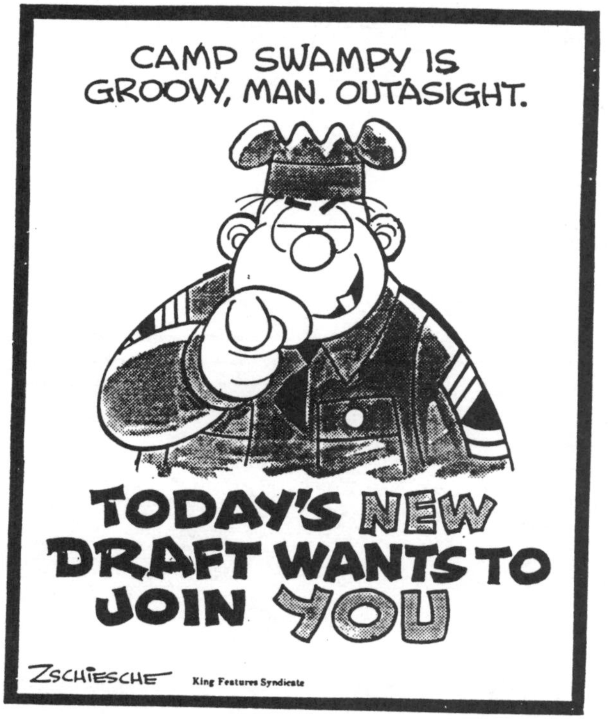
CAMP SWAMPY IS GROOVY, MAN. OUTASIGHT.
TODAY'S NEW DRAFT WANTS TO JOIN YOU
ZSCHIESCHE
King Features Syndicate

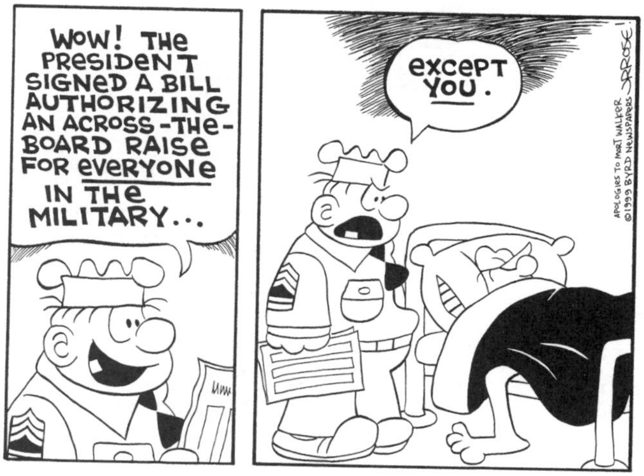
WOW! THE PRESIDENT SIGNED A BILL AUTHORIZING AN ACROSS-THE-BOARD RAISE FOR EVERYONE IN THE MILITARY...
EXCEPT YOU.
APOLOGIES TO MORT WALKER
©1999 BYRD NEWSPAPERS

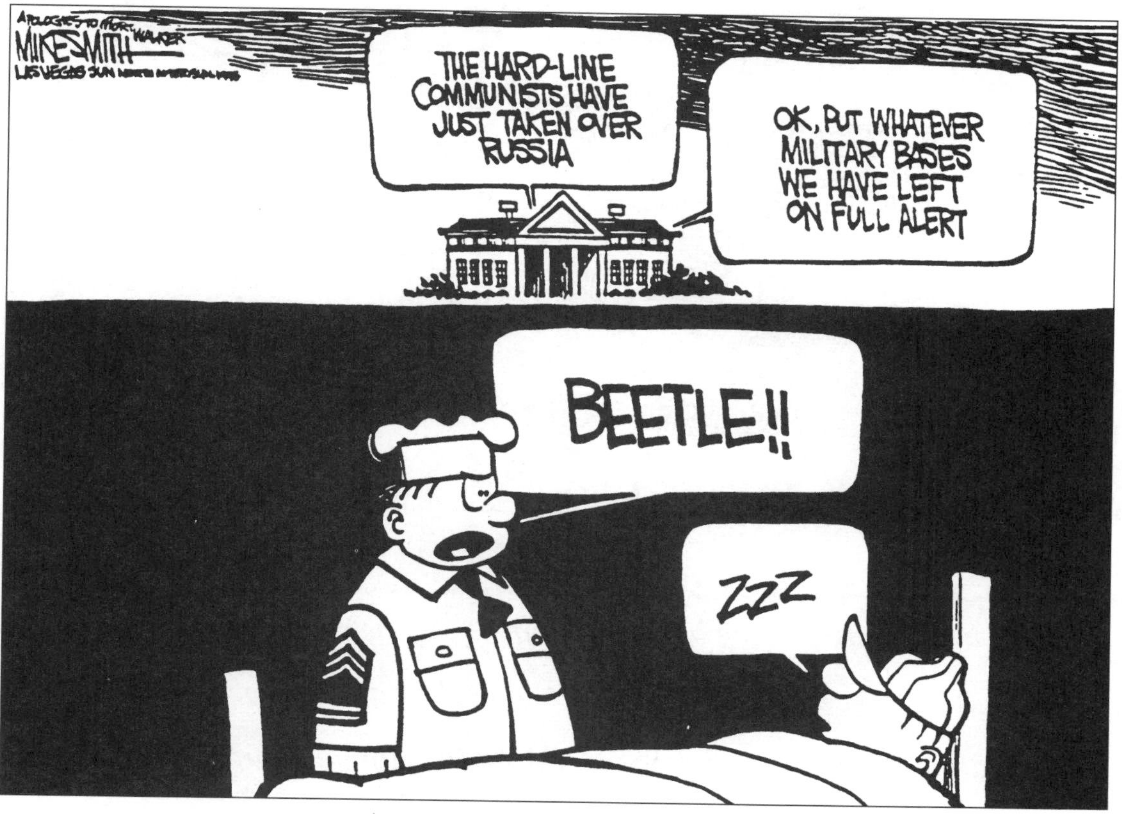
APOLOGIES TO MORT WALKER
MIKE SMITH
LAS VEGAS SUN
THE HARD-LINE COMMUNISTS HAVE JUST TAKEN OVER RUSSIA
OK, PUT WHATEVER MILITARY BASES WE HAVE LEFT ON FULL ALERT
BEETLE!!
ZZZ

My wife and I were passing by a church in Greenwich. The sign said SECOND
CONGREGATIONAL CHURCH. *Cathy: "What's the difference between the First*
Congregational Church and the Second Congregational Church?" Me: "One."

CHAPTER NINE

Cartoon Art

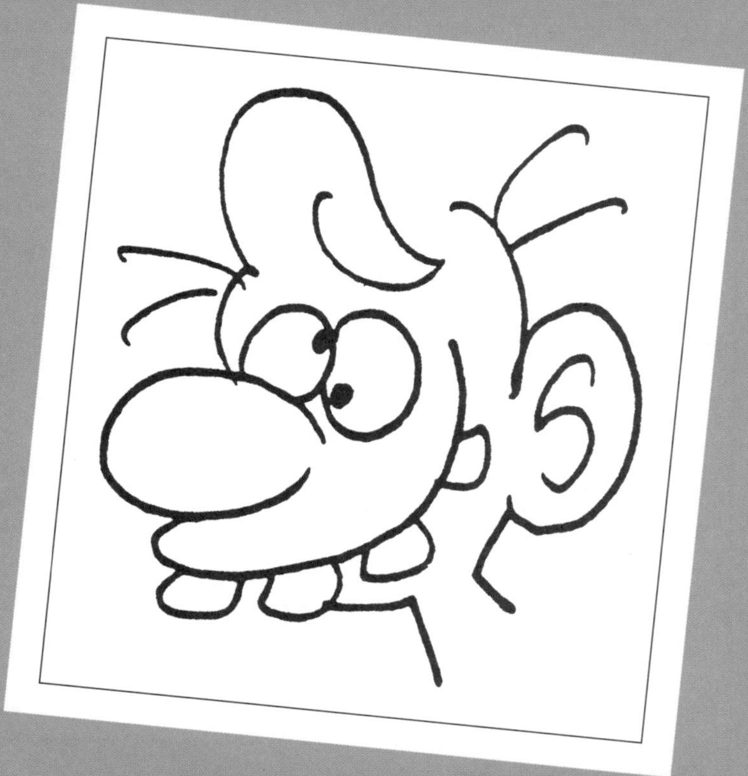

Cartooning is as old as the hills. Man has been drawing cartoons since he drew his first breath. We've found drawings on cave walls dating back five thousand years. They're on Egyptian tombs, Greek vases, Aztec temples, French tapestries, Chinese scrolls—they're everywhere. They tell stories of people's exploits, make fun of their foibles, and ridicule their leaders. Our written language began as little cartoon sketches, or pictographs. Later on, these drawings on stone became lithographs, which allowed cartoons to be printed and distributed. Daumier, the famous French satirist, was thrown in the pokey for five months in 1832 for drawing King Louis Philippe as a frog.

The wonderful thing about comic strips is that they take the mundane, the humdrum, and the failures of everyday life and transform these minor happenings into humor, philosophy, adventure . . . and eventually into history. Comic strips have become the prime chronicler of the common man and woman, mirroring the way they dress and talk and the social climate at their moment in time. The early newspaper comics showed the life of immigrants and were all written in dialect. Then comic characters strove to make money any way they could.

Women went to work for the first time. There were boardinghouses, orphans, hillbillies, and boxers. We saw the country fall in love with the automobile and the airplane and saw our funny friends go to war. There is not a movement or an event that occurred in the last hundred years that has not been recorded, dissected, and brought into focus by our comic artists. Most comics today are about family life. Even *Beetle Bailey* was diagnosed as a family strip by the *New York Daily News,* with Sarge as the mother of a bunch of unruly kids. ❖

IDEOGRAPHIC	"I killed			5 lions"
LOGOGRAPHIC (reconstructed)	"I	kill(ed)	5	lion(s)"
LOGOSYLLABIC (Assyrian cuneiform)	a — du — uk "I killed		5 5	naše lions"
SYLLABIC (Phoenician)	ʾ R Gⁿ T "I killed		H M Sⁿ Tⁿ five	e Bⁿ ⁿMⁿ lions"
ALPHABETIC (Greek)	ʾΑΠΈΚΤΟΝΑ apéktona "I killed		É 5 5	ΛΈΟΝΤΑΣ léontas lions"

Our written language began as cartoons.

A special drawing done to protest the shrinking space given to the comics by newspaper editors

As we see ourselves . . .

As editors see us. By Mort Walker.

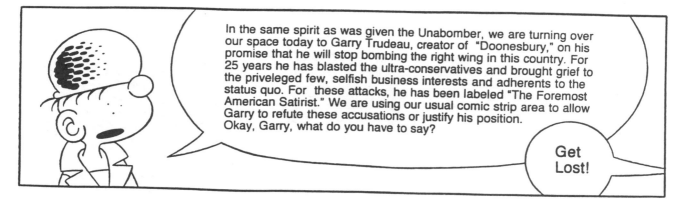

In the same spirit as was given the Unabomber, we are turning over our space today to Garry Trudeau, creator of "Doonesbury," on his promise that he will stop bombing the right wing in this country. For 25 years he has blasted the ultra-conservatives and brought grief to the priveleged few, selfish business interests and adherents to the status quo. For these attacks, he has been labeled "The Foremost American Satirist." We are using our usual comic strip area to allow Garry to refute these accusations or justify his position. Okay, Garry, what do you have to say?

Get Lost!

Be true to your art, and your art will be true to you.

FUNNY THING ABOUT CARTOONS

Cartoons are funnier than you think, except most people don't think seriously about them. It's a fantasy world where we accept everything without question. For example:

Betty Boop began life as a dog. Gradually, she metamorphized into a beautiful woman, but her dog boyfriend, Bimbo, stayed a dog. Is that fair?

Maggie and Jiggs have survived 80 years of marriage without a last name.

Charlie Brown's sister, Sally, was born and grew up to Charlie's size while he remained the same.

On the other hand, Skeezix was born 72 years ago making Uncle Walt about 104 today.

Blondie and Dagwood's "Baby Dumpling" has grown into a teen-age "Alexander" and they haven't aged a bit. Good trick.

Beetle's sister is Lois of "Hi and Lois." The only crossover we know of.

Tweety Bird is of no known gender although "It" began as a female, colored pink. She looked too naked in that color so she changed to yellow androgynous.

Same with Krazy Kat. Krazy is sometimes referred to as "he" and other times as "she," although she reacts ardently when hit by Ignatz's bricks, saying, "My li'l dollink."

Goofy was introduced as "Dippy Dawg," a dog that dresses as a human and walks on two feet while Mickey, a mouse, has a dog, Pluto, who walks on four paws and is a <u>dog</u>. You figure.

In another name change "Bluto" in Popeye is now "Brutus."

Donald Duck wears a shirt and no pants, but Mickey wears pants and no shirt.

Is Lois Lane really so dumb that she can't recognize that Clark Kent is Superman, or are those glasses he wears some super Krypton disguise?

Wouldn't it be a wonderful world if we were all cartoon characters?

SO MUCH FOR PREDICTIONS

In a 1909 interview with "Editor & Publisher" magazine, R. F. Outcault, creator of "The Yellow Kid" and "Buster Brown," predicted the demise of comic sections in newspapers.

He said, "The public is losing interest in comics and the cartoonists have written so continually and so well that they have finally become exhausted. The public is getting comic indigestion and will soon demand a change of comic diet. No new men in this field have appeared to startle the editors or the public."

Obviously Outcault was better at cartooning than at prognosticating.

SCIENTISTS MAKE FUNNY DISCOVERY

After centuries of hitting our funny-bones in our elbows or laughing our tails off, researchers have discovered that our laugh center is actually in the brain. Unfortunately, cartoonists will have to get more intellectual.

The Chinese had four tests to distinguish the greatness of a work of art. The first was chiao *(clever); the second,* miao *(wonderful); the third,* shen *(divine); the fourth* I *(effortless).*

Thinking that Beetle *would not survive after the Korean War, I tried taking him home to get involved with his sister Lois's family. It didn't work.*

I Sue the U.S. Government

In 1960, Syracuse University decided to start a popular-culture collection for their library. They were asking writers, musicians, artists, and cartoonists to donate work. They pointed out that donations (at that time) were tax deductible. I had 1,000 of my drawings appraised at $50 each and gave them to the university. I went to Washington first, conferred with IRS officers, and was assured that the $50,000 deduction was entirely acceptable. Four years later, they disallowed it. My lawyers told me to pay the money and sue for a refund. This would get me into a federal court with a jury.

What a time we had! We showed up in a courtroom in Bridgeport, Connecticut, with a jury sitting there and heard the booming voice declare, "Mort and Jean Walker *vs.* the United States Government." It was a sobering moment.

The trial lasted a week. I brought in famous cartoonists like Milton Caniff, an appraiser, and other authorities on cartooning. They showed my strips and read them. The jury and the judge were laughing all week. We won. The judge told me later it was the best trial he'd ever had. The jury poured out into the hall and told me how much they'd enjoyed their week. It was another triumph for cartooning.

Several years later, some senators tried to stop Lyndon Johnson and Hubert Humphrey from donating their papers to a museum and taking tax deductions. They passed a law that says you can't get a deduction from anything you created yourself. Johnson and Humphrey predated their donations and got away with it, but the rest of us were caught. It doesn't make any difference if I give a cartoon to a charitable auction and they sell it for $500 (the going price now for the same $50 drawing in 1960), I can't benefit from it. However, if I *die,* the drawings left in my estate will be *taxed.* It's no wonder I attack bureaucracy with such a vengeance every day in my strip. ❖

Collections

I used to collect anything that had to do with cartoons. I think I had every *Big Little Book* that was published. I had the very first comic books ever published. I usually got them by gathering deposit bottles around the neighborhood and trading them in at the drugstore. I found a used-magazine store that sold old humor magazines, *Life, Judge, College Humor,* and others. I bought every issue I could find. The central library in Kansas City had a huge newspaper room with reading stands holding papers from all over the country. I think men used

them to find jobs during the Depression. I talked the library into saving the papers for me, and every week my father and I would pick them up. I'd cut out all the comic strips, tie strings around them, and store them in our attic. I had a collection of every comic strip published in the United States. I also had many original cartoons given to me by professionals. When I went off to the army during the war, I was gone for almost four years. During that time, my father underbid on the building of a church. They held him accountable and he had to sell

our house. When I came back, my collection was gone; they had had no place to store it. After participating in a war for mankind to have freedom, justice, and a comic collection, I was crushed. Since then I've heard of many other guys who came back from the war and found their collections cleaned out by mothers who said, "I thought you'd outgrown those comic books." In addition to the several hundred thousand dollars the collection would be worth today, the thing I regret most is the loss to history. ❖

Collecting Al

Al Hirschfeld took a train to Boca Raton to attend the opening of his exhibit at the International Museum of Cartoon Art. It was a dynamite exhibit, one of the best we've ever had, and Al and his wife, Louise, were charming and sweet. In my welcoming speech I recalled that many years ago I had asked Al to donate one of his drawings to our museum. "What museum?" he asked. "The Museum of Cartoon Art," I told him. "Oh, I'm not a

cartoonist," he replied. I thought about that for a few years and then realized he was indeed unique. He had created his own genre. Nobody else on the face of this earth was doing what he was doing. Al's gimmick has always been to hide his daughter Nina's name in his drawings and state the number of times it appears beside his signature. In honor of this occasion I drew a picture of Beetle with Al's name hidden fifty times.

Comics have proven to be one of the best-read parts of the paper and are enjoyed by people of all ages. Many people read the headlines and skip right to the comics. It is estimated that over 300 million people read at least one comic every day. King Features syndicates its comics to seventy-two different countries. It would seem, then, that cartoonists are the best-read authors in the world. ❖

Photo by
George
Mayernik

BOY! THE PAPER IS JUST ONE TRAGIC STORY AFTER ANOTHER

THEY SAY BAD NEWS IS REPORTED 20 TIMES OFTENER THAN GOOD NEWS

9-26

IS THAT WHY THE COMICS ARE ON PAGE 21 ?

MORT WALKER

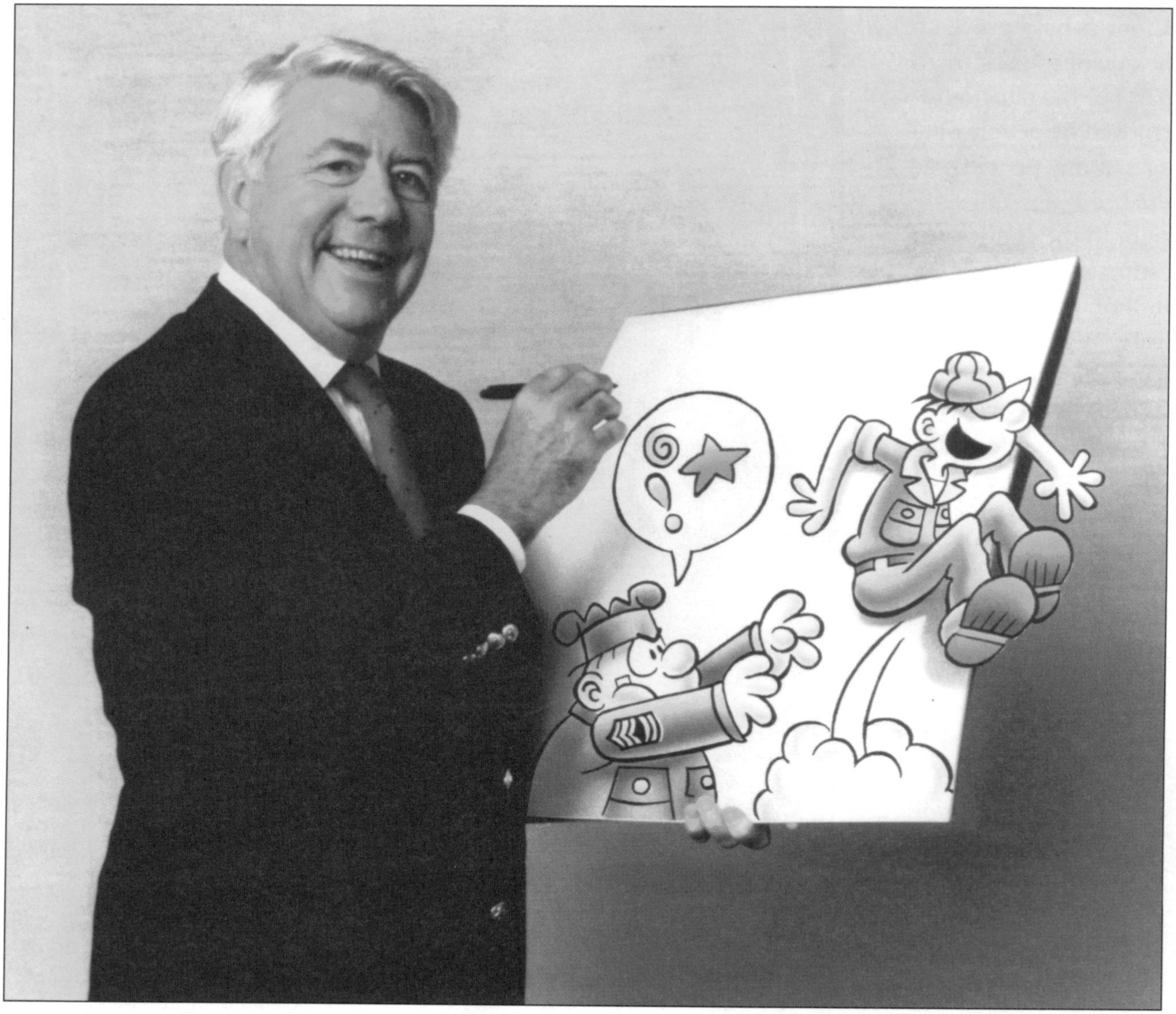

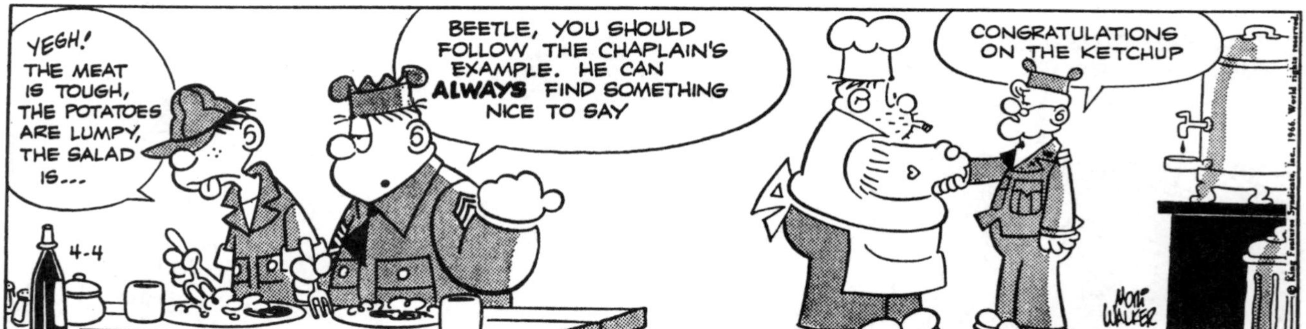

YEGH! THE MEAT IS TOUGH, THE POTATOES ARE LUMPY, THE SALAD IS...
BEETLE, YOU SHOULD FOLLOW THE CHAPLAIN'S EXAMPLE. HE CAN **ALWAYS** FIND SOMETHING NICE TO SAY
CONGRATULATIONS ON THE KETCHUP
4-4
MORT WALKER

William Randolph Hearst toasts some of his comic creations, in a 1904 Puck *cartoon by J. S. Pughe.* Beetle *was the last strip Hearst put his okay on. (*Puck, *June 29, 1904)*

TAKE A PEN LINE FROM WALT DISNEY... SOME GAG STYLE FROM SMITTY, BLONDIE, AND HUBERT... A BIT OF FLAVOR FROM SAD SACK... A FEELING OF CHARACTER DEVELOPMENT FROM LI'L ABNER... SOME COMPOSITION TRICKS FROM MILTON CANIFF... SPRINKLE WITH A LUSTY BROADNESS FROM MOON MULLINS... STIR IN A HUNDRED OTHER INGREDIENTS FROM A HUNDRED OTHER FAVORITES... AND YOU HAVE **ONE** MAN'S COMIC HERITAGE

THANKS

The Beginning of the Cartoon Museum

Dik Browne and I were in Jamaica in 1960 at a cartoonists' golf tournament that we had just won. We were celebrating with a few cool ones, watching the sun set into the Caribbean, and talking about the state of cartooning. "Why don't cartoonists get more

Greenwich, Connecticut: the museum's first home, 1974–77

respect?" I said. "Because museums don't exhibit cartoons," Dik answered. "Let's start a cartoon museum then," I said.

That casual statement was the beginning of a thirty-five-year pursuit that would cost me millions of dollars and countless days of work. I started by forming a committee of the most famous cartoonists in the country. We went to foundations, corporations, and government agencies to get support. After several years the committee fell apart, but I didn't give up the dream.

At a banquet I found myself sitting next to a member of the William Randolph Hearst Foundation. I said, "The Hearst Foundation should help fund our museum. After all, Hearst was the one who created the comic section of the newspaper." He nodded his head, and a year later, with the help of Joe D'Angelo, president of King Features Syndicate, we were given $100,000 to get us going. I rented an old mansion near my house in Greenwich, Connecticut, and began fixing it up. My son Brian had just finished college, and he got a friend to join the cause. The house had been empty twenty-five years and needed a lot of refurbishing.

Jack Tippit, a cartoonist friend, came on to be director, and we opened on August 11, 1974. It was an immediate success. School buses brought kids, groups came from many foreign countries, and cartoonists swarmed to see it. It was a happy situation. Then, after a year, the owner announced that he was not going to renew our lease because we were "wearing out" his house. I went into the staff meeting that morning and broke the news. The tears started flowing. Trying to rescue the situation, I said enthusiastically, "Let's treat this as an opportunity to improve ourselves. Let's find a *castle* to move to."

A year later we had found our castle. It sat high on a hill above the Byram River with a view of Long Island Sound to the east and New York City to the west. It was a one-hundred-year-old landmark built entirely of concrete: roof,

The museum staff: left to right, Jack Tippit, director, and Charles Green, assistant curator, with Brian and me

floors, walls, stairs, all fireproof concrete. It too had been empty for years and needed a lot of repairs. But this time I bought it so we couldn't be thrown out. We opened November 12, 1977.

We were there for fifteen years before repairs began heading toward the million-dollar mark, and we decided to move to a larger and more modern facility. We searched the area from Boston to Washington, D.C. In Connecticut, we came close to getting buildings in Stamford and Norwalk.

Ward's Castle, November 12, 1977–June 30, 1992

Then the Cultural Council of Palm Beach County heard about our quest and invited us to come down for a look. Florida was experiencing a boom, and a lot of corporations were locating there. People needed things to do besides go to the beach. Local governments were trying to build museums, performing arts centers, and discovery centers and were helping with the funding.

Before we started the Museum of Cartoon Art, cartoonists were giving their work away to anyone who asked. The *New York Daily News* syndicate put piles of originals in their lobby, free for the taking. Animation studios washed the drawings off their cels so they could reuse the plastic. I remember Hal Foster telling me he had so many requests for his art he was beginning to ask $5 for them to discourage fans; today his *Prince Valiant* strips sell for over $10,000. Disney cels have sold for over $500,000. The six-panel Disney storyboard with the first-ever drawings of Mickey Mouse that we display in the museum for the *Plane Crazy* film was appraised at $3,750,000. When I first held those drawings in my hand, a chill went up my back. Disney in his wildest fantasies would never have imagined that these simple little pencil drawings would result in a major movie studio, theme parks all over the world, and billions of dollars of licensed products.

The mandate of the museum is to spread knowledge, incite pleasure, and stimulate curiosity. We want to create an archive of collective memory, a bank of popular culture to have a broad appeal to people of all ages, genders, and ethnic backgrounds. Museums are an important alternative to formal education and can fill many gaps between what is taught and what needs to be learned. Museums have been called the savings banks of the soul. We want to collect and present information in an inviting way, connecting enlightenment and entertainment, formal and informal education, and elite and popular culture. Our education center teaches reading skills, history, philosophy, and the value of laughter in our lives. Disney has been called the greatest educator of our times, because you are having fun without knowing you're learning at the same time. We want to expand on that idea and use our bank of cartoons as a teaching tool for the world.

The city of Boca Raton offered us a beautiful piece of land worth over a million dollars. We accepted and went to work raising money. We figured we needed $15 million to build. Joe D'Angelo, Cathy, and I were now the prime movers to find the funds, make the plans, and get support. I did a lot of the architectural work, Cathy ran the temporary office and staff, and Joe told our story to everyone he came in contact with.

We had many disappointments and setbacks, but we wouldn't allow ourselves to get discouraged. In March 1996 we opened with one of the best parties ever thrown. Disney

Marcia and Joe D'Angelo aboard the presidential yacht with me and Cathy, hosting the Japanese Nemoto Group, contributors to the museum

sent costumed characters and props. We had characters from all the major strips and a sell-out crowd of cartoonists and important people from the area. We're very proud of what we have done.

When we originally opened in 1974, we were the first cartoon museum of its kind in the world. There had been a few small museums in foreign countries devoted to one cartoonist, but this was the first Hall of Fame and the first museum that included all genres: comic strips, comic books, animation, caricature, editorial cartoons, illustration, advertising, and greeting cards from many countries. Now there are around thirty museums like ours in the world. On November 21, 1998, I was given an award as guest of honor at the first convention of cartoon museum executives in Angoulême, France. I'm happy that cartoons have finally been recognized as a legitimate art form.

Jim Davis, with Beetle, Garfield, and me, breaking ground to start construction of the International Museum of Cartoon Art in Boca Raton, Florida. Jim was our national fund-raising chairman.

In 1978 I got a call from a kid named Jim Davis who told me he had just signed a contract with United Features to do a strip called *Garfield*. He wondered if he could get on a train from New York and visit me in Greenwich, forty-five minutes away. "Sure," I said, "come on up for lunch; I'll meet you at the station." I went to meet the train and didn't see him get off. I went home and waited till the next train was due. Still no Jim. I went home again and had lunch, disappointed that I couldn't take him to the club. The phone rang. Jim said he was waiting at the station. It turned out he had got off the train by a small waiting room and seen the main station across the tracks, so he crossed over and had been waiting over an hour for me there, on the inbound side. I brought him back, gave him a scotch, a balogna sandwich, and an Oreo cookie. We've been friends ever since. ❖

Rye Brook, New York

*Cathy Jr. and Priscilla, who did most of the packing
and shipping (portraits by Ward Brackett)*

A Moving Story

On June 30, 1992, the Museum closed its doors in Rye Brook, NY for the last time. The task of sorting out 20 years of acquisitions, of labeling, boxing and getting everything ready for moving to Florida fell to Mort and Cathy Walker and Cathy's two daughters Cathy and Priscilla. Priscilla, a student at the Rhode Island School of Design, had worked for a moving company and during school vacations worked at the Museum. She was eminently qualified to be the on-site moving supervisor. She prepared for this move working with a curatorial moving consultant associated with the international museum consulting firm, LORD Cultural Resources.

Each drawing was packed with tissue paper in acid free boxes and labeled, keeping the inventory on computers. In all, over 100,000 drawings, thousands of books and hundreds of viewing hours of tapes and films were shipped. It took six weeks. The professional moving company North American Van Lines carried the precious cargo to Florida treating it as well as the Matisse exhibit they had just deposited at the Museum of Modern Art.

Several months later, the Museum's beloved castle was sold to a family from Scotland.

Building the Museum

Our plot of land was leased from the city for fifty years at $1 a year.

The construction took six months and cost over $6 million.

The tower is hauled up to finish the construction.

Cathy and I share the view from the deck with Beetle and Sarge.

*Two of my sketches
for the museum . . .*

*. . . and the
architect's
version*

Opening Day at the Museum

March 10, 1996

Cathy and I were the first ones

through the door, followed by

a flood of cartoon characters.

Cathy was so happy!

The museum hired a psychologist to do a study of new employees. Candidates were asked a list of simple questions, and deductions were made from their answers. The psychologist asked if I'd like to answer the questions, to see how it worked.

He came back with a fifteen-page analysis. In essence, he said, my big problem was that I wanted everyone to like me. I scratched my head. "That's a *problem?*" ❖

SUNSHINE

Beetle's Buddy

Mort Walker's
Comic Vision Comes
To Boca Raton

> *The most healing, friendly force for good human relations and ease of mind that we are blessed with is laughter and humor.*

Philosophy in the Comics

Al Capp once said, "You cain't draw a picture of a dog without making a statement on the condition of dogs." All cartoons therefore contain observations on mankind and society. Some cartoons are just more obvious in this regard.

Oct. 9, 1936

Dear Mr. Walker:
   I am sorry I haven't time to do something better for you & when you get to be a professional cartoonist you will understand.

Sincerely,
Webster

The Lexicon of Comicana

It started out as a joke for the National Cartoonists Society magazine. I spoofed the tricks cartoonists used, like dust clouds when characters are running or lightbulbs over their heads when they get an idea. My son Brian thought I should expand the idea and make a book of it. I spent many hours at the museum going over old cartoons and recording their "language." I created pseudoscientific names for each cartoon cliché, like the sweat marks cartoon characters radiate. I called them "plewds" after the god of rain, "Joe Pluvius." I considered it a humor book. When it came out, I looked for it in the humor section of the bookstore and finally found it in Art Instruc-tion. I inquired and they said, "What's funny about it?" I said, "The names." They said, "We didn't know what those things were called." I said, "They weren't called anything till I called them that." It was another case of satire falling flat. I gave up and am selling it now as an instruction book.

Teteology

Often we relate to people more through facial expressions than through language. If someone says, "You jerk!" you must look at his face to see if he's being affectionate or insulting. It is important, therefore, to master the most basic aspects of "teteology."

Happy

Sad

Mad

I don't get any of this.

Hites

"Hites" indicate speed and are drawn horizontally.

The more hites, the more speed. Add a few "briffits" (dust clouds) for better effect.
Note that briffits are permissible even if the floor is marble and highly polished.

Lucaflect

How can you tell if an area or object is round, wet, or shiny? One very common gimmick is to show a window reflected in the object. This is "lucaflect." It doesn't matter if a window is nowhere near. You will probably never be questioned about it. If you are, clam up and give only your name, rank, and serial number . . . or go out and rent a window.

Emanata

Now that we have our characters, there's a lot more we can do with them to show what's going on inside them. Those of you who believe in mental telepathy should not be at all surprised at the things cartoonists have emanating from their characters. For instance:

Lady discovers her slip is showing.

A few more plewds—her shoulder strap broke.

An eight-plewded lady. We'll leave her plight to your imagination.

"Emanata" can come from things as well as people to show what's going on. Here are a few:

Waftarom
Shows that the pie smells good

Indotherm
The coffee is hot.

Solrads
You can almost feel the warmth radiating from the sun.

How to draw a circle:

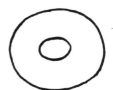  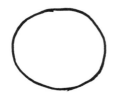 

Draw a man with a round face.   *Eliminate eyes.*   *Eliminate moustache.*   *Eliminate nose.*

How to draw smoke:

1.   **2.**   **3.**   **4.**   **5.**

How to draw feet:

  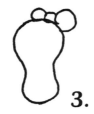 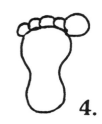 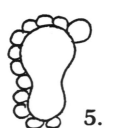

1.   **2.**   **3.**   **4.**   **5.**

Drawing feet is easy and fun. Just start with the basic shape and add toes. The trick is knowing when to stop.

How to draw eyes:

1.   **2.**   **3.**

How to draw ears:

Wrong   Wrong   Wrong   Wrong   Wrong   *Right*

How to draw stick figures:

How to draw caricatures:

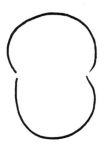

Photo of subject

1. Exaggerate shape of head.

2. Choose outstanding feature and exaggerate it.

3. Fill in other features.

Symbolia

There are a number of uncategorized indicia that must be memorized if one is to become a true expert in comicana.

Person getting an idea must have a lightbulb overhead.

Snoring is dramatized by a log being sawed . . .

. . . or merely with a Z or lots of Z's if he's really asleep.

Maladicta

Even in today's permissive society many four-letter words are not permissible in the comics. Even though profanity may be used in other sections of the paper, people feel that, since children read cartoons, the comic section should be inviolate.

Cartoonists, therefore, have had to develop acceptable substitutes. A first sergeant would lose a lot of his charm if he said, "Gee whiz, Beetle. You make me so terribly mad!" So the creative mind came up with a variety of "jarns," "quimps," "nittles," and "grawlixes" to help convey a sergeant's strong emotion and add color and dimension to his personality.

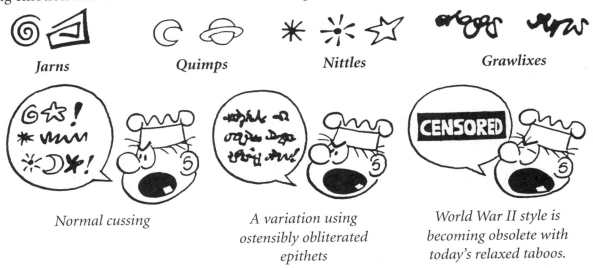

Jarns   *Quimps*   *Nittles*   *Grawlixes*

Normal cussing   *A variation using ostensibly obliterated epithets*   *World War II style is becoming obsolete with today's relaxed taboos.*

Blurgits

Various components can be combined at times, such as "hites," "reverbatrons," "agitrons," etc., to produce other effects. "Blurgits" are produced by a kind of stroboscopic technique to show movement within a single panel, or to produce the ultimate in speed and action.

BERRY'S WORLD

"Worst case of Russian flu I've seen!"

The full book of the lexicon of comicana is now available from iuniverse.com. ❖

CHAPTER TEN

Public Life
and Service

*Receiving the Reuben from Rube Goldberg as the
best all-around cartoonist of the year, 1954*

Awards & Honors

1953 National Cartoonists Society "Cartoonist of the Year," and the Billy De Beck Award

1955 Banshee Silver Lady Award, "Outstanding Cartoonist"

1966 National Cartoonists Society "Best Humor Strip of the Year"

1969 National Cartoonists Society "Best Humor Strip of the Year"

1972 Italy Il Secolo XIX Award

1975 Sweden "Best International Cartoonist," Adamson Award

1977 Segar Award, King Features, "Lifetime Achievement"

1977 Power of Printing Award, Printing Industries of Metropolitan New York

1978 American Legion Fourth Estate Award

1979 The Newspaper Features Council, Jester Award

1979 San Diego Comic Convention, Inkpot Award

1980 University of Missouri Faculty Alumni Award

1981 William Penn College, Doctor of Letters

1987 National Conference of Christians and Jews "Man of the Year"

1988 Sweden "Best International Cartoonist," Adamson Award

1988 Kappa Sigma Fraternity "Man of the Year"

1989 Newspaper Features Council, National Chairman of Cartoonists for Literacy

1989 Museum of Cartoon Art, Hall of Fame

1990 The Pentagon, Certificate of Appreciation for Patriotic Civilian Service

1991 University of Missouri, Scholar in Residence

1992 National Cartoonists Society, Reuben Award Statuette Presentation

1995 Boca Raton Chamber of Commerce, Award of Excellence

1998 Cystic Fibrosis Foundation, Palm Beach County Leading Men Award (one of thirteen men to receive)

1999 Gold T-Square Award, National Cartoonists Society, "Lifetime Achievement"

1999 Super Segar Award, King Features

2000 Chevalier in Arts and Letters, from the French Government for Establishing the International Museum of Cartoon Art in 1974

2000 Distinguished Civilian Service to the United States Army, Presented to Mort Walker by Secretary of the Army Louis Caldera at the Pentagon in Washington, D.C. (This is the highest award that can be given to any civilian by the army. The previous recipient was journalist Walter Cronkite.)

When I was getting my medal at the Pentagon for Distinguished Civilian Service

from the secretary of the army, I told him that a month before I had gotten the

Chevalier medal from the French Embassy in New York. I told him that the

ambassador pinned on the medal and kissed me on both cheeks.

The secretary said, "This is the army. We don't ask and we don't tell."

The Reuben

I have been a member of the National Cartoonists Society for over fifty years. I served on

Best Comic Strip Artist plaque (1966, 1969)

the board for many years before I was elected president. In its early years, the society had few members and was mostly a social organization. I tried to make it more professional, with exhibits and shop talks, and the membership grew. Later on I wrote the monthly newsletter, produced the quarterly magazine, and edited the annual publication. I created the Album, members writing their own bios. I won the coveted Reuben as best cartoonist of 1954 and two plaques as the "best humor strip" artist of

1966 and 1969. I am currently Ethics Chairman and try to help other cartoonists who have problems, and I am chairman of the Milt Gross fund, which helps indigent cartoonists. ❖

The Reuben (1954)

Icon If Ucon

One night I became an Icon, and I'm not sure I feel good about it. At a banquet in New York, the great writer Tom Wolfe referred to me as an "American icon." First of all, I assume that means I'm old or dead. I'm approaching both those things but hopefully haven't arrived. I know you can't become an Icon overnight, or even in six lessons. It takes years of either pestering people or greasing a lot of palms.

I'm sure there are some rights and privileges that go with being an Icon besides

being able to go to bed before 9 P.M. I'd like to think that people would listen respectfully when an Icon spoke and see that his glass was kept full. I'd like to think he'd be able to get a good table, at least in a third-rate restaurant. Most of all I would like to see my cat pay some attention to me and not walk away when I try to pet her. And I certainly hope there are no responsibilities to being an Icon. I've got my hands full being mediocre.

I already feel the weight of the office very heavily, like I should be doing something

important, saying profound things, or learning to program my VCR. It's the unknown that plagues an Icon. Who am I? What is the meaning of it all? Why does a chicken cross the road?

I went around for a week with my lower jaw stuck out, speaking with a Boston accent, assuming the icon role. All I got were looks of disgust. I wonder if real icons can change a lightbulb without an entourage.

Of course, if we knew all those things, we'd be able to figure out Jerry Lewis. ❖

We Lampoon the President

Bill Mauldin, Don Sherwood, me, Milton Caniff,
and George Wunder stand behind Lyndon Johnson.

The National Press Club asked a few cartoonists who did military strips to put on a show for them. The day before we were to go to Washington I was at a golf outing. I got a call at the bar. A woman said, "This is the White House." "Yeah," I said. "Who is it really?" "Really. President Johnson heard you were coming to Washington and would like you to come and visit him."

We went to his office the next day and talked for half an hour, got some pictures taken, and, as we were leaving, Milton Caniff, a fellow cartoonist, asked the president if he'd join us for lunch. He said yes, to everyone's surprise. It threw the Press Club into a panic; Johnson had never been there before. He had a great time, even though we murdered him at the easel. ❖

I draw big ears on Johnson as he sits in the crowd and howls.

I've been involved with various projects through the years. Here are just a few. . . .

Richard Nixon launching the program to encourage people to hire the handicapped

My poster launching the new ZIP codes, with Postmaster General Red Blount and his wife

Judging a worldwide army art contest

Waiting to put on a show at the Waldorf-Astoria: Milton Caniff (Steve Canyon), *Allen Saunders* (Mary Worth), *a model, Chester Gould* (Dick Tracy), *and me*

With Dik Browne at a book fair

We had so many strips going at once that people used to joke that we were "King Features East." Here I am going along with the gag, tacking up a sign on my old barn studio.

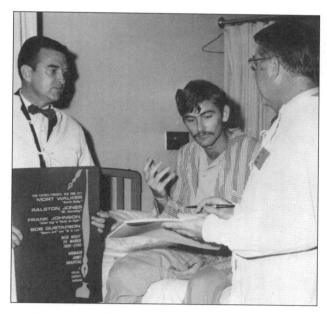

Cartoonists have always been generous with their talent. Many made regular trips overseas to entertain the troops, and we visited hospitals frequently. Here I am drawing for a patient in a septic ward at Fort Bragg back in 1977.

At the State Department

The End of the Act

One night Cathy and I went to Sardi's with another couple. At that time, Sardi's was the "in" restaurant on Broadway where the stars hung out; their caricatures covered the walls.

We decided to see if we could spot any celebrities. We were all busy looking when a man came up behind me and said, "Mr. Walker?" I turned in shock and said, "Yes?" He said, "Can

my wife have your autograph? She saw you on the Phil Donahue show." The celebrity status of Sardi's, in our eyes, hit rock bottom at that point. ❖

Speaking Tours

I make about twenty speeches and public appearances a year around the country. It keeps me in touch with my audience and I enjoy their response. I do a lot of drawing rather than talking because people are fascinated by seeing a blank piece of paper being turned into something. I've had to cut down

on the travel lately because of my busy life. This was Albany, New York, in 1955.

Dik Browne and I went on tour for a few years with our "act." I'd draw while he would insult me, then I'd attack him while he drew. We went all over the country performing this theatrical gem. The biggest

laughs we got were when an easel fell over or when Dik's mike would slip down into his pants and he'd dance around trying to retrieve it. We gave up after assessing that we weren't getting anything out of it except hotel bills. ❖

We have several balloons that can be rented for special occasions.
Here's Beetle in San Diego. Sarge has been in Chicago and New York.

NIAGARA FALLS

'Beetle Bailey' strikes again

Suspect robbing banks at rate of one every day

By DIANNE CHOMA
Standard Staff

The so-called Beetle Bandit struck his third bank in as many days Thursday with the holdup of a Royal Bank branch in Niagara Falls.

Around 4 p.m., police responded to the Royal Bank at 3499 Portage Rd. where a man had just fled on foot with an undisclosed sum of money.

"Oh no, not another one!" said one female customer after police told her she could not enter the bank because there had just been a robbery.

For the third day in a row, a man has entered a bank, handed the teller a note demanding cash and indicating he was carrying a gun. In each robbery, no weapon was actually seen.

> **"Oh no, not another one!"**
> female customer

Police believe the man is the same suspect who robbed the Canada Trust branch just down the street at 3646 Portage Rd. on Wednesday and the Niagara Credit Union on Highway 55 in Virgil on Tuesday.

"It fits the pattern," said Constable Neal Orlando.

The suspect could also be responsible for the robbery of the Bank of Montreal at 6841 Morrison St. on Aug. 27 and of the Royal Bank at 5733 Victoria Ave.

Please see Beetle page A2

The suspect, left, in a least five bank robberies bears a striking resemblance to King Features cartoon character Beetle Bailey, right, being bailed out by Sarge.

Niagara Regional Police officers turn away customers after a robbery at the Royal Bank branch on Portage Road in Niagara Falls Thursday.

staff photo by Dianne Choma

A bank bandit in Niagara Falls got stuck with the Beetle Bailey moniker because the poor man looked like my cartoon character. Anybody whose name is Bailey or who wears his hat over his eyes is automatically stuck with the "Beetle" nickname. Sorry about that, guys.

I was grand marshal of the University of Missouri homecoming parade around 1977. All the dorms, fraternities, and sororities decorated their lawns with Beetle Bailey themes. Jean decided not to go at the last minute, but they had a sign on my lead jeep that said MR. AND MRS. MORT WALKER, *so they had last year's beauty queen ride with me. We heard someone in the crowd say, "Why would a pretty young girl like that marry that old fart?"*

I've always donated my talents for good causes, probably doing at least two free drawings a week. Here are a few. . . .

I worked on a book with Al Capp for President Eisenhower's People-to-People program to teach good behavior on foreign travel.

Cover of a booklet for the Army and Air Force Exchange Service

More than 200 color receivers will be spotted throughout the Fair — almost anywhere.

The Red Cross

The New York World's Fair, 1964

Hi and Lois

One of the many drawings made for the President's Committee to Employ the Handicapped. They were used as posters on trains and buses.

Helping the U.S. Postal Service
launch ZIP codes

McGeorge Bundy headed the Ford Foundation, and I was trying
to get a grant for the museum. Unfortunately, it didn't work.

For the army and air force post exchanges

For the Greenwich, Connecticut, Arts Council

For the Child Welfare League of America, Inc.

A poster I did for the Red Cross

A Beetle insignia for an air force group

I had been trying unsuccessfully for years to get the U.S. Postal Service to issue a cartoon stamp. When the hundredth anniversary of the comic strip approached, we made a major effort with Cathy at the helm. Three years later, twenty stamps were issued, representing the first fifty years. They were launched at a huge ceremony in front of the museum in Boca Raton, Florida. We expect an issue of the second fifty years soon.

Unveiling our stamps at the museum

With Secretary of State Sandra Mortham

Cathy Walker with "Annie"

Mike Peters with me, Jim Davis, and Dean Young

The "Kings of the Comics" marched into the World Trade Center to open an exhibit, "Masters of Cartooning." Marching with me, left to right: Bil Keane (Family Circus), *Dean Young* (Blondie), *and Hank Ketcham* (Dennis the Menace).

I was honored at the Pentagon in appreciation for patriotic civilian service. The commanding general handed me the award and said, "Now maybe you'll be kinder to us." I replied, "Don't count on it."

I have been a member of the Newspaper Features Council from its beginning in 1954 as the Newspaper Comic Council. The organization consists of the top cartoonists, presidents of syndicates, newspaper publishers, and a few columnists. I served as vice president for many years and declined the presidency many times because I thought an editor would be better for the job. I edited the newsletter for several years, recruited cartoonists to do chalk talks at our meetings, put together numerous exhibits, started the Cartoonists for Literacy program, and helped create several books and print projects. I have been on the board for about forty years. I was given the Jester Award for service. It's a bronze sculpture of a boy reading the comics. ❖

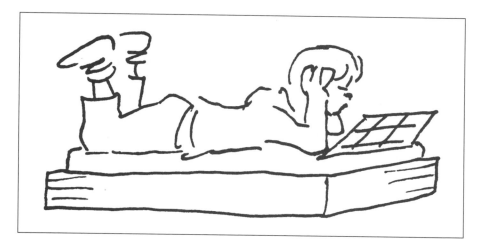

The Jester Award for outstanding contributions to the profession

Longtime friend and former assistant Bob Gustafson shares a smile with Mort in 1988.

The National Cartoonists Society

When I joined the National Cartoonists Society (NCS) in 1950 I was twenty-seven, and almost all the other members were old established cartoonists whose comics I'd read during my childhood. They used to call me "the kid," as in, "We're going to Washington for a war bond show. Let's take the kid with us."

There were only a few members, so we had monthly meetings. I remember meetings where less than a dozen guys would show up and all we did was sit around and drink and tell stories.

The old Founders Society took turns being president. There weren't any elections. They'd just say, "It's your turn, Otto." All the work was done by our secretary, Marge Devine. The president would just show up, and Marge would hand him the agenda and tell him what to say.

One evening I was at home feeding one of my babies when the phone rang. It was Rube Goldberg. They wanted me to be the next president. I told them I couldn't possibly do it. I had three little children under four years old and two comic strips. I was frantically busy. Rube said, "Here, Milton Caniff wants to talk to you." They kept passing the phone to the next guy until I gave in.

Once I became president I decided to organize the society the way I felt it should be. I had an agenda for the board meetings. I built up the membership and had name tags. I hired my own secretary to help with the work. I had exhibits and shop talks at every meeting.

I don't know how well the old-timers liked it. They were used to their easygoing routine, but I wanted us to be more professional. The younger guys seemed to subscribe to it, though; most of the ideas stuck and are around today. There are more than 500 members now, from many countries, and our meetings are held all over the country through regional chapters. ❖

THE NATIONAL CARTOONISTS SOCIETY: WHAT IT WAS, IS, AND WILL BE

THIS, THE OCCASION OF OUR FIFTEENTH ANNUAL AWARD DINNER, IS A GOOD TIME FOR RECASTING THE PAST AND FORECASTING THE FUTURE OF A SOCIETY CREATED IN 1946 BY FIVE WORKING CARTOONISTS (RUBE GOLDBERG, RUSSELL PATTERSON, GUS EDSON, CLARENCE RUSSELL AND OTTO SOGLOW) WHO WERE CLAD IN LONG UNDERWEAR AND BILLETED IN QUANTICO, WHERE THEY HAD BEEN ENTERTAINING SOME OF THE FORCES OF THE UNITED STATES MILITARY ESTABLISHMENT. THE LONG UNDERWEAR HAS SINCE BEEN DONATED TO THE SMITHSONIAN INSTITUTION BUT THE MAJORITY OF THE WEARERS OF THAT HISTORIC RAIMENT ARE HERE IN THIS HALL TONIGHT.

PERHAPS THE MOST ASTONISHING THING ABOUT THE NATIONAL CARTOONISTS SOCIETY IS THE TARDINESS OF ITS FORMATION — AS LATE AS 1946. FOR THE TRADITION OF THE CARTOONIST GOES BACK A LONG, LONG TIME. BEFORE MAN COULD WRITE, OR EVEN TALK, THERE WERE CARTOONISTS AROUND. THOSE LOVELY DRAWINGS OF BISON AND BOARS ON THE ROCK WALLS OF THE CAVES IN PERPIGNAN WERE THE FIRST FUMBLINGS AT A COMIC STRIP, WHEN THOSE CORPORATE BODIES NOW KNOWN AS MAGAZINES AND NEWSPAPER SYNDICATES WERE NOT YET IN EXISTENCE TO EXPLOIT THEM. THEY HAD NEITHER BALLOONS NOR CAPTIONS; IT WAS FIRST NECESSARY FOR THAT ANCIENT CARTOONIST TO INVENT ALPHABETS AND WRITING BEFORE HE COULD COMMUNICATE HIS GAG.

Caricature of me in The Cartoonist *by John Reiner*

...and about "Reuben"...

In looking around for appropriate design for the Society's annual award, all pseudo-heroic statuary was discarded, such as Winged Victory, draped goddesses holding lighted torches, and Pegasus rampant on a sea of scrollwork. Too phony. Our profession is dedicated to puncturing such foolishness. As a breed we are irrèverent needlers of pomp and pomposity. But what should our award be?

Years ago, Rube Goldberg, our leader in lampooning, had designed a lamp base for people weary of cupids and curlycues on their lighting fixtures. It was a horrible-looking creation consisting of four nude gnomes doing acrobatics, or something. Nightmarish.

The minute we recoiled from the sight of it we knew we had the design we'd been searching for. It was hideous and disrespectful and honest enough that no cartoonist would feel finky handing it to another and saying, "Here. Take the stupid thing. You won it by majority vote of the members who think you're the outstanding cartoonist of the year. You deserve this."

Bill Crawford removed the lamp socket from the topmost gnome's rear end and replaced it properly with a model of a Higgins Ink bottle. He had it cast in bronze and set on an onyx base. We liked it so well we decided to allow non-members to win it as well as members. We're generous that way.

We call it the "Reuben" and it has served us well for the past ten years. There has been lots of grumbling about its lack of beauty, which makes us very proud. It fits us. So does grumbling.

Nevertheless, it is our highest tribute to the top men in our craft. And it is the greatest thrill to be voted by your colleagues to receive it.

At least no one has ever returned one.

— Mort Walker

The issue celebrating the Roaring Twenties

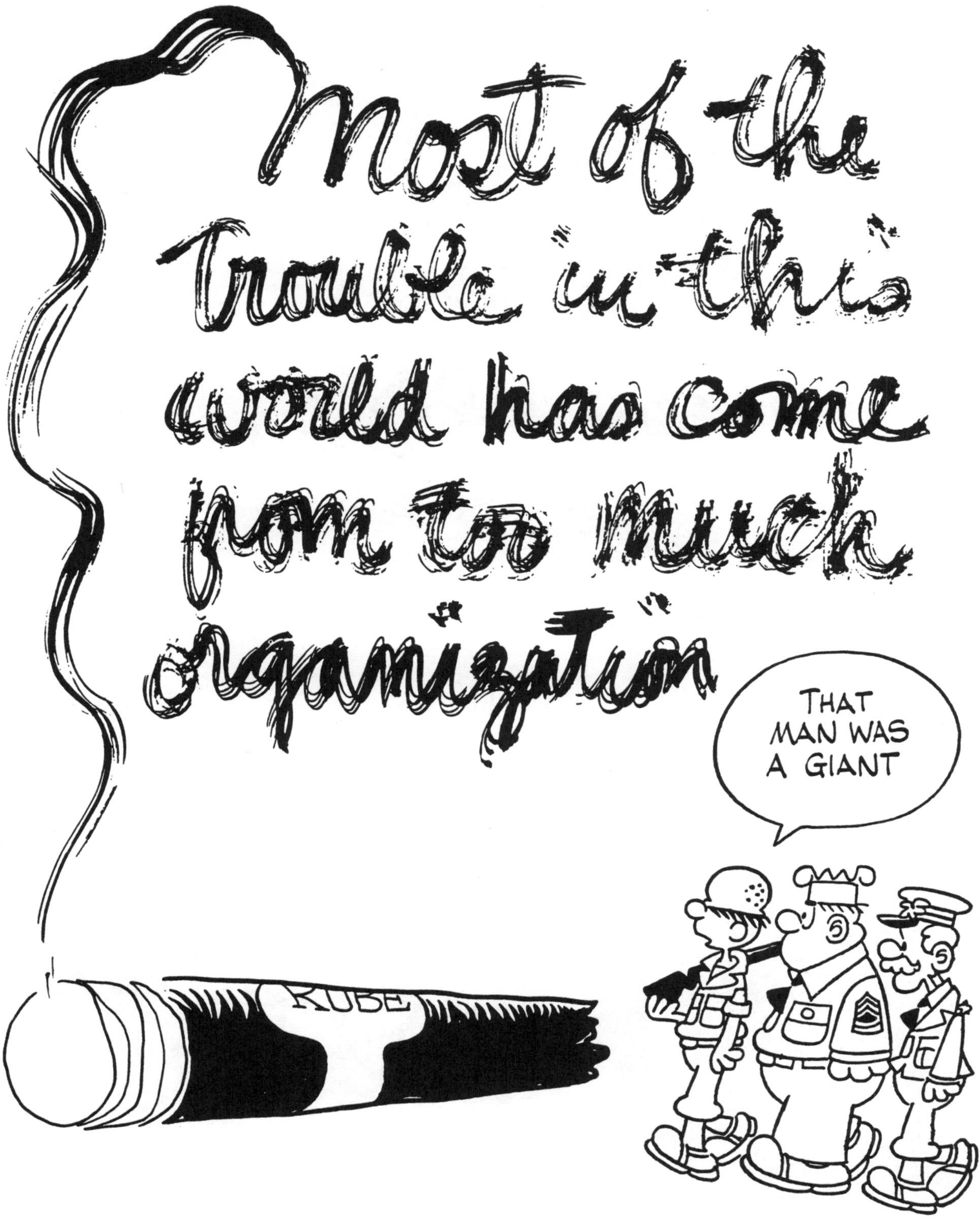
Most of the trouble in this world has come from too much organization
THAT MAN WAS A GIANT
RUBE

A Rube Goldberg quote

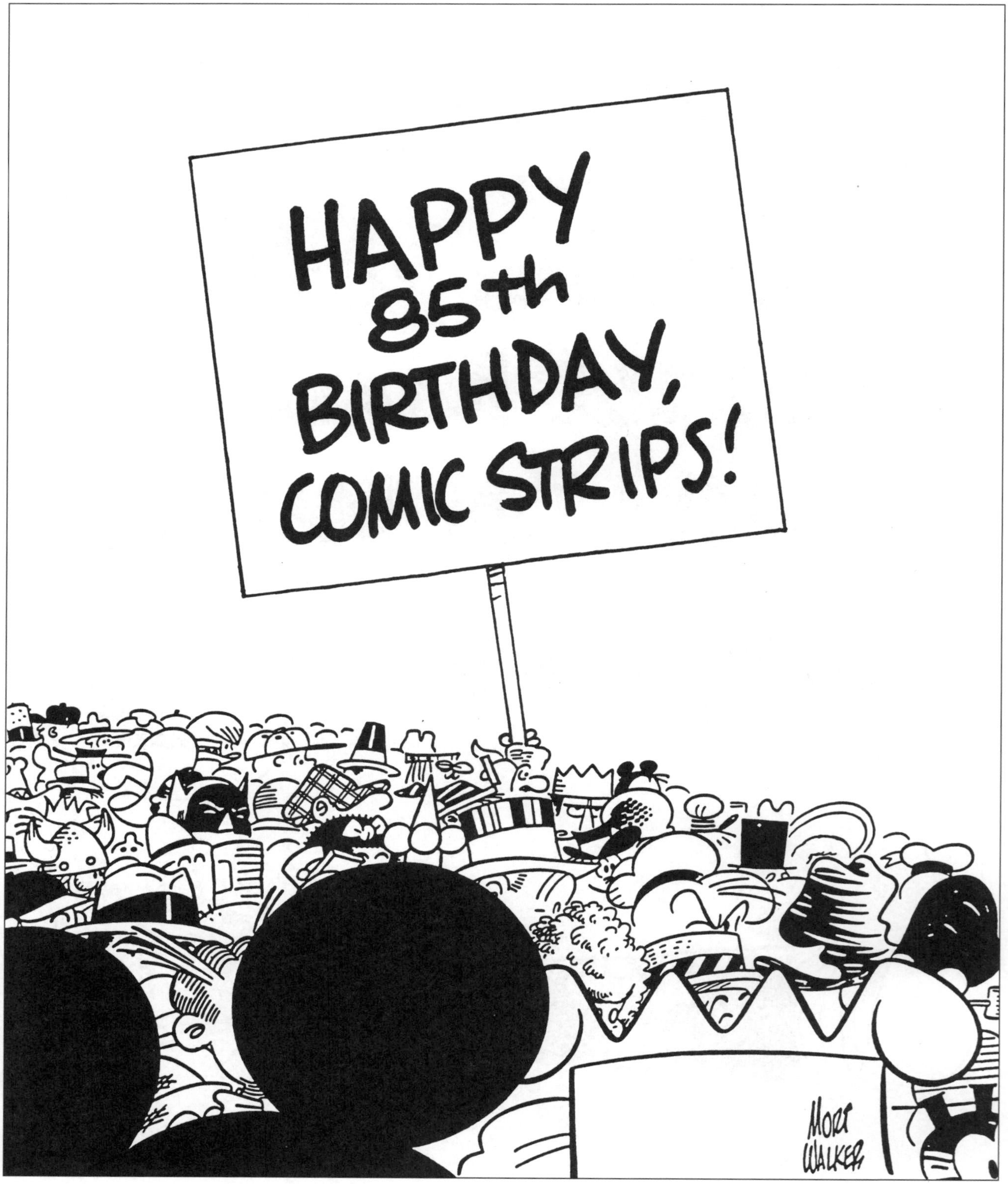
HAPPY 85th BIRTHDAY, COMIC STRIPS!
MORT WALKER

1980

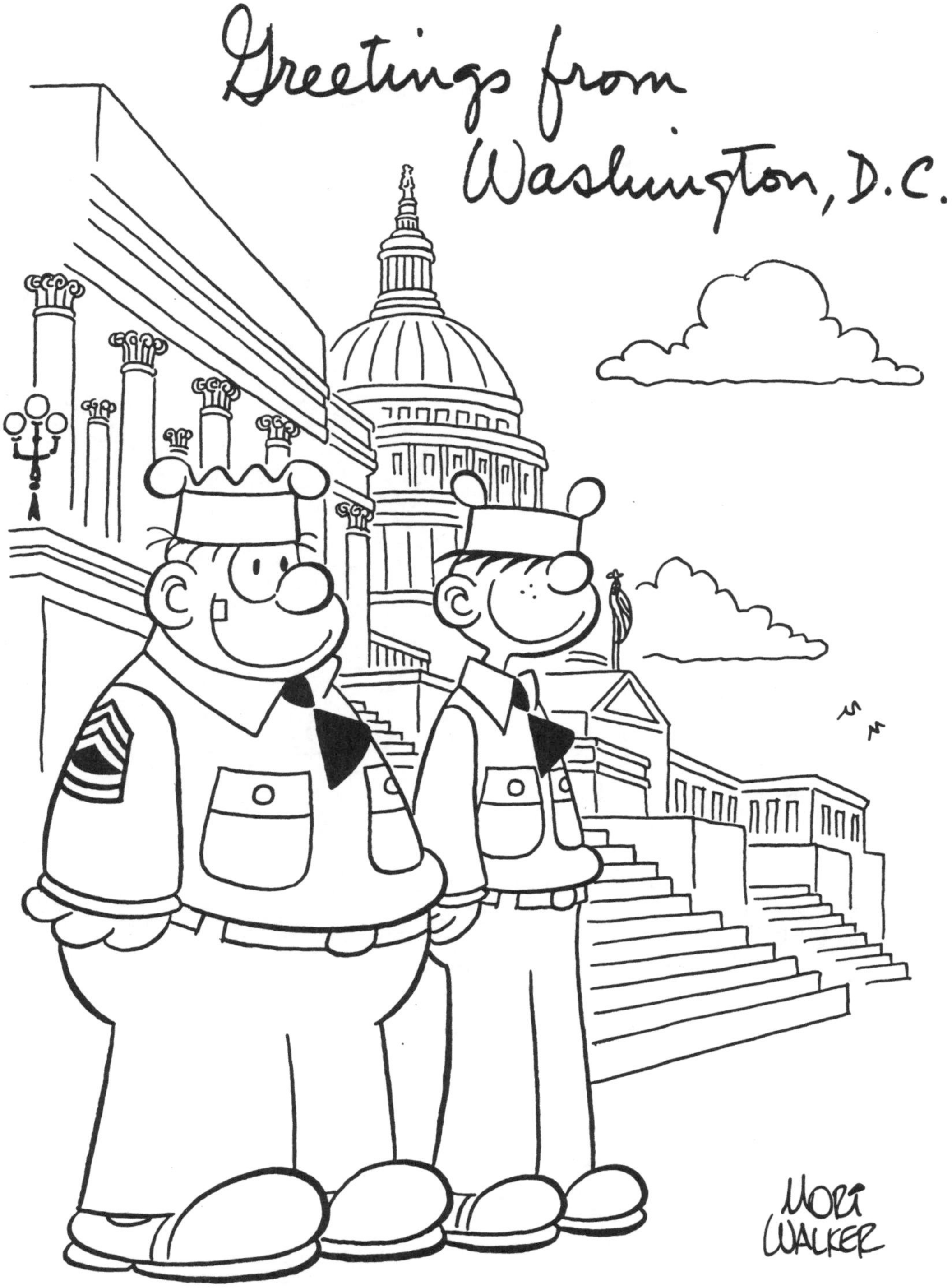
Greetings from Washington, D.C.
MORT WALKER
Where everyone gets along.

NCS's twenty-first birthday

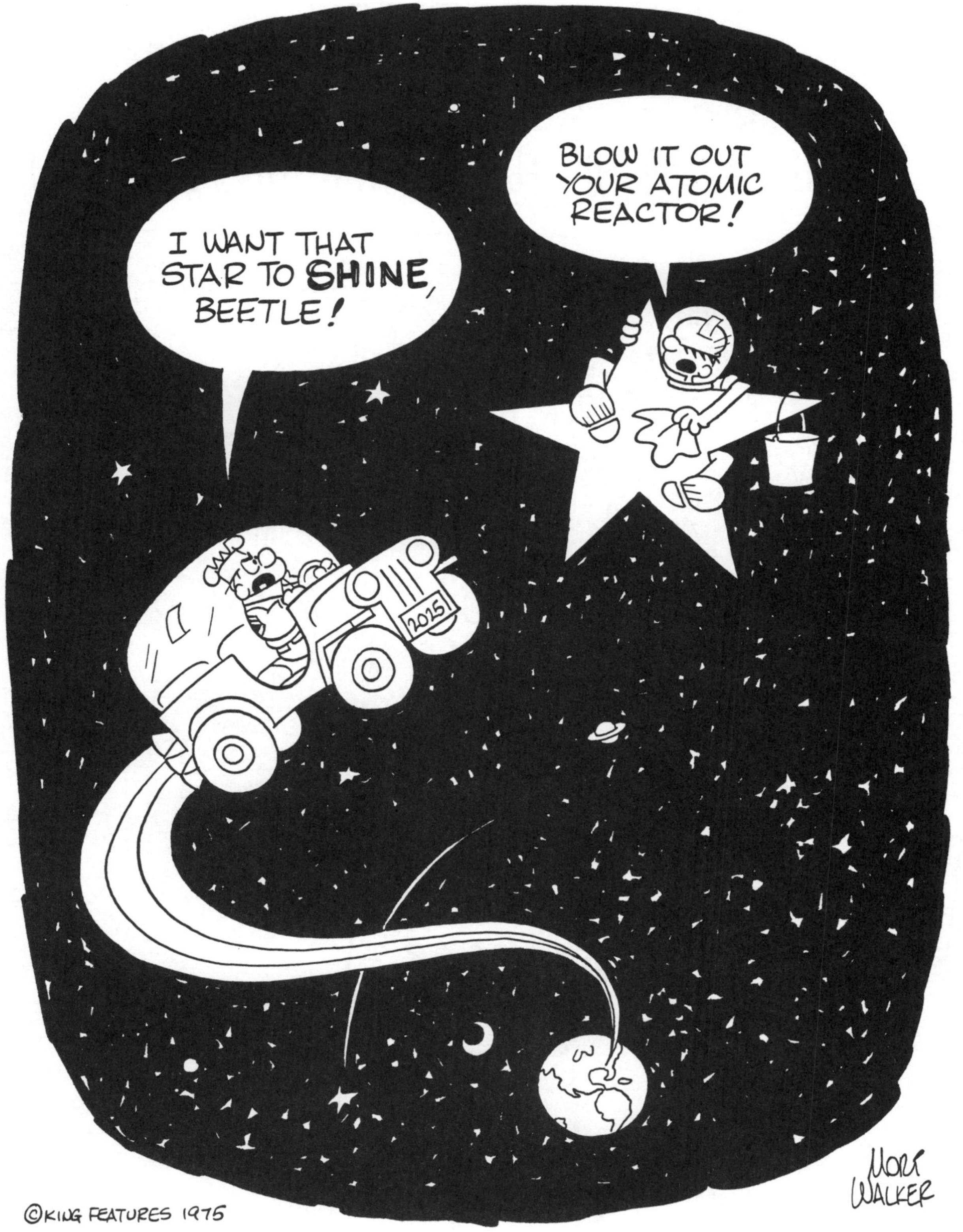
I WANT THAT STAR TO SHINE, BEETLE!
BLOW IT OUT YOUR ATOMIC REACTOR!
2015
©KING FEATURES 1975
MORT WALKER

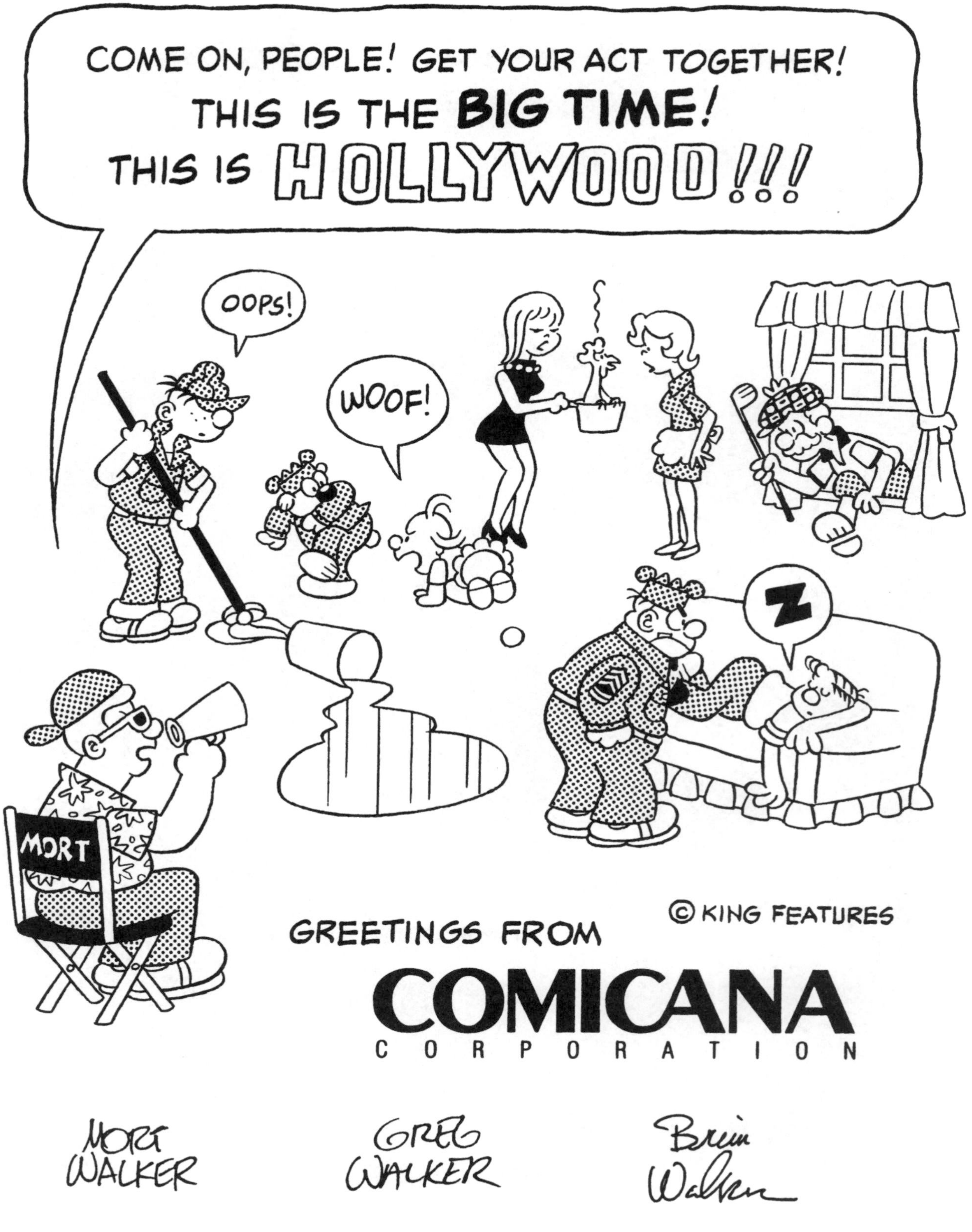
COME ON, PEOPLE! GET YOUR ACT TOGETHER!
THIS IS THE BIG TIME!
THIS IS HOLLYWOOD!!!
OOPS!
WOOF!
Z
MORT
© KING FEATURES
GREETINGS FROM
COMICANA
CORPORATION
MORT WALKER
GREG WALKER
Brian Walker

HAPPY BIRTHDAY, NCS!!

GREG WALKER, BRIAN WALKER

MORT WALKER
MEMBER 1950

"I CAN'T UNDERSTAND WHY I'M THE ONLY PERSON WHO CAN GET ANYTHING DONE AROUND HERE!"

CHAPTER ELEVEN

Oh! And One More Thing

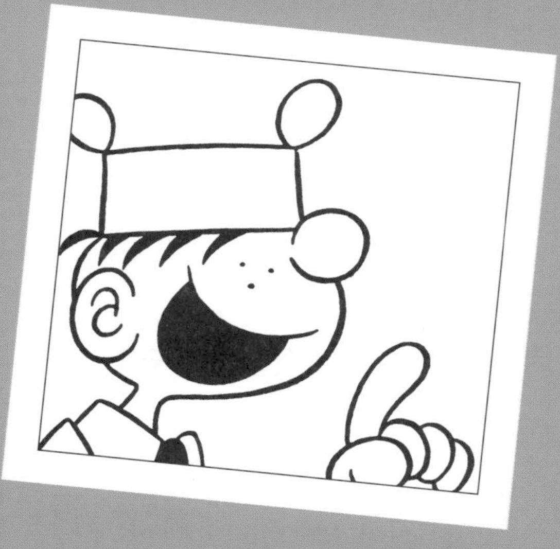

My father got up every morning at five and wrote a poem. He had been named Poet Laureate of Kansas, and his poems appeared regularly on the front page of the *Kansas City Star,* often with his illustration or one by my mother. It was only natural that I grew up writing poems, too. Here are a few in the Edgar A. Guest doggerel style.

Water Boy

A hearty "hail"
To the unsung hero
Who totes the H_2O,
This lowly gridiron
Gunga Din
This hero of T.O.*
(*Time Out)

The Benefits of Kraft Fat-Free Cheese

Eat a lot of fat-free cheese, and your bones will stay together.
The dishes that it's served on (if cracked) will weather any weather.
Sandwiches won't fall apart, they stick to both your hands.
Your marriage, once beyond repair, now has cheesy wedding bands.

Blessings on you, new
  attendant.
Saddle-footed, cheeks
  resplendent.
Come unto the columned
  sward,
Learn of life . . . and room
  and board.

Home

Ferny stuff is not enough
To make a house a home.
You need some clocks
And shiny rocks
And pencils by the phone.
Doilies on the armchairs,
Baskets by the fire,
Artistic prints on every wall
Which show a little wire.

Some fish and figurines are
  nice
And photos by the score,
Will show you care,
It can't be bare . . .
It's better if it's more.
Drapes and lamps and many
  books
A picture of a pigeon,

With spots upon the fireside
  rug
To look like it's been lived in.
It's picture perfect to the point
That Mother looks and swears,
"We'll keep it for the company,
And don't you dare go in
  there."

Killer Garbage Trucks

You can hear them coming,
From great distances you can hear them
    coming, coming after us.
Grinding their gears, slamming doors, eating
    things up, churning.

They are coming to our place
And there is no way they can be stopped.
Humongous trucks in the dark of the morning,
Making angry noises in our ears and in our face.

They are devouring the residue of our lives,
Destroying our peaceful sleep, our quiet dreams,
Descending on us to take away a part of us
To return again and again in hungry reprise.

Medical Checkup

I pee
and then
I pee some more.

    It seems
    I can always
    pee some more

        until the
        nurse says
        Pee in this jar.

Homecoming

Thy locks are growing grayer,
And thy paunch is growing, too . . .
Thy trophies growing greener,
Since you played for old Mizzou.

BEETLE BAILEY

by MORT WALKER

To the Newspaper Readers Association

There are many things for fun today.
I like them all, and yet . . .
I think the daily newspaper
Is still the world's best bet.

For instance, would your radio
Keep you from getting wet?

Or can you wrap your garbage
In your television set?

Or could you use your movie film
When you paint the cabinet?

There must be more advantages
That I've not thought of yet.
So I'll take the news, and while
I think, I'll set and set and set.

Yours truly,
Beetle Bailey

©K.F.S.

We dipped into the future far as *Showme* eyes could see,
Saw the vision of the world, and all the wonders that would be,
Saw the campus filled with creatures looking strangely specialized.
Man's aptitudes had changed him to befit the job he tried.

While there's much to be said about skating and skiing,
There's another sport lately that we have been seeing.
Now there's naught we consider more pleasant than being
Engaged in a tourney of "he-ing" and "she-ing."

The endless game of "boy and girl"
Has kept the world in motivation.
But here the ratio three to one
Decreases the acceleration.

Some far-off god sits idly
Turning nimbus spouts in play,
Watching raindrops pitter-patter
On the guy who's making hay.

A Big Order for President Clinton

Hillary, Chelsea, and Bill
All of my dreams will fulfill,
From Medicare, and helping the poor,
The budget, and one thing more:
I'd like a Big Mac and a dill.

Shed the sedentary irons and move,
Transport the heart, the suit, the toothbrush case,
Nomad device, your trunk, that takes you home
Wherever whim and bus check motivates.

Early Thoughts

My favorite time
Is just at dawn
When the sky is fresh
And watered down.
Where everything's
In packages
Of dewy film
Like sparkled gloves
Before the noise
And dirt and grit
And people wake
And ruin it.

Dear Ann: After reading your column on the subject of leaving the toilet seat up or down, I thought I'd send this little poem I created just for you. I hope you like it.

Mort Walker, creator of the
Beetle Bailey comic strip

Dear Mort Walker: I loved it.
Thanks for sending it on.

To Ann Landers

Is the seat up or down?
She cannot tell.
She'll sit down and try it,
And if it's up, she'll yell,
"Ann Landers! Ann Landers!
I'm not feeling well.
Please send all the men
On this earth straight to hell!"

There was a Cartoonists' Day at the New York World's Fair. A bunch of us were having dinner, and Dick Cavalli, who draws *Winthrop,* excused himself to go to the bathroom. He never came back. The next day I asked him where he had gone. He said the zipper on his fly got stuck and he worked a long time with it with no success. He asked someone to send a maintenance man with pliers and finally got it fixed. When he came out, we were gone. I wrote this poem.

The Stuck Zipper

Who stands and tugs
With pants half on
While friends go in
And out the john
And meet and drink
And then are gone?

Who pulls the tab
With vexed despair
As lights go off
Across the fair
And when the dawn comes
Still is there?
The man with zipper stuck.

Who struggles there
With metal track
While soldiers in
Viet Nam attack
And droughts cause earth
To dry and crack?
The man with zipper stuck.

When everything is
Done and said
And all his friends
Are finally dead,
Who'll still be
Stranded in the head?
The man with zipper stuck.

Dick Cavalli showed up to play golf one day with a very colorful floral hat. We razzed him all around the course, which prompted this poem.

The Hat

Who's off that tee
In nothing flat,
And sometimes even
Quicker than that?
Not Palmer, or Nicklaus,
Or Billy the Fat, it's
The man in the Lady's Hat.

Who swings a driver
Like it was a bull fiddle?
Who hits fifty yards
But right down the middle?
Whose follow-through ends
With him flat on his prat?
The man in the Lady's Hat.

Who takes a big divot
But misses the ball?
Whose waggle is sexier
Than Arlene Dahl?
Who reads three-way breaks
When the green is flat?
The man in the Lady's Hat.

When that day comes
As it must, by and by,
When we all go to meet
The Head Pro in the sky,
And St. Peter, glaring, cries,
"Who the hell is that?"
It'll be,
The man in the Lady's Hat.

Who Has Time for a Senior Moment?

Give us old folks a break. When I can't remember a name immediately, everyone says, "He's having a senior moment." Have you ever heard of a baby moment? Of course not. A baby only has two names to remember, Mommy and Daddy. Babies know where their milk is coming from. But give the baby a few years in grade school, then college and beyond, and the names begin to accumulate.

In high school I knew almost everybody. They tested me by lining people up and having me go name by name down the line. In college and the army I knew more and more people, and in the wide world of my career the fog began to set in. I must have half a million names in my mental computer by now. It gets tougher and tougher to blurt out the right names all at once.

Someone showed me a picture recently. "Who's that?"

I said, "Oh . . . um . . . I know the face."

They said, "Are you having a senior moment?"

"No," I said, "it's coming to me. . . . I know. . . . It's Mommy."

See? I'm still sharp as a Tic-Tac. ❖

THE SATURDAY EVENING POST

"I don't even have on a shirt."

I must have had a senior moment when I drew this in 1949 at age twenty-six. The man says he doesn't have a shirt on, but I showed a cuff below his coat sleeve.

Dubious Achievements

At the University of Missouri in 1947 there were experimental sessions with something called facsimile. It was the first fax machine. Someone put one of my cartoons through it as a test. It worked, and I have the distinction of drawing the first faxed cartoon in history.

The government was sending a submarine to explore the North Pole. It was the first time anyone had gone *under* the Pole. The crew liked one of my cartoons and asked if they could hang it on their wall. I don't know what it's worth, but have *you* ever had one of your cartoons go under the North Pole? ❖

Opportunities

I guess I set a course for myself early in life without really knowing it, because I turned down a number of good opportunities.

I wrote some songs in high school and a friend said, "Let's go to Hollywood." I didn't want to go, but one of the songs was recorded. I heard it on the radio and didn't like it.

"You have a good job at Hallmark if you want to come back after college." I said no.

"I want to finance a greeting card company in Puerto Rico to take advantage of the tax laws. You know greeting cards. Do you want to run it?" I didn't.

"My backers think a sex-oriented magazine would be a hit. Would you like to edit it?" I wouldn't. (I often wondered if Hugh Hefner was the next interview.)

"You've done well in real estate. Could we form a partnership?" No.

Another greeting card company in New York made an offer. I said no.

A syndicate man said, "I like your work and I'd like to make some money off you. Could we do a comic strip together?" No. I wanted to do my own.

I'm glad I stuck to my course, but I'll never know what the other offers might have brought and I hope I never will. ❖

My Brush with Art

I think I was drawing before I was walking. At least, I can't remember *not* drawing or painting. It was more fun than walking. I guess I had a natural talent for the easy life.

My parents liked my work, which is par for parenthood, and my friends liked it because I drew stuff on their arms and jackets. It wasn't until I took some art courses in college that I encountered the truth.

"That's not art, that's a cartoon," my professor said. I looked at what I'd done. "I'm painting it just like it looks," I replied. "It's a cartoon," he insisted.

Later on, when I was in New York, I was asked to do a painting to exhibit in a gallery on Park Avenue. I was rather proud of what I produced and was anxious to get a reaction. I saw two men "admiring" my painting, so I worked my way behind them just in time to hear one of them say, "You have to realize he's just a cartoonist."

I was asked to do drawings preceding a fancy charity ball at the Waldorf. I began sketching the first lady in line, when she flared at me. "What's that you're drawing?" she demanded. "Your nose," I replied. "I didn't come here to be insulted," she yelled, and stalked off. The next lady got even huffier in the middle of her "portrait," and I quit forever trying to be something I'm not.

My eye or brain has a funny filter that won't allow the serious side of life to get through . . . and to tell you the truth, I enjoy it.

A college attempt at "art"

In high school I won a national art contest with an oil painting of a black man working on the Missouri River with a riverboat behind him.

I did a lot of oil paintings over the years, which simply reinforced my conviction that I was really a cartoonist. Here are two of my paintings.

This painting of my Greenwich, Connecticut, studio was exhibited at Lever House on Park Avenue.

While on vacation in Vermont it rained every day. I went to the local art store and bought supplies. Using the music holder on the piano as an easel, I painted this scene of Marblehead, Massachusetts, in one day.

THE AMERICAN YOUTH FORUM · 250 PARK AVENUE · NEW YORK

ESTABLISHED BY THE AMERICAN MAGAZINE

Dear Mort:

Here's news to make you happy! Our Judges have awarded you the enclosed <u>Certificate of Merit</u> and check for ten dollars for your entry in the art division of The 1939-40 American Youth Forum competition.

We heartily congratulate you upon your success and call your attention to the fact that you ranked among the first 121 students in a total of 494,456 competitors. Thus, your <u>Certificate of Merit</u> will serve as a permanent reminder of your success in a national field.

Your name along with the names of the other art award winners will be printed in the August issue of <u>The American Magazine</u> which comes out July 5. The results in the article division will be contained in the September issue of <u>The American</u>, out August 2.

Sincerely yours,

John Dungan
DIRECTOR

JD:WD

I won $10 in a national contest for oil painting.

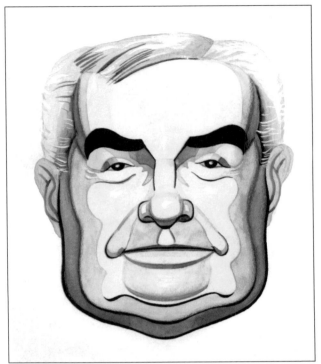

In a college art class assignment we were told to draw a realistic portrait of a person, then a poster version, a line drawing, and an abstract. I chose the famous Judge Learned Hand.

I *try my hand at a few caricatures from time to time.*

Ed Sullivan

E. G. Marshall

Remember her? This was how Hedy Lamarr looked to a fifteen-year-old in 1938.

Bob Hope

Special Drawings Cartoonist Friends Did for Birthdays, Anniversaries, and Other Occasions

Cartoonists are always quick on the draw when it comes to doing a drawing for a friend. Whether it's a birthday, anniversary, special occasion, or get-well message, they haul out their pens to express their feelings. It got to the point where we were all in a limo to go to a cartoonist's funeral and someone said, "Did you do your cartoon?" We all laughed, but who knows? Maybe someday we'll be asked to do funny drawings when someone dies. These special drawings, which the public never sees, are sometimes the most hilarious creations you will never see . . . till now. I have hundreds of them, and I'd like to share a few with you. I took a lot of them off my wall, where they warm my heart every morning when I walk into my studio. I hope you enjoy them as much as I do.

TO MORT WALKER — CONGRATULATIONS ON THE 50TH ANNIVERSARY OF BEETLE BAILEY

AMONG ALL THE GREAT ONES, YOU AND BEETLE ARE A CLASS ACT. CONGRATULATIONS.

Curt Swan (the venerable Superman artist)

Jim Davis (Garfield)

Fred Lasswell (Snuffy Smith)

Chuck Saxon (The New Yorker)

Hank Ketcham (Dennis the Menace)

Bill Yates (Prof. Phumble)

Charles Schulz (Peanuts)

Roy Doty

Stan Drake (Blondie)

Johnny Hart (B.C.)

Jim Davis (Garfield)

Orlando Busino (Gus)

Dik Browne (Hagar)

Mike Peters
(Mother Goose
and Grimm)

Gill Fox

Chris Browne (Hagar)

Tom Armstrong (Marvin)

My assistant, Bill Janocha

Mike Peters (Mother Goose and Grimm)

" HE'S DISAPPOINTED BECAUSE IT DOESN'T HAVE
CHOCOLATE FILLING"

Dik Browne

Jack Davis

Chance Browne and Brian Walker (Hi and Lois)

Bud Blake (Tiger)

Roy Doty

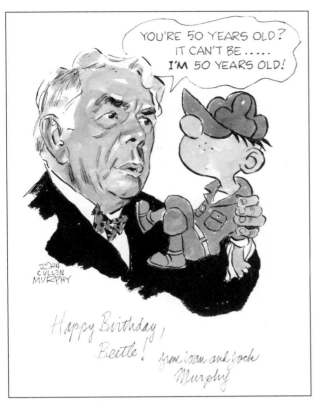

Jack Murphy (Prince Valiant)

Hy Eisman (Popeye)

Patrick McDonnell (Mutts)

Dean Young and Denis Lebrun (Blondie)

Mort's big break happened during World War II, when he met another struggling cartoonist, Bill Mauldin. Mort talked Bill into collaborating on a strip called *Beetle and Joe*. It never worked out — Bill wanted captions and Mort wanted bubbles. But King Features saw Mort's character and the rest is history.

Although Mort is getting the Gold T-Square, not every strip he's drawn has been successful.

For instance, he drew a feminist strip about a buxom blond living in the old west. It was called *Blondie and Deadwood*, but it just never went anywhere.

Then he did an environmental strip, about how man and nature should live together — *Nancy and Slug*. The wildlife people loved it, but it didn't sell. So, finally in desperation he tried to draw a social commentary strip about the royal family and how they were having problems with prescription drugs. That one he called *Prince Valium*.

Mort always had trouble drawing eyes. He tried everything: Little Orphan Annie eyes. Wall eyes. Seven little dwarf eyes. *Rip Kirby*, Richard Nixon, even Bette Davis eyes.

Then one day Mort made a revolutionary discovery — no eyes! He brought the hat down low enough to hide the eyes.

It was so simple and yet so brilliant! It was his ticket to fame and fortune: hide the eyes by just using his hat — think of the money you'll save on ink alone!

Unfortunately this worked against him when he started apprenticing for other strips. Like when he worked on *Steve Canyon*. Milton Caniff was a saint. Milton let Mort work in his studio for three weeks, but finally had to tell him, "I'm sorry, kid, you're just not working out." Mort was crushed, but he knew he could make a living by not drawing eyes.

Then he got a job working on *Dick Tracy*. Once again Mort drew this character as only he knew how. Chester Gould fired him that first day, but Mort kept pushing on.

He even tried working on *Mandrake*. Mort once said that Lee Falk was such a perfectionist — "No, I want his eyes to show!" he would yell. It just kept getting worse, but Mort could not tell Lee Falk his dreaded secret.

In fact years later, Mort even tried to help young Cathy Guisewite develop her main character, Cathy. But since he didn't draw eyes and she didn't draw noses all they came up with was a talking mouth.

A satirical presentation by Mike Peters during my Gold T-Square Award dinner

Jerry Scott and Jim Borgman (Zits)

Bil Keane (Family Circus)

Barbara Dale

Dik Browne (Hagar)

Milton Caniff (Steve Canyon)

John Newcomb

I think humor is God's greatest gift to man (besides that other activity). Humor saves us from so many lousy situations and disappointments. It makes reality palatable. Humor is sanity, the fearful truth. It strips pomposity to the bone and shakes out the sham. When the kids start to overcome you, I like Jean Kerr's philosophy: "It's *our* house and we're *bigger*." Humor heals. When you laugh, the endorphins go to every part of your body, providing a feel-good effect. Norman Cousins used humor to overcome a serious illness. We make friends with laughter. Humor is used by politicians, ministers, and corporate leaders to win over their audience. I'm not suggesting that cartoonists are doing a public service when they draw their strips, but it's a hell of a lot better bringing joy to the world than collecting taxes. ❖

Someone asked me what it was like to get old.

I said the worst part was that most of your good friends have

died and the ones that are left you can't tell the difference.

The Curse of Creativity

Sometimes I feel like taking my Magic Marker and writing across the mirror, "Stop me before I create again!" In the past few years I've written a novel, three children's books, two new comic strips, a stage musical, a TV special, and a number of movie and TV treatments; created sculptures, greeting cards, a newspaper, a quarterly magazine, architectural plans, song lyrics, and a Web site; invented stuff, wrote poems, created games and products, written articles, made speeches, and run annual golf tournaments, as well as met my weekly deadlines.

I love it, but I can't stop it. I wake up almost every day with another idea. I drive everyone nuts. "Oh, God! Not another idea! Don't you ever sleep?" people tell me. It's a curse, and the worst part is, I'm so busy creating, I don't have the time to follow through and complete my ideas. There's no one to pick up the torch and bear it.

They say you have to present an idea five times before anyone ever takes it seriously or begins to understand it. *Five times?* I think I need to take some cold showers.

On the rocky road of life, pause occasionally and pet a pebble.

I feel like I've had a good day when I end up with a full wastebasket.

At an early age I learned how to turn an enemy into a friend. If someone attacked me or spoke unkindly, I went right over and said, "I want to be your friend. Let's talk things over." It almost always worked, and I've ended up with hundreds of friends. Who needs enemies?

I have learned to use everyday words in my work. Nobody should have to run to the dictionary to find out what my comic strip is saying. They wouldn't do it and I'd lose my audience. I need to communicate, not impress people with my vast intelligence and erudition. (Oops! A big word.) "Good words" get the idea across as well as "big words," so that millions of people every day can understand and nobody's left out. After all, when you tell a joke, you want to be sure everyone gets it.

As society becomes more spread out, with families living miles away from each other and with life becoming more impersonal, comic strips help fill the void in people's lives by creating the illusion of friends and shared experiences.

The comic strip is one of the few mediums that allow one person to express his philosophy, his anger, his joy, and his disappointment in mankind without restriction. It is one of the purest forms of art and expression that exists. ❖

Deadlines are like living with a nymphomaniac.

You enjoy what you're doing, but it never stops.

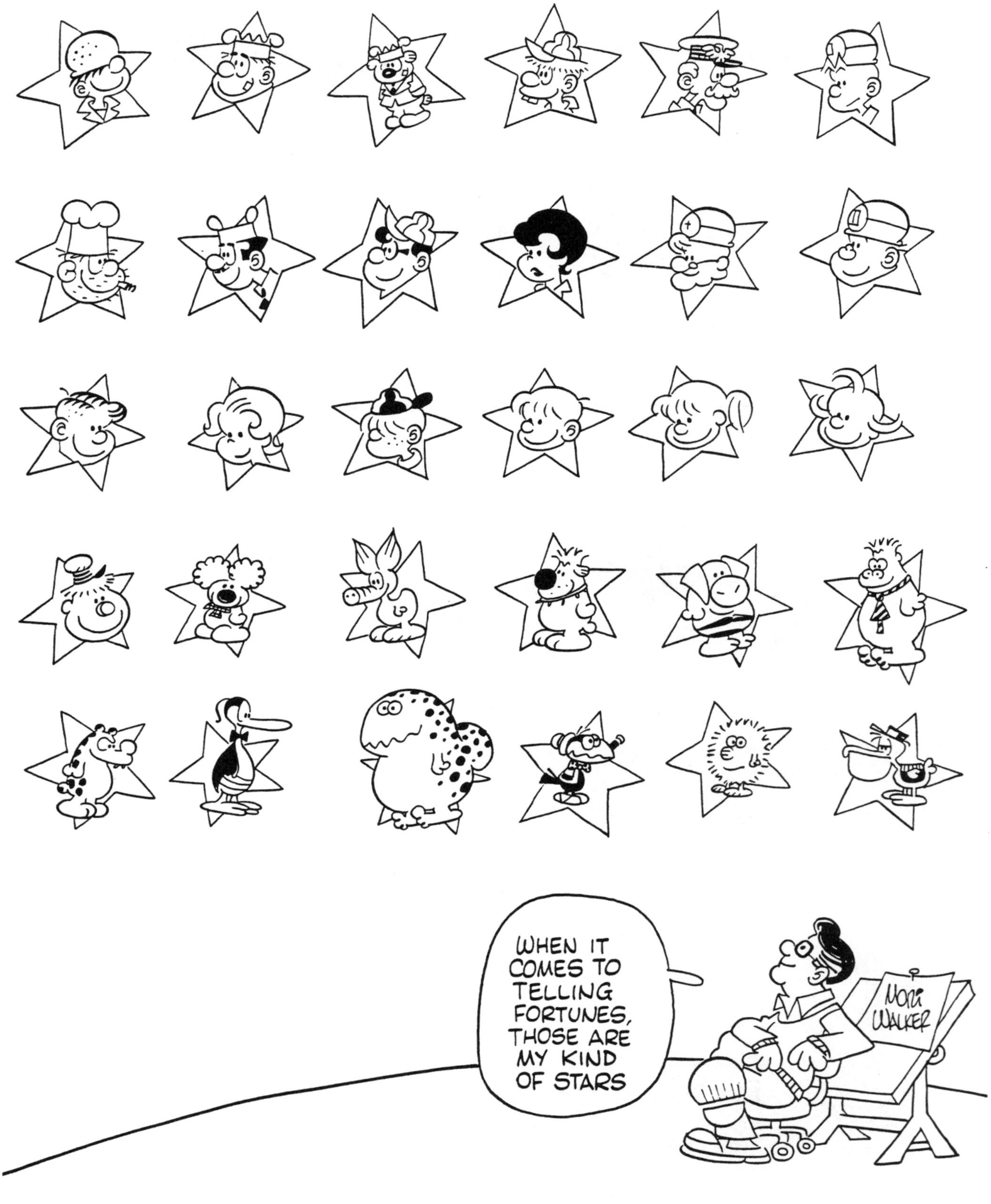
WHEN IT COMES TO TELLING FORTUNES, THOSE ARE MY KIND OF STARS
MORT WALKER

A truckload of my characters

A Fifty-Year Parade of Strips

In all, I have had nine comic strips in syndication. *Mrs. Fitz's Flats, Sam's Strip, Boner's Ark, Betty Boop and Felix, The Evermores,* and *Gamin and Patches* are no longer published. *Beetle Bailey* is currently in 1,800 newspapers; *Hi and Lois,* 1,100 newspapers; and *Sam and Silo,* 100 papers. In adding up the numbers, it has been said that I am the most widely syndicated cartoonist in history.

I have had over a hundred books in print with sales of around 10 million copies, and more are on the way. I've had a TV special, fifty animated films in syndication, and a stage musical. It's been a great career. I have the longest running strip by the same creator. ❖

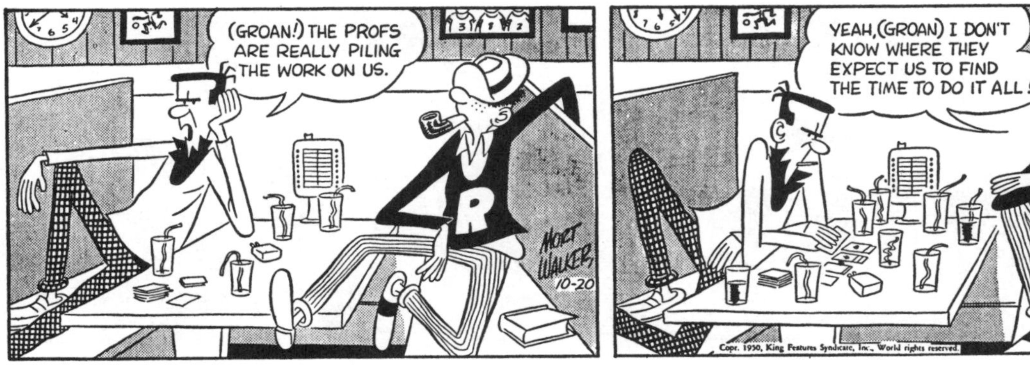
(GROAN!) THE PROFS ARE REALLY PILING THE WORK ON US.
MORT WALKER, 10-20
YEAH, (GROAN) I DON'T KNOW WHERE THEY EXPECT US TO FIND THE TIME TO DO IT ALL!
Copr. 1950, King Features Syndicate, Inc., World rights reserved.

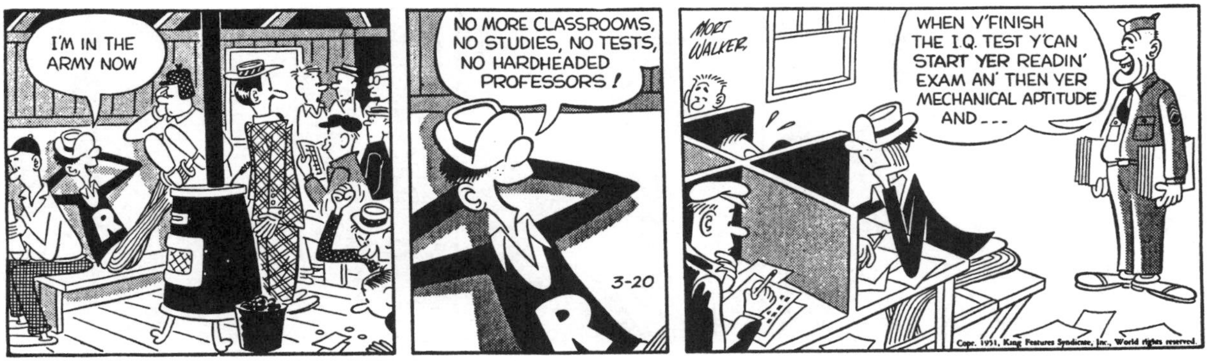
I'M IN THE ARMY NOW
NO MORE CLASSROOMS, NO STUDIES, NO TESTS, NO HARDHEADED PROFESSORS!
3-20
MORT WALKER,
WHEN Y'FINISH THE I.Q. TEST Y'CAN START YER READIN' EXAM AN' THEN YER MECHANICAL APTITUDE AND---
Copr. 1951, King Features Syndicate, Inc., World rights reserved.

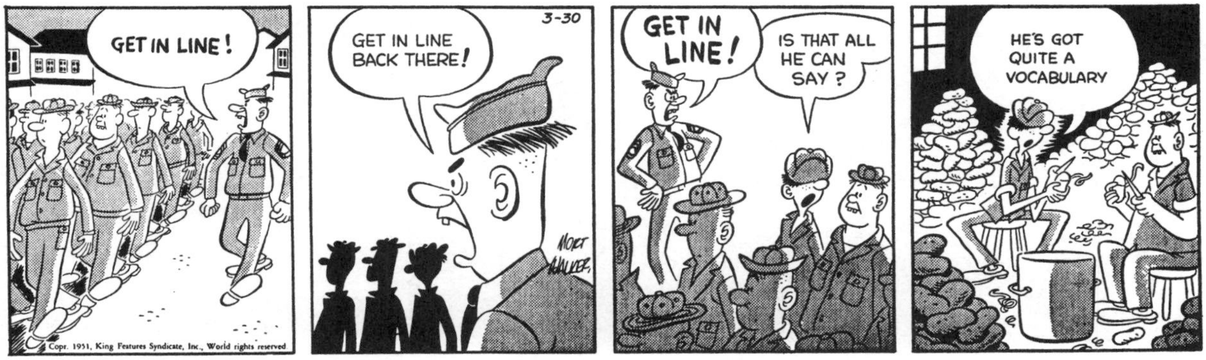
GET IN LINE!
Copr. 1951, King Features Syndicate, Inc., World rights reserved
3-30
GET IN LINE BACK THERE!
MORT WALKER,
GET IN LINE!
IS THAT ALL HE CAN SAY?
HE'S GOT QUITE A VOCABULARY

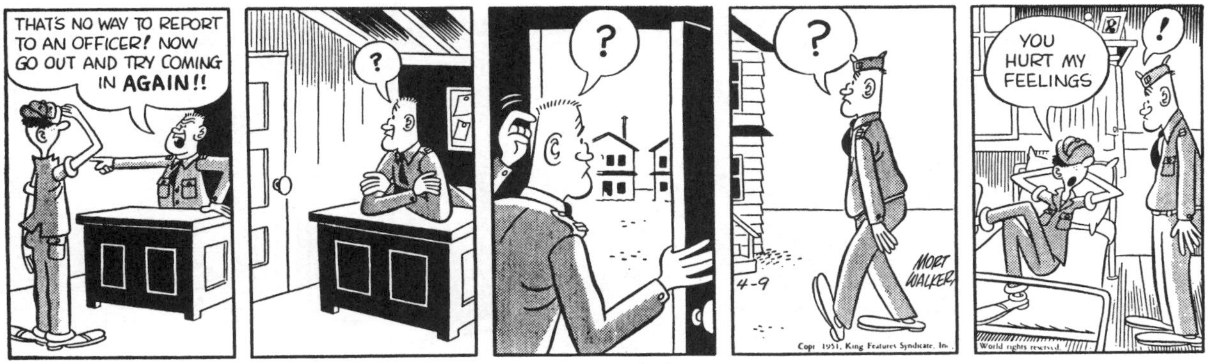
THAT'S NO WAY TO REPORT TO AN OFFICER! NOW GO OUT AND TRY COMING IN AGAIN!!
?
?
?
MORT WALKER,
4-9
Copr. 1951, King Features Syndicate, Inc.
YOU HURT MY FEELINGS
!
World rights reserved.

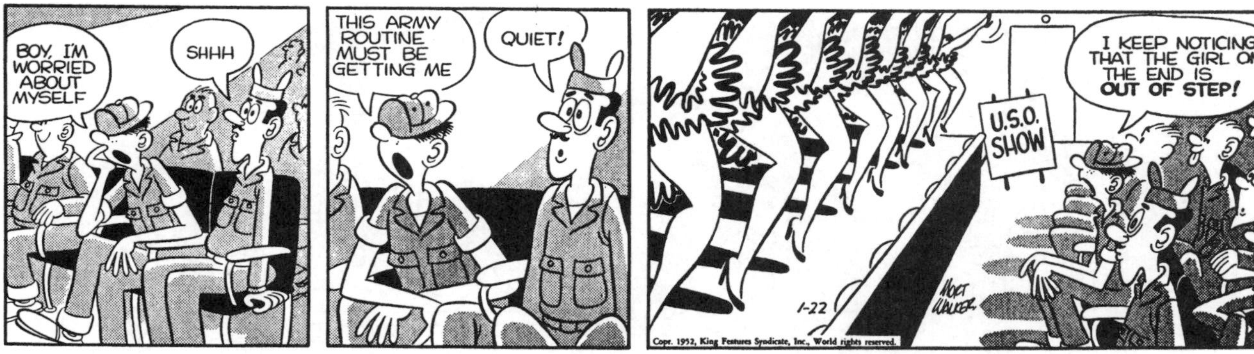
BOY, I'M WORRIED ABOUT MYSELF
SHHH
THIS ARMY ROUTINE MUST BE GETTING ME
QUIET!
I KEEP NOTICING THAT THE GIRL ON THE END IS OUT OF STEP!
U.S.O. SHOW
1-22
MORT WALKER
Copr. 1952, King Features Syndicate, Inc., World rights reserved.

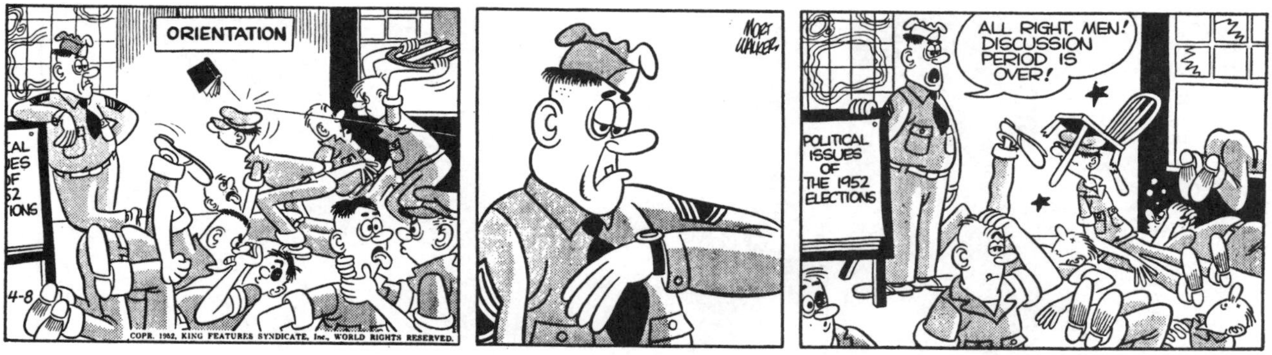
ORIENTATION
4-8
COPR. 1952, KING FEATURES SYNDICATE, Inc., WORLD RIGHTS RESERVED.
MORT WALKER
ALL RIGHT, MEN! DISCUSSION PERIOD IS OVER!
POLITICAL ISSUES OF THE 1952 ELECTIONS

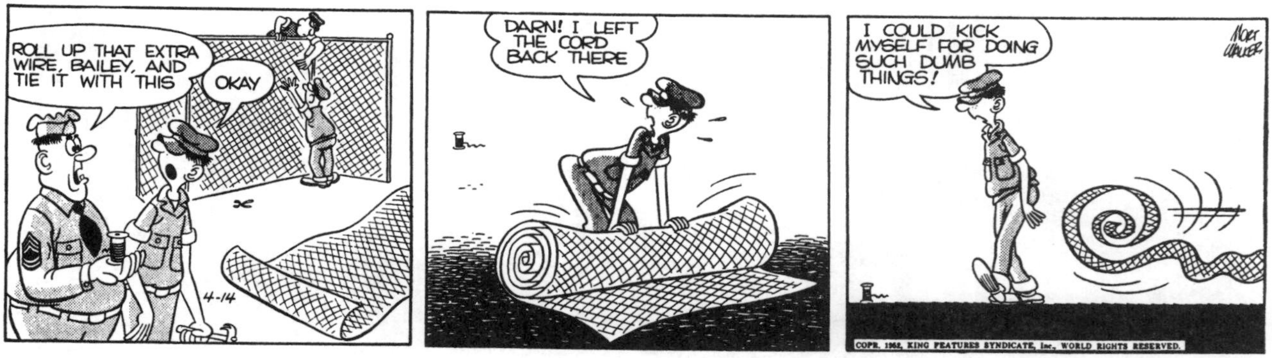
ROLL UP THAT EXTRA WIRE, BAILEY, AND TIE IT WITH THIS
OKAY
4-14
DARN! I LEFT THE CORD BACK THERE
I COULD KICK MYSELF FOR DOING SUCH DUMB THINGS!
MORT WALKER
COPR. 1952, KING FEATURES SYNDICATE, Inc., WORLD RIGHTS RESERVED.

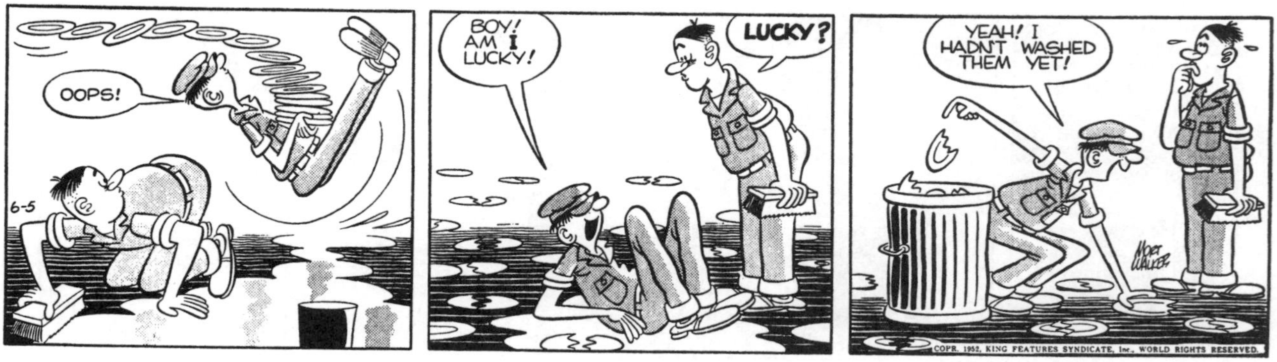
OOPS!
6-5
BOY! AM I LUCKY!
LUCKY?
YEAH! I HADN'T WASHED THEM YET!
MORT WALKER
COPR. 1952, KING FEATURES SYNDICATE, Inc., WORLD RIGHTS RESERVED.

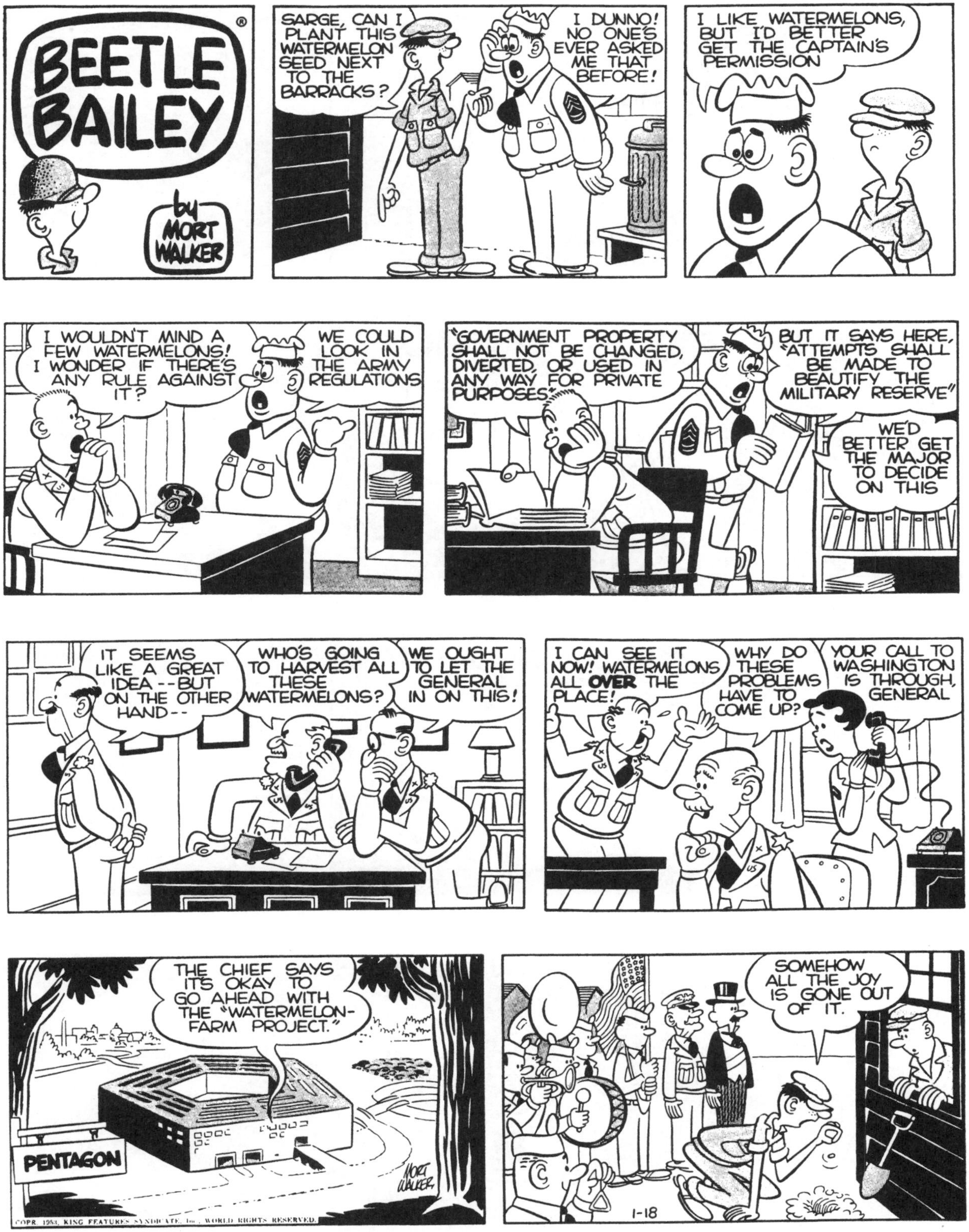
BEETLE BAILEY
by MORT WALKER
SARGE, CAN I PLANT THIS WATERMELON SEED NEXT TO THE BARRACKS?
I DUNNO! NO ONE'S EVER ASKED ME THAT BEFORE!
I LIKE WATERMELONS, BUT I'D BETTER GET THE CAPTAIN'S PERMISSION
I WOULDN'T MIND A FEW WATERMELONS! I WONDER IF THERE'S ANY RULE AGAINST IT?
WE COULD LOOK IN THE ARMY REGULATIONS
"GOVERNMENT PROPERTY SHALL NOT BE CHANGED, DIVERTED, OR USED IN ANY WAY FOR PRIVATE PURPOSES"
BUT IT SAYS HERE, "ATTEMPTS SHALL BE MADE TO BEAUTIFY THE MILITARY RESERVE"
WE'D BETTER GET THE MAJOR TO DECIDE ON THIS
IT SEEMS LIKE A GREAT IDEA--BUT ON THE OTHER HAND--
WHO'S GOING TO HARVEST ALL THESE WATERMELONS?
WE OUGHT TO LET THE GENERAL IN ON THIS!
I CAN SEE IT NOW! WATERMELONS ALL **OVER** THE PLACE!
WHY DO THESE PROBLEMS HAVE TO COME UP?
YOUR CALL TO WASHINGTON IS THROUGH, GENERAL
THE CHIEF SAYS IT'S OKAY TO GO AHEAD WITH THE "WATERMELON-FARM PROJECT."
PENTAGON
MORT WALKER
COPR. 1953, KING FEATURES SYNDICATE, Inc., WORLD RIGHTS RESERVED.
SOMEHOW ALL THE JOY IS GONE OUT OF IT.
1-18

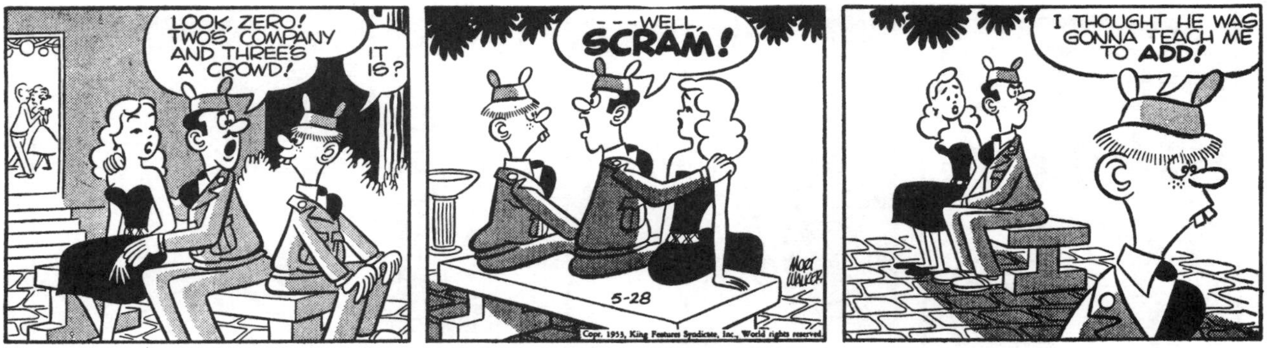
LOOK, ZERO! TWO'S COMPANY AND THREE'S A CROWD!
IT IS?
---WELL, SCRAM!
I THOUGHT HE WAS GONNA TEACH ME TO ADD!
MORT WALKER
5-28
Copr. 1953, King Features Syndicate, Inc., World rights reserved.

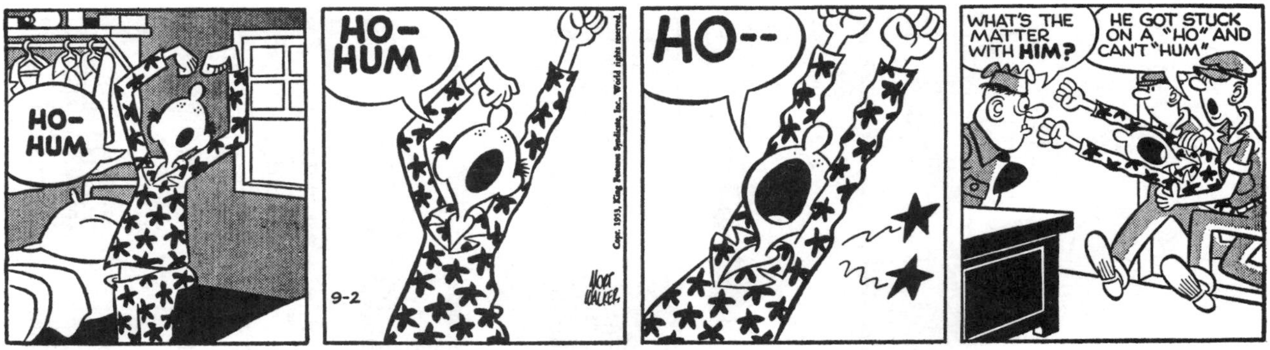
HO-HUM
HO-HUM
HO--
WHAT'S THE MATTER WITH HIM?
HE GOT STUCK ON A "HO" AND CAN'T "HUM"
9-2
MORT WALKER
Copr. 1953, King Features Syndicate, Inc., World rights reserved.

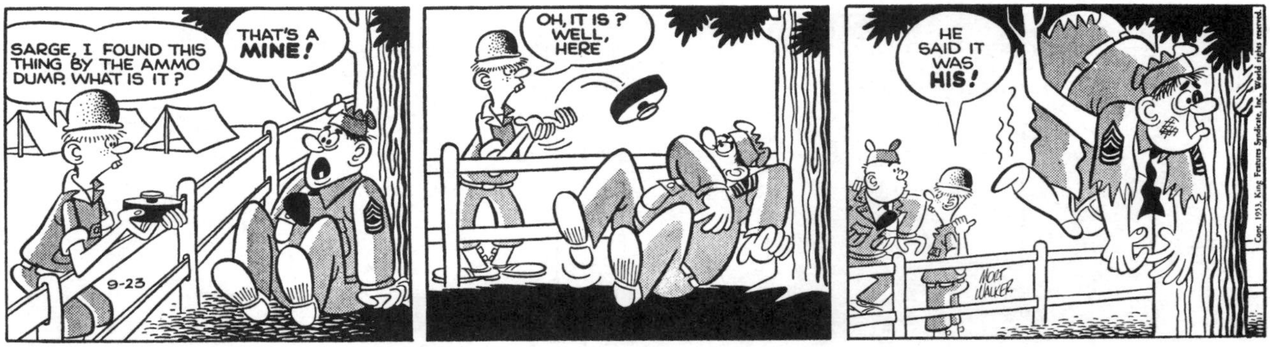
SARGE, I FOUND THIS THING BY THE AMMO DUMP. WHAT IS IT?
THAT'S A MINE!
OH, IT IS? WELL, HERE
HE SAID IT WAS HIS!
9-23
MORT WALKER
Copr. 1953, King Features Syndicate, Inc., World rights reserved.

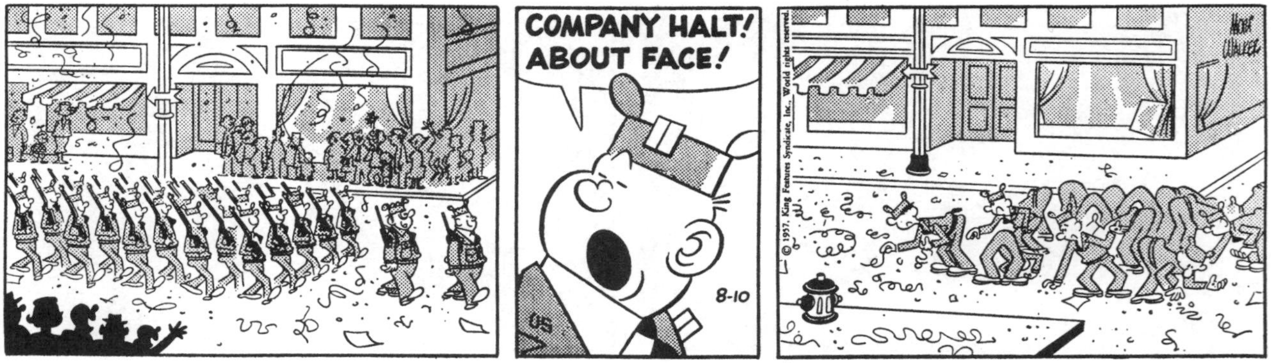
COMPANY HALT! ABOUT FACE!
8-10
US
MORT WALKER
© 1957, King Features Syndicate, Inc., World rights reserved.

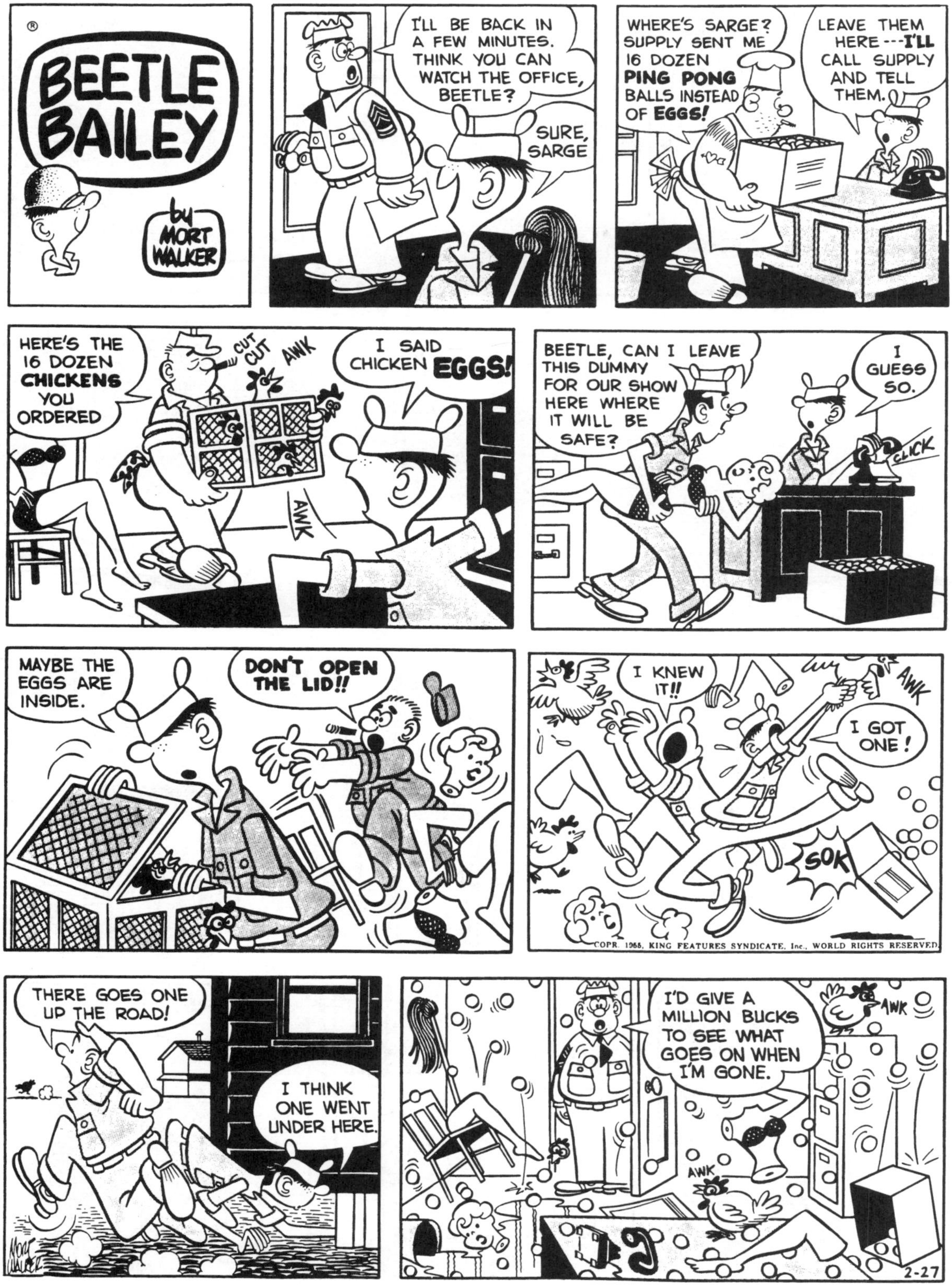

BEETLE BAILEY
by MORT WALKER
I'LL BE BACK IN A FEW MINUTES. THINK YOU CAN WATCH THE OFFICE, BEETLE?
SURE, SARGE
WHERE'S SARGE? SUPPLY SENT ME 16 DOZEN PING PONG BALLS INSTEAD OF EGGS!
LEAVE THEM HERE---I'LL CALL SUPPLY AND TELL THEM.
HERE'S THE 16 DOZEN CHICKENS YOU ORDERED
CUT CUT
AWK
I SAID CHICKEN EGGS!
AWK
BEETLE, CAN I LEAVE THIS DUMMY FOR OUR SHOW HERE WHERE IT WILL BE SAFE?
I GUESS SO.
CLICK
MAYBE THE EGGS ARE INSIDE.
DON'T OPEN THE LID!!
I KNEW IT!!
AWK
I GOT ONE!
SOK
COPR. 1958, KING FEATURES SYNDICATE, Inc., WORLD RIGHTS RESERVED.
THERE GOES ONE UP THE ROAD!
I THINK ONE WENT UNDER HERE.
I'D GIVE A MILLION BUCKS TO SEE WHAT GOES ON WHEN I'M GONE.
AWK
AWK
2-27

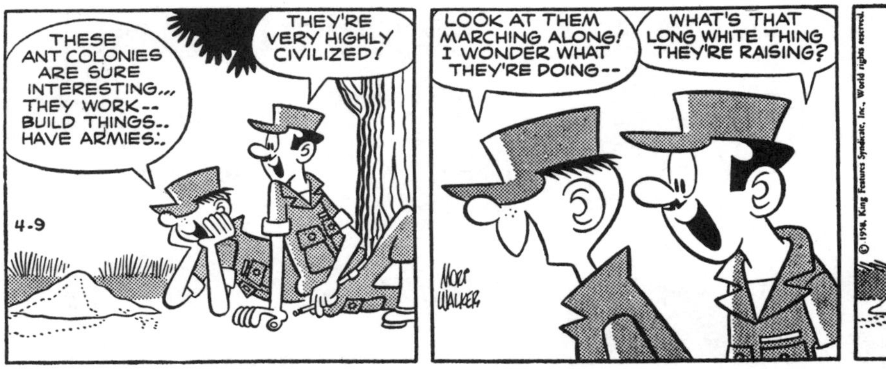
THESE ANT COLONIES ARE SURE INTERESTING... THEY WORK-- BUILD THINGS.. HAVE ARMIES..
THEY'RE VERY HIGHLY CIVILIZED!
4-9
MORT WALKER
LOOK AT THEM MARCHING ALONG! I WONDER WHAT THEY'RE DOING--
WHAT'S THAT LONG WHITE THING THEY'RE RAISING?
© 1958, King Features Syndicate, Inc., World rights reserved.
BOOM

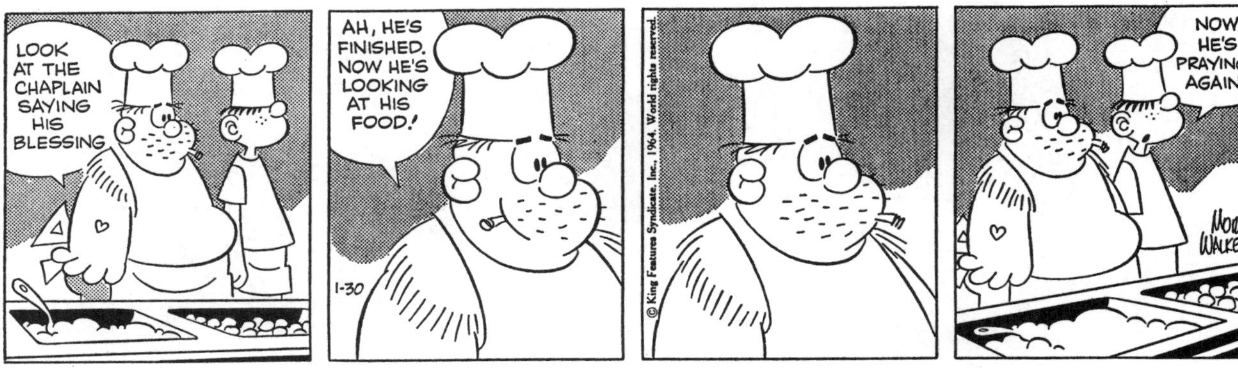
LOOK AT THE CHAPLAIN SAYING HIS BLESSING
AH, HE'S FINISHED. NOW HE'S LOOKING AT HIS FOOD!
1-30
© King Features Syndicate, Inc., 1964. World rights reserved.
NOW HE'S PRAYING AGAIN
MORT WALKER

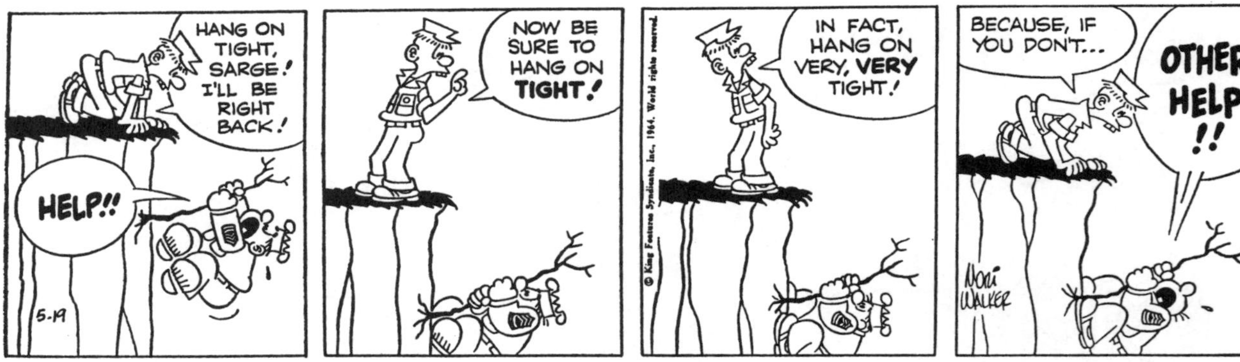
HANG ON TIGHT, SARGE! I'LL BE RIGHT BACK!
HELP!!
5-19
NOW BE SURE TO HANG ON TIGHT!
© King Features Syndicate, Inc., 1964. World rights reserved.
IN FACT, HANG ON VERY, VERY TIGHT!
BECAUSE, IF YOU DON'T...
OTHER HELP !!
MORT WALKER

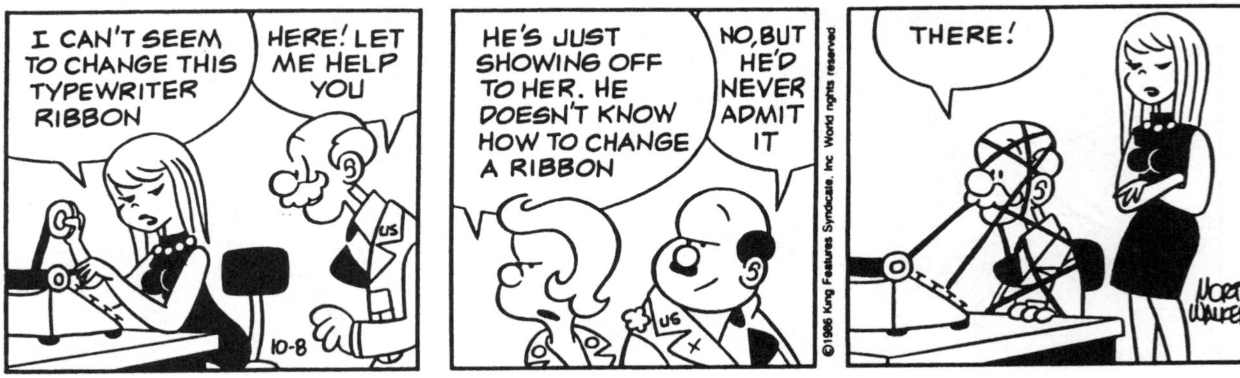
I CAN'T SEEM TO CHANGE THIS TYPEWRITER RIBBON
HERE! LET ME HELP YOU
10-8
HE'S JUST SHOWING OFF TO HER. HE DOESN'T KNOW HOW TO CHANGE A RIBBON
NO, BUT HE'D NEVER ADMIT IT
©1986 King Features Syndicate, Inc World rights reserved
THERE!
MORT WALKER

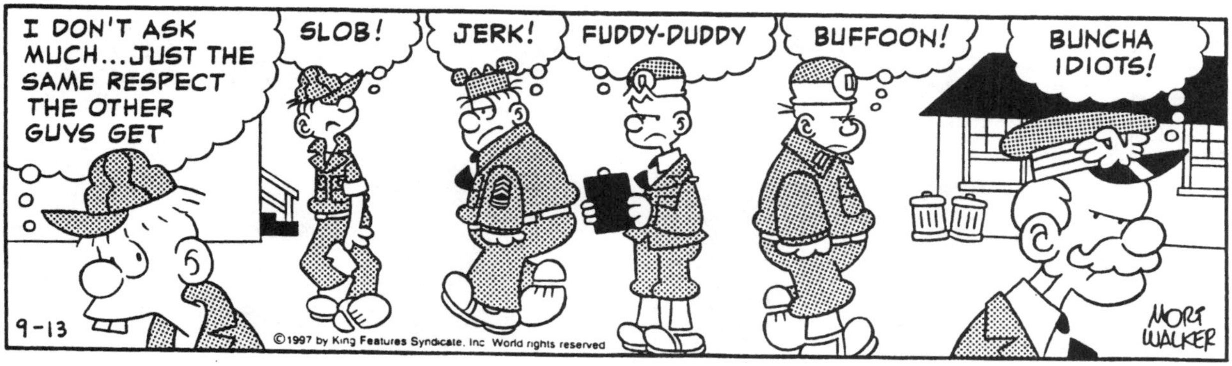
I DON'T ASK MUCH...JUST THE SAME RESPECT THE OTHER GUYS GET
SLOB!
JERK!
FUDDY-DUDDY
BUFFOON!
BUNCHA IDIOTS!
9-13
©1997 by King Features Syndicate, Inc. World rights reserved
MORT WALKER

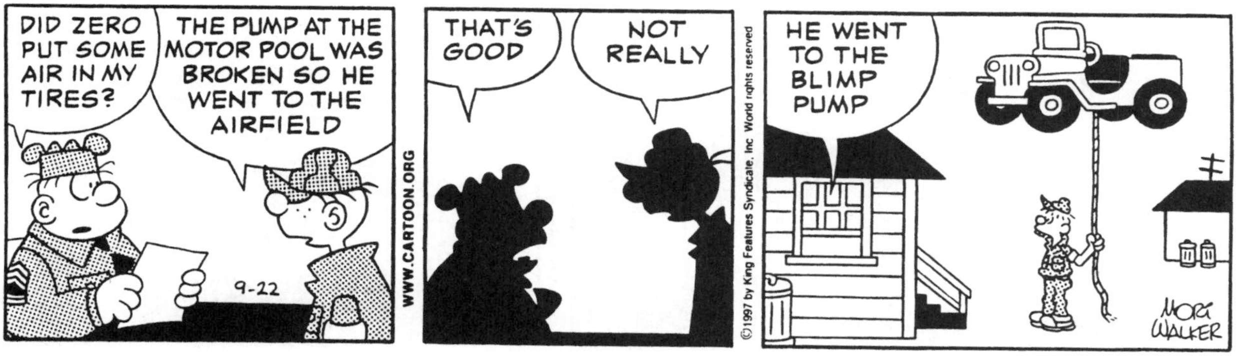
DID ZERO PUT SOME AIR IN MY TIRES?
THE PUMP AT THE MOTOR POOL WAS BROKEN SO HE WENT TO THE AIRFIELD
9-22
WWW.CARTOON.ORG
THAT'S GOOD
NOT REALLY
©1997 by King Features Syndicate, Inc. World rights reserved
HE WENT TO THE BLIMP PUMP
MORT WALKER

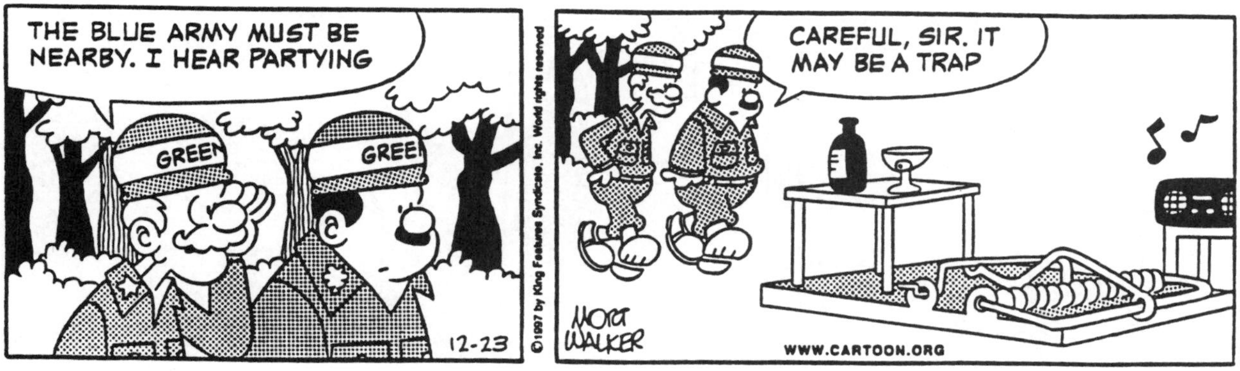
THE BLUE ARMY MUST BE NEARBY. I HEAR PARTYING
GREEN
GREE
12-23
©1997 by King Features Syndicate, Inc. World rights reserved
CAREFUL, SIR. IT MAY BE A TRAP
MORT WALKER
WWW.CARTOON.ORG

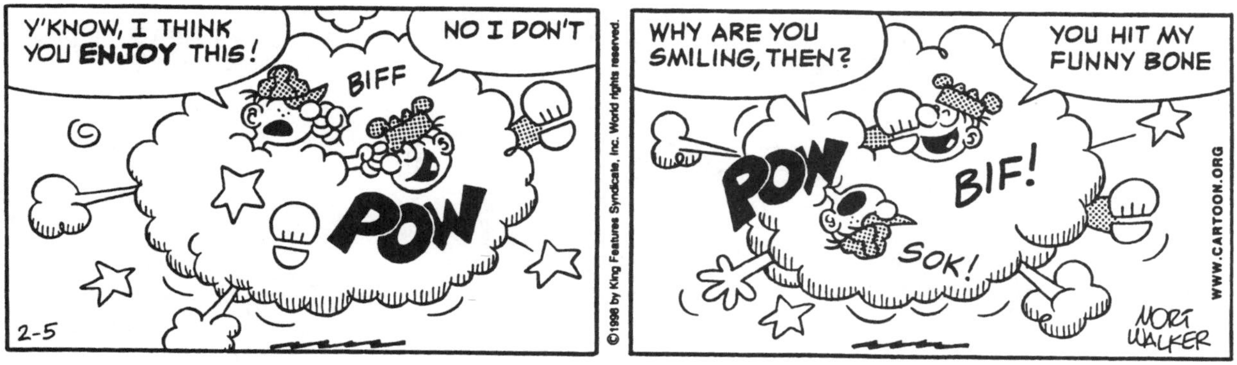
Y'KNOW, I THINK YOU ENJOY THIS!
NO I DON'T
BIFF
POW
2-5
©1998 by King Features Syndicate, Inc. World rights reserved.
WHY ARE YOU SMILING, THEN?
YOU HIT MY FUNNY BONE
POW
BIF!
SOK!
WWW.CARTOON.ORG
MORT WALKER

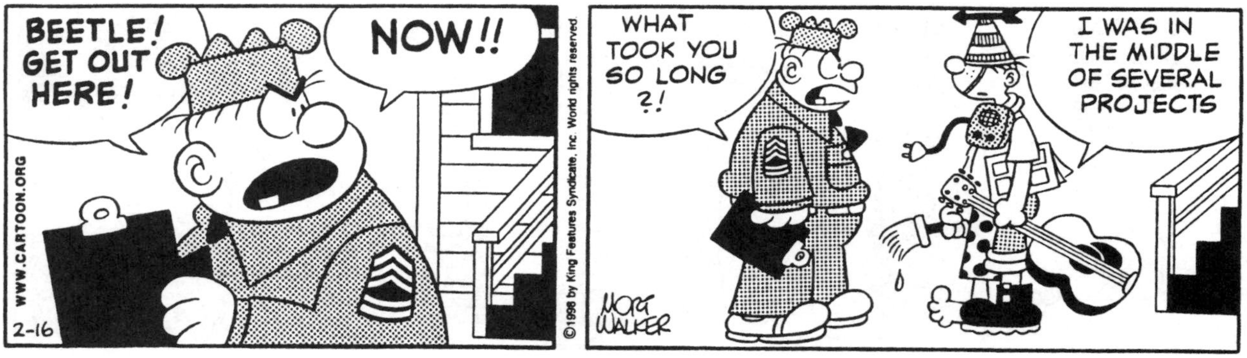
BEETLE! GET OUT HERE!
NOW!!
WHAT TOOK YOU SO LONG ?!
I WAS IN THE MIDDLE OF SEVERAL PROJECTS
2-16
WWW.CARTOON.ORG
©1998 by King Features Syndicate, Inc. World rights reserved.
MORT WALKER

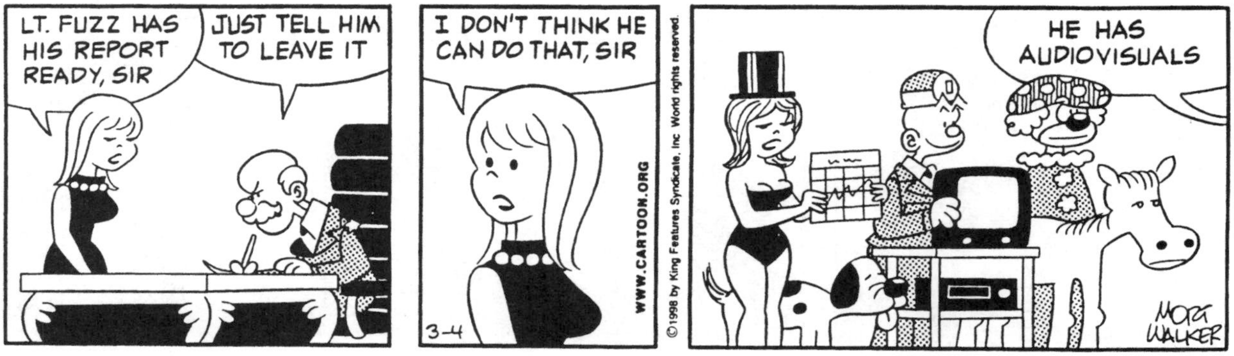
LT. FUZZ HAS HIS REPORT READY, SIR
JUST TELL HIM TO LEAVE IT
I DON'T THINK HE CAN DO THAT, SIR
HE HAS AUDIOVISUALS
3-4
WWW.CARTOON.ORG
©1998 by King Features Syndicate, Inc. World rights reserved.
MORT WALKER

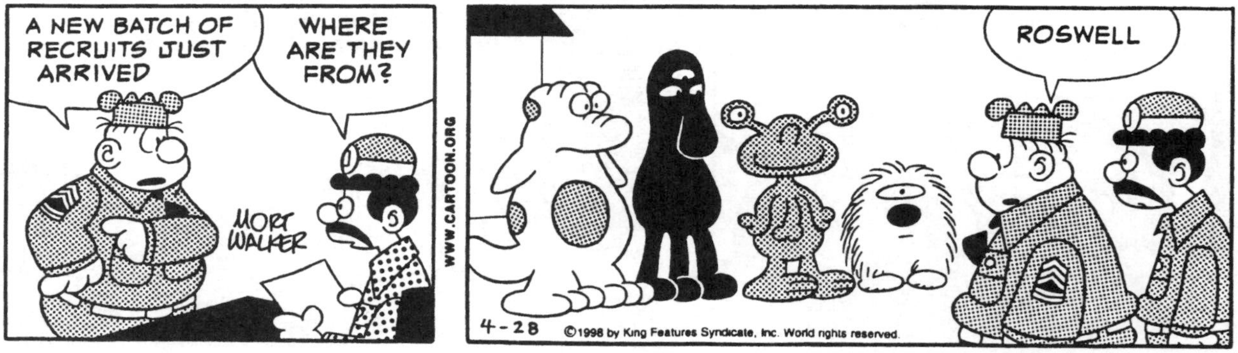
A NEW BATCH OF RECRUITS JUST ARRIVED
WHERE ARE THEY FROM?
ROSWELL
MORT WALKER
WWW.CARTOON.ORG
4-28
©1998 by King Features Syndicate, Inc. World rights reserved.

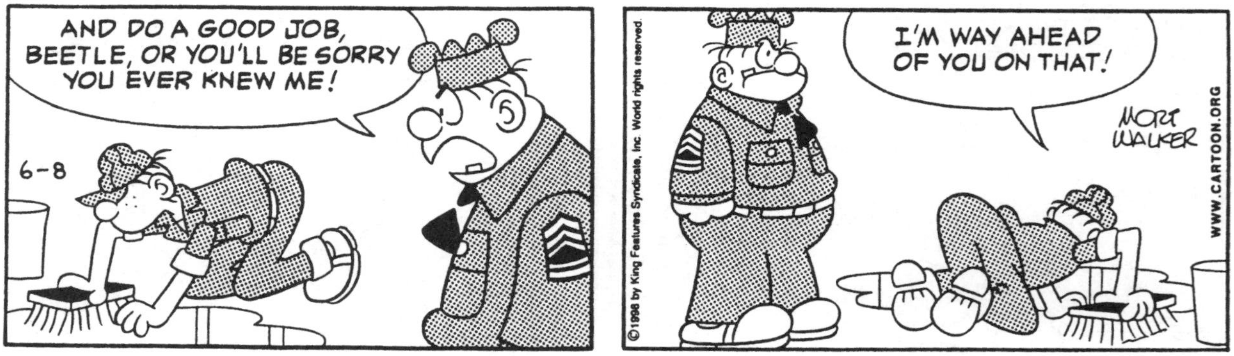
AND DO A GOOD JOB, BEETLE, OR YOU'LL BE SORRY YOU EVER KNEW ME!
I'M WAY AHEAD OF YOU ON THAT!
6-8
©1998 by King Features Syndicate, Inc. World rights reserved.
MORT WALKER
WWW.CARTOON.ORG

EXCITED ABOUT YOUR DATE, KILLER?

YEAH, SHE SAID TONIGHT I'D GET THE THRILL OF MY LIFE

7-1

READY?

MORT WALKER

DO YOU HAVE TO WEAR THAT OUTFIT TO GO ROLLER-BLADING?

NO

7-7

I'M GOING ROLLER-BLADING SO I **CAN** WEAR IT!

MORT WALKER

I'VE BEEN WONDERING

IF I GET AN IDEA WHEN MY WIFE IS OUT OF TOWN...

7-10

IS IT STILL A STUPID IDEA?

MORT WALKER

I'M LEAVING NOW, OTTO. WATCH THINGS FOR ME

9-10

IN AMERICA, A WATCHDOG WATCHES WHAT HE WANTS TO WATCH

MORT WALKER

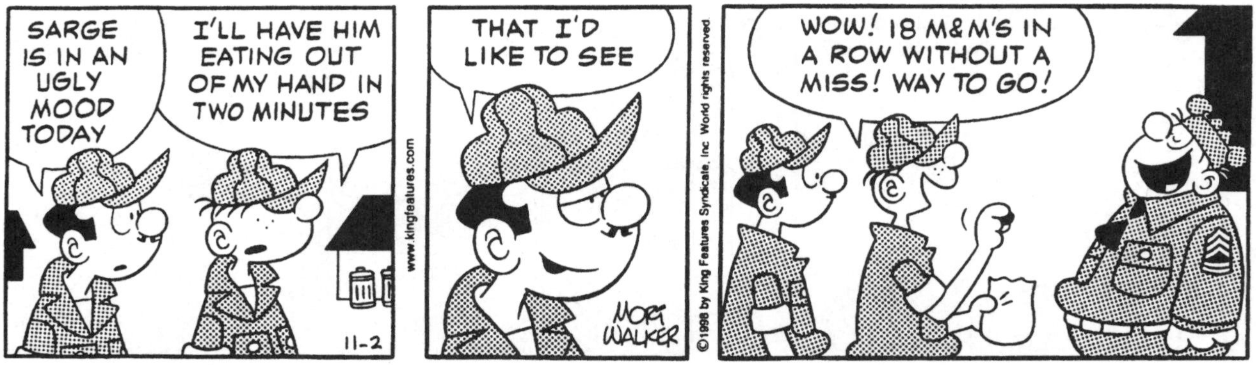
SARGE IS IN AN UGLY MOOD TODAY
I'LL HAVE HIM EATING OUT OF MY HAND IN TWO MINUTES
11-2
www.kingfeatures.com
THAT I'D LIKE TO SEE
MORT WALKER
©1998 by King Features Syndicate, Inc. World rights reserved
WOW! 18 M&M'S IN A ROW WITHOUT A MISS! WAY TO GO!

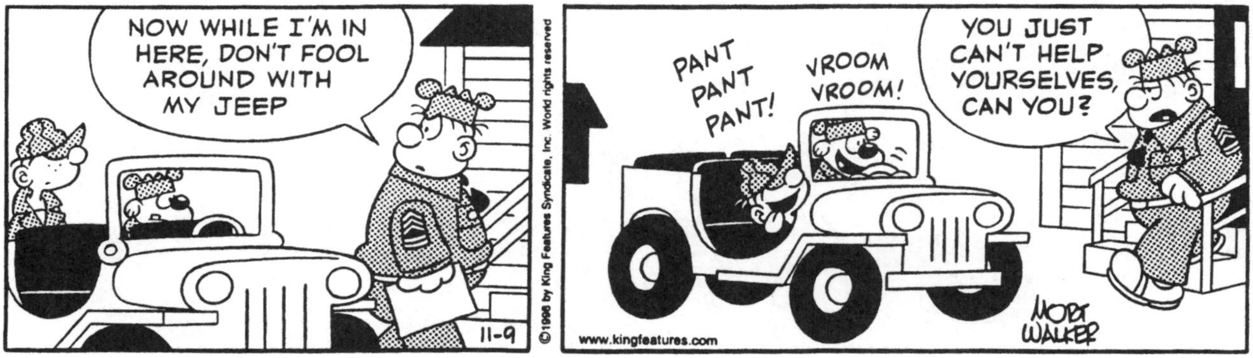
NOW WHILE I'M IN HERE, DON'T FOOL AROUND WITH MY JEEP
11-9
©1998 by King Features Syndicate, Inc. World rights reserved
PANT PANT PANT PANT!
VROOM VROOM!
YOU JUST CAN'T HELP YOURSELVES, CAN YOU?
www.kingfeatures.com
MORT WALKER

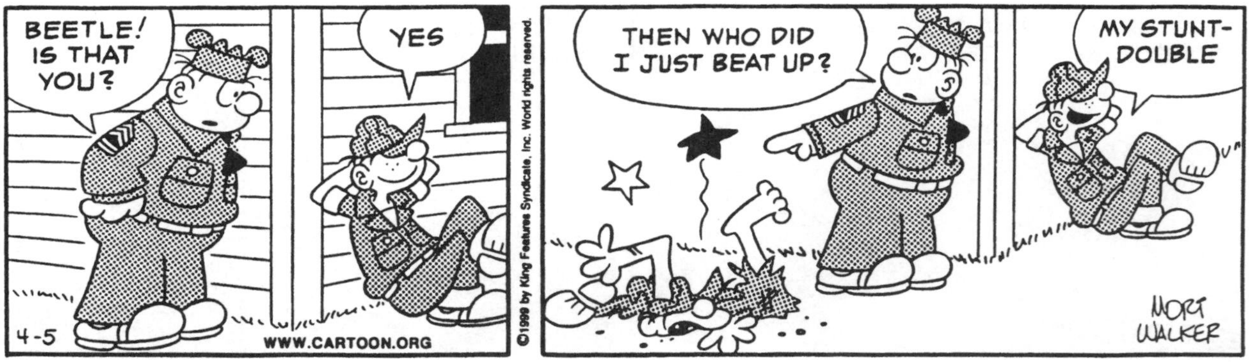
BEETLE! IS THAT YOU?
YES
4-5
WWW.CARTOON.ORG
©1998 by King Features Syndicate, Inc. World rights reserved.
THEN WHO DID I JUST BEAT UP?
MY STUNT-DOUBLE
MORT WALKER

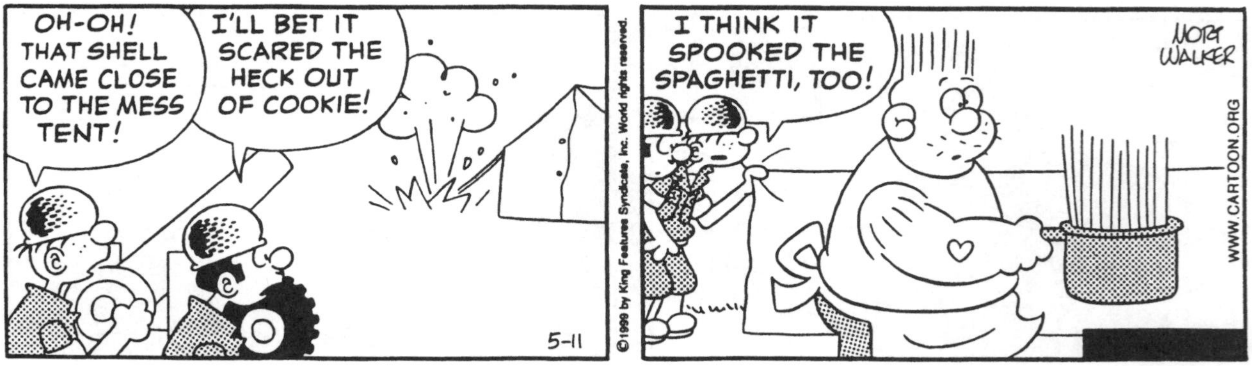
OH-OH! THAT SHELL CAME CLOSE TO THE MESS TENT!
I'LL BET IT SCARED THE HECK OUT OF COOKIE!
5-11
©1998 by King Features Syndicate, Inc. World rights reserved.
I THINK IT SPOOKED THE SPAGHETTI, TOO!
MORT WALKER
WWW.CARTOON.ORG

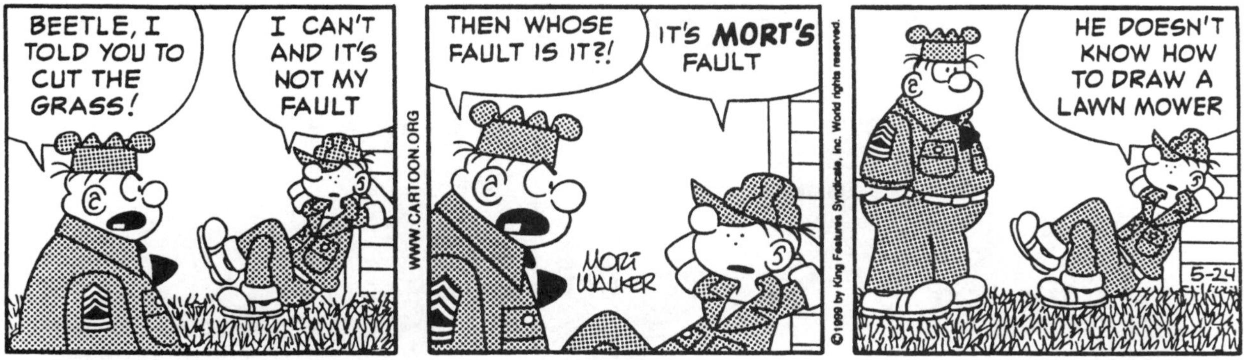
BEETLE, I TOLD YOU TO CUT THE GRASS!
I CAN'T AND IT'S NOT MY FAULT
WWW.CARTOON.ORG
THEN WHOSE FAULT IS IT?!
IT'S MORT'S FAULT
MORT WALKER
©1999 by King Features Syndicate, Inc. World rights reserved.
HE DOESN'T KNOW HOW TO DRAW A LAWN MOWER
5-24

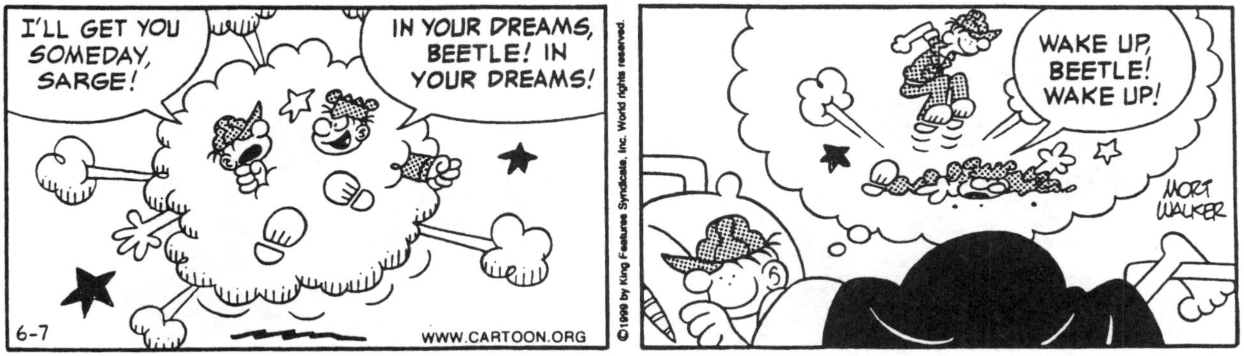
I'LL GET YOU SOMEDAY, SARGE!
IN YOUR DREAMS, BEETLE! IN YOUR DREAMS!
6-7
WWW.CARTOON.ORG
©1999 by King Features Syndicate, Inc. World rights reserved.
WAKE UP, BEETLE! WAKE UP!
MORT WALKER

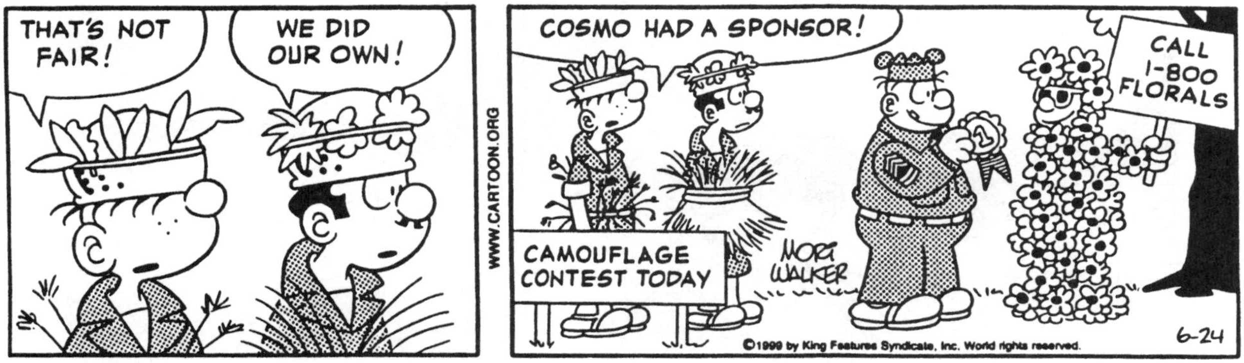
THAT'S NOT FAIR!
WE DID OUR OWN!
WWW.CARTOON.ORG
COSMO HAD A SPONSOR!
CALL 1-800 FLORALS
CAMOUFLAGE CONTEST TODAY
MORT WALKER
©1999 by King Features Syndicate, Inc. World rights reserved.
6-24

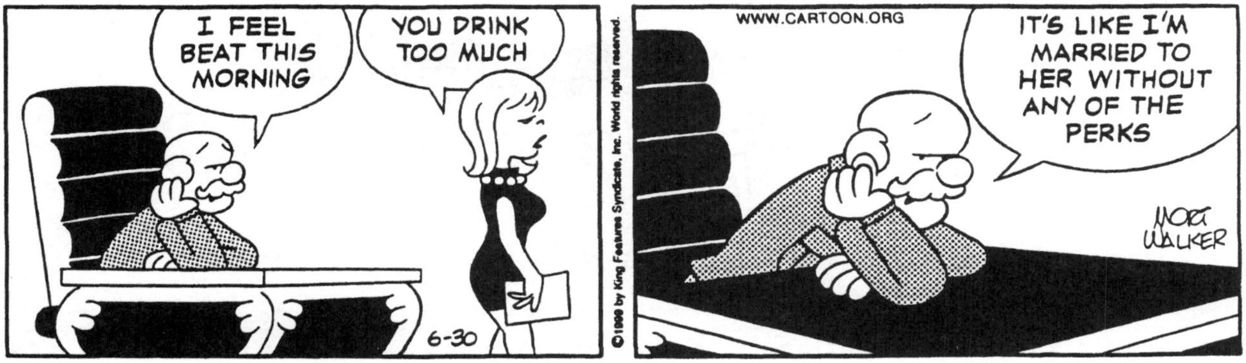
I FEEL BEAT THIS MORNING
YOU DRINK TOO MUCH
6-30
©1999 by King Features Syndicate, Inc. World rights reserved.
WWW.CARTOON.ORG
IT'S LIKE I'M MARRIED TO HER WITHOUT ANY OF THE PERKS
MORT WALKER

The Cartoon!st

1950   2000

INSIDE: Mort Walker on 50 years of cartooning

The Newsletter of the National Cartoonists Society ■ September-October 1999

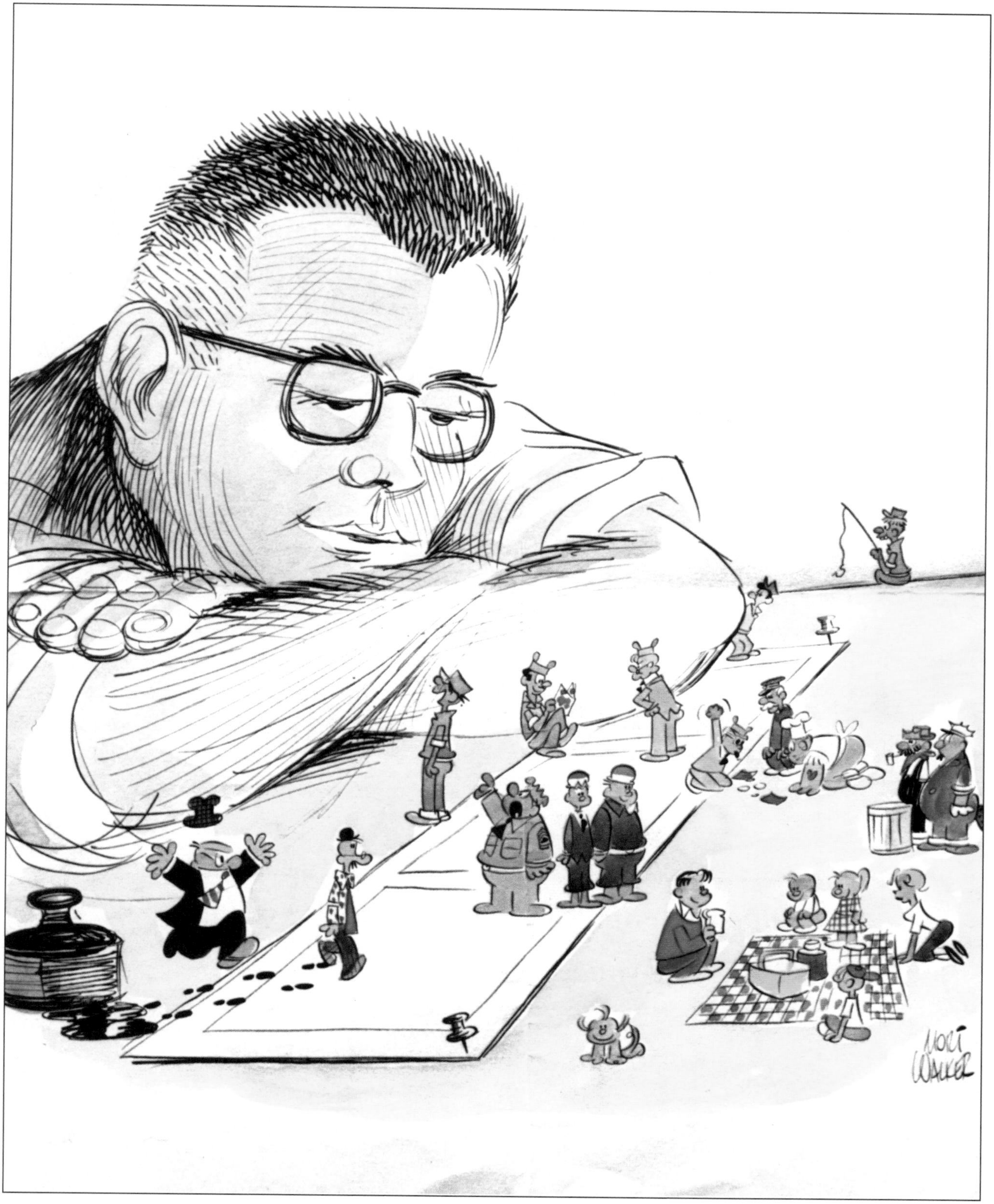
MORT WALKER

I *hope you enjoyed my life as much as I have.*
See you in the funny papers.

The group who worked on this book, from left to right: Brian Walker, editing and organizing; Mort Walker, writing, research, and bragging; Cathy Walker, editing and moral support; Cathy Jr. Deutsch, putting copy on disk; Bill Janocha, copying and restoration; Neal Walker, scanning artwork.

OLD CARTOONISTS
NEVER DIE,
THEY JUST
ERASE AWAY. . . .

Thanks to Rocky Shepard, president of King Features, for his help in getting this book to market.